Brenda Bisho
Hugh Peabody Bishop

# Marblehead's
# FIRST
# HARBOR

Hi Dick,
I think you will enjoy
this !!
My best,
Hugh

# Marblehead's FIRST HARBOR

• *The Rich History of a Small Fishing Port* •

Hugh Peabody Bishop &
Brenda Bishop Booma

Charleston — London
THE
History
PRESS

Published by The History Press
Charleston, SC 29403
www.historypress.net

All images are from the authors' collection unless otherwise noted.
*Facing page*: Gretchen Peabody Bishop and Robert Hugh Bishop.
A sailing dory designed and built by Will Chamberlain. *Courtesy of Peach Collection*

First published 2011

Manufactured in the United States

ISBN 978.1.60949.497.1

Booma, Brenda Bishop.
Marblehead's first harbor : the rich history of a small fishing port / Brenda Bishop Booma
and Hugh Peabody Bishop.
p. cm.
Includes bibliographical references.
ISBN 978-1-60949-497-1
1. Fishing ports--Massachusetts--Marblehead--History--20th century. 2. Fisheries-
-Massachusetts--Marblehead--History--20th century. 3. Harbors--Massachusetts--
Marblehead--History--20th century. 4. Fishers--Massachusetts--Marblehead--Biography. 5.
Marblehead (Mass.)--History--20th century. 6. Marblehead (Mass.)--Biography. I. Bishop,
Hugh Peabody. II. Title.
SH222.M4B66 2011
725'.34097445--dc23
2011042754

*To our parents, whose effort on our behalf enabled us to live the lives we have*

*And all I ask is a merry yarn from a laughing fellow-rover,*
*And quiet sleep and a sweet dream when the long trick's over.*

# Contents

# CONTENTS

# Acknowledgements

At a neighborhood Christmas party in 2008, I told Arlene Briggs Willard how well I remembered her father and how much I thought of him. She then related the story told in the book about how her father signed up for duty in World War I in April 1917. I decided that this type of Marblehead history, along with my varied experiences from a lifetime of commercial fishing, should be put in writing to pass on to my children. The stories started to grow, and I enlisted my sister Brenda's help. She has never been one to give a halfhearted effort. The end result is this book, which involved much more time and effort than either of us anticipated.

Brenda and I would like to thank the offspring of the old-timers for their generous help. These Marbleheaders include Arlene Briggs Willard, Joyce Conner Thibodeau, Betty Cloutman, Virginia Bates Williams and Dave, Karen, Tom and Ted Peach.

Others who spurred us on with their interest in our project include Harriet Brown Bull, Suzanne Brown, Dave Hildreth, Jeff Tutein and Wayne Butler of the Marblehead Historical Commission.

There were many people with whom we held conversations, who came forward with a useful bit from their pasts and offered moral support. We appreciate their thoughtfulness and assistance.

Our good friend and one-time employee, Peter Schalck, has been exceedingly helpful with graphic design and computer support. Once our shipping manager at the Lobster Company, he now uses his considerable talents running his own company, Flat Rock Creative in Salem, Massachusetts.

Without the professionalism of The History Press, this book could not have come to fruition.

We would like to thank Hugh's wife, Judy Bishop, who has earned unlimited appreciation from both of us for her effort, support and patience.

Ed Hawkes.

There are two people without whom the job never could have been accomplished. They are Ed and Jean Hawkes. They earned our special thanks and admiration. Ed is mentioned extensively in the book and is an extraordinary individual. He is a patriot, successful businessman and good family provider, a perfect example of the "Greatest Generation." Now ninety-one years old, his stories, material and personal writing helped sustain and encourage us when even Brenda would get a little down. Without Ed and Jean's inquiries about, "How's the book coming?" it's possible a partly completed pile of paper would be gathering dust somewhere. Our thanks and love to both of them.

# Aerial View of Little Harbor

## *(originally called First Harbor)*

1. Fisherman's Beach
2. Hildreth/Percival House
3. Molly's Rocks
4. Gashouse Beach
5. Bates Boat Yard
6. Baay's Yacht Yard
7. Burgess Airplane Factory
8. Hood Enterprises
9. Beachcomber Club
10. Barber's/Marblehead Lobster Company
11. Graves Float
12. Fishermen Shanties
13. Old Victorian House
14. Crowninshield House

# MARBLEHEAD CHART

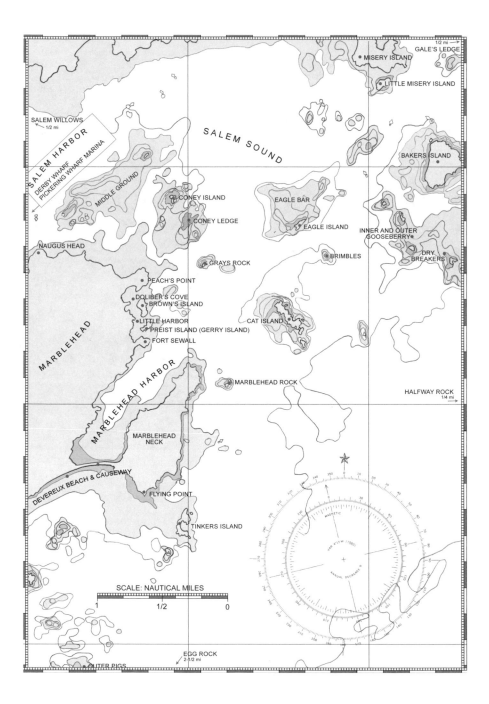

GALE'S LEDGE

MISERY ISLAND

LITTLE MISERY ISLAND

SALEM SOUND

BAKERS ISLAND

SALEM WILLOWS
1/2 mi

SALEM HARBOR
DERBY WHARF
PICKERING WHARF MARINA

MIDDLE GROUND

CONEY ISLAND

EAGLE BAR

CONEY LEDGE

EAGLE ISLAND

INNER AND OUTER
GOOSEBERRY

NAUGUS HEAD

GRAYS ROCK

BRIMBLES

DRY
BREAKERS

PEACH'S POINT

DOLIBER'S COVE
BROWN'S ISLAND

MARBLEHEAD

LITTLE HARBOR
PREIST ISLAND (GERRY ISLAND)
FORT SEWALL

CAT ISLAND

MARBLEHEAD HARBOR

MARBLEHEAD ROCK

HALFWAY ROCK
1/4 mi

MARBLEHEAD
NECK

DEVEREUX BEACH & CAUSEWAY

FLYING POINT

TINKERS ISLAND

SCALE: NAUTICAL MILES

1        1/2        0

MAGNETIC

OUTER PIGS

EGG ROCK
2-1/2 mi

# GULF OF MAINE CHART

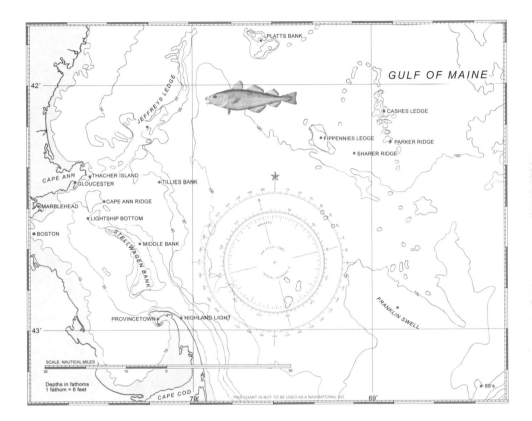

PLATTS BANK

GULF OF MAINE

JEFFREYS LEDGE

CASHES LEDGE

FIPPENNIES LEDGE

PARKER RIDGE

SHARER RIDGE

100

CAPE ANN

THACHER ISLAND

GLOUCESTER

TILLIES BANK

MARBLEHEAD

CAPE ANN RIDGE

100

LIGHTSHIP BOTTOM

BOSTON

50

STELLWAGEN BANK

MIDDLE BANK

45

30

10

FRANKLIN SWELL

100

PROVINCETOWN

HIGHLAND LIGHT

43°

10

SCALE: NAUTICAL MILES

30          10          0                                    30

Depths in fathoms
1 fathom = 6 feet

88's

CAPE COD

THIS CHART IS NOT TO BE USED AS A NAVIGATIONAL AID

70°

69°

42°

# CANYONS OF THE CONTINENTAL SHELF AND NANTUCKET SHOALS CHART

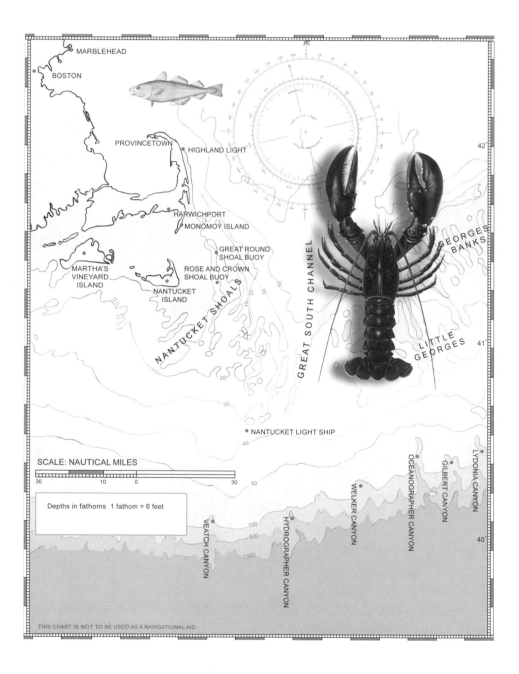

MARBLEHEAD

BOSTON

PROVINCETOWN

HIGHLAND LIGHT

42°

HARWICHPORT

MONOMOY ISLAND

GREAT ROUND
SHOAL BUOY

MARTHA'S
VINEYARD
ISLAND

ROSE AND CROWN
SHOAL BUOY

NANTUCKET
ISLAND

NANTUCKET SHOALS

GREAT SOUTH CHANNEL

GEORGES
BANKS

LITTLE
GEORGES

41°

50

30

20

30

20

NANTUCKET LIGHT SHIP

40

SCALE: NAUTICAL MILES

30          10          0                    30

50

Depths in fathoms  1 fathom = 6 feet

100
500

1000

VEATCH CANYON

HYDROGRAPHER CANYON

WELKER CANYON

OCEANOGRAPHER CANYON

GILBERT CANYON

LYDONIA CANYON

40°

THIS CHART IS NOT TO BE USED AS A NAVIGATIONAL AID

# Prologue

In the 1600s, the early Marbleheaders followed the trail from the beach at First Harbor to their meetinghouse on Old Burial Hill. Their lives and deaths were resolved at this lookout, high above the Atlantic Ocean, but the heart and soul of their beings was intertwined with the sea. The growing season in New England being a short one, the ocean afforded the best opportunity for economic prosperity in those years.

Fishing became the trademark of the town. First Harbor was a refuge for the working folk, a safe haven for their vessels and a community of like-minded, independent Yankees. The Cove's notoriety, however, is usually overshadowed by that of Marblehead Harbor, a major yacht anchorage on the East Coast of the United States, and by the town itself, with its claim of "Birthplace of the American Navy." During the seventeenth century, Great Bay (the big harbor) was ancillary to First Harbor, the small inlet nestled between Fort Sewall and Peaches Point.

In the early days, Marblehead had more fishermen than Gloucester. The seventy-five years from the American Revolution to the middle of the nineteenth century were the golden age of fishing for the town. In 1809, there was a fleet of 116 fishing schooners that sailed to the Grand Banks twice a year between spring and fall. By 1879, however, there was only "a solitary vessel representative of the great industry from which for more than two centuries, a vast majority of the men and boys of Marblehead had gained a livelihood."

The Gale of 1846, near Newfoundland, brought devastation. Ten vessels went down, and sixty-five men were lost. A final death knell was dealt by the inception of the Civil War.

First Harbor (Little Harbor), view from Fountain Park, circa 1880. An inshore fishing craft is in the cove.

Fisherman's Beach, circa 1910, with the cupola and fence of Fountain Park on upper left. *Peach Collection.*

An early view of Little Harbor showing the cupola and fence at Fountain Park. *Marblehead Historical Commission.*

As Samuel Roads wrote in his *History of Marblehead*, "The first call for troops [on April 15, 1861] came late in the afternoon. By 8 a.m. the next day, three companies, arriving by train, were in Faneuil Hall, Boston, with the fifes and drums playing 'Yankee Doodle,' ready to proceed to the front. The other two arrived an hour later."

Marbleheaders claimed the honor of being the first responders. They certainly provided an enthusiastic enlistment of 1,048 men to the army and navy, but the postwar tally showed a dwindling population in Marblehead. Of the men who went to war, over 20 percent were either killed in battle or succumbed to sickness upon their return home.

My story is of First Harbor in the twentieth century, where the patriotism still raged as strongly as the northeast storms. The small group of fishermen approached their trade with the same passion that had been shown so many years before. A spirited individualism remained in this insular section of town. Slow to accept change, but quick to respond, the men at First Harbor, now known as Little Harbor, were to be admired for the character with which they had been instilled.

My contemporaries and I became the beneficiaries of the inner thoughtfulness of these men, which was often masked by well-calloused exteriors. This book is a tribute to the gift they offered, providing us with a strong foundation for the voyage we would undertake from our small anchorage.

# Chapter 1

# Reflection

anuary 8, 1998, at 2:15 a.m., my alarm goes off. When it's time to go commercial fishing, I'm ready to try to catch something. The anticipation of what I will catch is the motivating factor.

I look out the bedroom window into the darkness. The bare branches on the only visible tree are not moving—a good sign. Television weathermen on the evening news the night before promised that the strong northwest winds of the past couple of days would die out overnight, so today sounded like a "good chance." This meant small boat fishermen, like myself, up and down the New England coast would be heading to their vessels. Some of us would be lobstering, others gill net fishing, dragging for fish and shrimp or line trawling. Over the years, we had all found the type of fishing that suited us during a particular season and what worked best for the type of boat we owned.

As for me, I'm a line trawler. I fish with hooks and lines, more hooks and lines than a person on shore can visualize.

The previous afternoon, I had baited about sixteen hundred separate hooks with small pieces of squid and mackerel I had cut up. The process is as follows: attached to each hook is a piece of two-hundred-pound test (breaking strength) monofilament line about three feet long. On the other end of the monofilament line is what is known as a snap. It's about four inches long and looks like a very large safety pin. The design makes it easy to attach it to a line. The snap, monofilament and hook are known as a ganging. When I bait these gangings, I carefully place the baited hook in a five-gallon plastic bucket. The monofilament line comes up over the top edge of the bucket, and the snap hangs down over the outside edge. Each bucket holds about three hundred baited hooks.

When I get where I want to set out these hooks, I am going to throw out a surface buoy and run out an amount of line greater than the depth of the water. Then I will attach a small anchor and throw it overboard. As it sinks, I will start running my boat ahead. I will take each hook successively out of the bucket and attach the snap to the line, called ground line or back line, as it passes by my location at the steering station. I have developed a system unique to my boat where the line stored in a large former lobster holding area on the port side is pulled up and around through the pilothouse. The strain of first, the sinking anchor and, subsequently, the line trailing out behind the moving boat pull the line through a series of fair leads. As I snap the baited gangings on the constantly moving line, they pass into long sections of three-inch-diameter PVC pipe. The other end of the pipe extends about thirty feet from my setting location, along the edge of the starboard side deck to just past the stern of the boat. As the ground line and baited hooks come out of the PVC pipe, they sink to the ocean floor. There, the baited

The *Mistress* underway.

The *Mistress* and Hugh Bishop ready for winter fishing.

hooks will hopefully attract enough fish to put a smile on my face as I come around Eastern Point and head up Gloucester Harbor early this coming evening. There is about six miles of ground line to be set out. I divide it into at least two, and probably three, separate locations, depending on what my fish finder tells me when I arrive at the grounds. Setting out will take two to three hours.

The potential smile is a long way away at 2:30 a.m.

Shortly after setting out, haul back will commence. Six miles of ground line and the sixteen hundred gangings and hooks will be brought back inside the boat by means of a hydraulic line hauler, the speed of which I adjust at the rail with a control valve handle. My outlook on the day will improve with each caught fish. The whole retrieving procedure will take six to eight hours. On the way to Gloucester, the fish will have to be gutted (entrails removed) and the boat cleaned up. My girlfriend, the automatic pilot, will make it possible for me to do this work alone.

I've gone line trawling now for thirty-seven seasons. There was one exception. That was the winter of 1976. That year I spent the winter in East Boothbay, Maine, working with the crew who built the boat I'm going to be on in half an hour. The season runs from December to May. This is when colder water temperature drives small sharks called dogfish from the waters in which I fish. These waters have generally been from twenty to forty miles off the coast of eastern Massachusetts.

Dogfish eat the "good fish" like cod and haddock, snarling and damaging the gear. In the past, dogfish have been worthless, but in recent years, a market has developed for them, particularly in England, where the fillets are sold as part of "fish and chips." Even so, they don't command much of a price. As far as any fisherman, commercial or recreational, feels, the world would be better off without them. I know I have a long day ahead, but in January, I won't have to worry about getting "dogged up."

In the winter, day boat fishermen are totally dependent on the weather, and often only two or three days a week are available for production. The United States government has forced its ugly presence into our lives in the form of the National Marine Fisheries Service. When these bureaucrats came along in the 1970s, they had a small degree of reason, but that has long since departed. Confusing and contradictory regulations have taken much of the enjoyment and satisfaction away from commercial fishing, but even these government employees can't control my anticipation for the day ahead.

Because of the restrictions and regulations, I have chosen to downsize, and my fifty-foot line trawler, on which I used to have a crew of two, is now operated by me alone. I'm the captain, cook, deckhand and any other title that is needed. With this option, I now only have to support myself. I sell my fish at the Gloucester Fish Auction. Generally, when I tie up at the end of a trip to unload my fish, someone of the ever-changing unloading personnel will say, "Where's your crew?" When I tell them, "I'm it," there is a comment to the effect of (I've heard it many times), "You must be crazy fishing that size boat alone in the winter."

Always in my head and sometimes to the questioner, if I'm in the mood, I say things like, "When I fish alone I always have good company." I'm going to spend the day alone. The weather looks good for January, and I'm looking forward to it.

After buying a cup of coffee at Dunkin' Donuts in Salem, I park my truck at Pickering Wharf and walk down the gangway. My fifty-foot boat, the *Mistress*, is tied up and sitting peacefully at her winter berth in front of Victoria Station Restaurant. The water in the marina area is like a sheet of glass, flat and still. Thin ice has formed overnight around the boat due to the fourteen-degree temperature.

I jump aboard and slide open the back door to the pilothouse, as I have done so many times before. The pilothouse is warm from the diesel-fired

**Spirit of '76 Bookstore & Card Shop**
107 Pleasant Street
Marblehead, Massachusetts 01945
781.631.7199
Thank you for being a
shop-local hero!

Date: 12-17-2011
Sale: 176614
Time: 02:52 PM

Marblehead's First Harbor: The Rich History of a S
1609494970      Retail Price: $23.99
                Item Price: $23.99        $23.99

1 Items                  Subtotal: $23.99
              Sales Tax ( 6.250 % ): $1.50
                            Total: $25.49

                  Cash Payment: $26.00

                Amount Tendered: $26.00
                   Change Due: $0.51

Printed by: Hilary          Register: Cash Drawer 1

December 17, 2011 02:52 PM

Store credit, *WITH RECEIPT*,
within 30 days of purchase.
Calendars & holiday cards are not returnable.

STORE HOURS: Mon-Fri 8-8,
Sat 8-6, Sun 11-5
www.hugobookstores.com

Friend us on Facebook:    Spirit-Bookstore Staff!
Follow us on Twitter:     Spiritof76books

My wife had packed the food for me
ag, along with the other necessities
.

me a shot of adrenaline. The VHF
unnel used by myself and the only
formation. The two lorans and two
he boat's position, and radar reveals
onditions, the radar will show objects
n-up period, I cast off the lines and
h and down the channel past Derby

or; the engine is up to temperature.
settle into my chair, which mounts
I have a good view of everything to
one step away, are my hard-wired
. I put the boat on autopilot, which
hout this, I could never fish alone.
aving exact steering ability, it never
t the end of a trip. It also never says,
ng out for an extra day—things of
If it was a person, I could fall in love

of fishing over thirty-five years ago. I
ugh thick fog with visibility of twenty-
s to reach my destination. I relied on
luck and loud fognorns required by large vessels. While I had several close encounters, I accepted it as part of the business, as did all other fishermen. Small boat radars were unheard of in the early 1960s.

The lights of Marblehead pass to starboard, and I am going down Salem Sound toward Baker's Island. Any nice weekend day in the summer, there would be hundreds of recreational vessels, all sizes, rushing in every direction, but this morning the *Mistress* is the only boat moving. That's the way I like it—my boat and me "going fishing."

The blinking light of Baker's Island Lighthouse passes to starboard, and about a mile ahead, I can see on my radar Gales Ledge Nun, marking dangerous water just inside it. That passes to port. My planned fishing area for the day is now about thirty or so miles ahead on Jeffreys Ledge. To reach there, I plan to pass along the east side or "back shore" of Cape Ann and past Thacher Island with its two light towers.

As I approach the Eastern Point Whistle Buoy off the entrance to Gloucester Harbor, several vessel lights are visible. These are day boat fishermen coming out of Gloucester. There are very few of us left in Marblehead these days, but the fleet in Gloucester, while less than former years, is still quite substantial. Around 4:00 a.m. on a nice winter's morning, there is always significant fishing boat traffic. Some are heading southeast to Stellwagen Bank and will intersect my course, which is about east-northeast. This morning, there are three or four vessels that are going to come very close to me. I alter course slightly and allow them to pass in front of me, even though I have the right of way under maritime rules.

Eastern Point Light passes to port. Ahead, I can see the flashing light of one of the Thacher Island towers. My next and last visual aid is Thacher Island Whistle Buoy, seven miles ahead, which I plan to pass nearby.

My Dunkin' Donuts coffee was finished in Salem Sound. Now it's time for a cup of my own and the foil-wrapped package marked "breakfast." I always have a kettle of hot water on top of the galley stove, so the coffee is quickly made. The packet, leftover scrambled eggs and ham from yesterday's breakfast in our kitchen, is popped into the oven for a quick reheat. Immediately, I feel an attachment to home.

Soon, I'm sitting in my chair enjoying the food. I'm getting my body and mind ready for the day ahead. The boats from Gloucester are spread out by now. All of us are heading to where we plan to start our individual day of fishing. Each skipper is, to some degree, wondering what the day will bring; uncertainty is one of the fuels of real living. Now I'm starting to get farther and farther away from other boats. A period of reflection starts. I often ask myself, "How much longer will I be able to do this?" The answer is always, "As long as I can!"

Thacher's Buoy passes about one hundred yards to starboard. The sky is full of stars, the wind northwest about ten knots. There is still no sign of first light in the eastern sky. I settle down for the hour-plus ride down Jeffreys Ledge. All is well with the world.

The radio has been completely silent since I left Salem. Suddenly, "*Lucky Strike* calling the *Mistress*," crackles over the radio on Channel 19. It is my very close friend, Jeff Tutein, a fellow line trawler from Gloucester. The time is 4:50 a.m. All is dark except the lights from other fishing boats. Aware of his schedule, I know he would have left his berth at Beacon Marine Basin in East Gloucester to arrive where he is planning to fish that day before first light. He is likely one of the half dozen or so boat lights visible from my position. Any confidential fishing information Jeff and I would have exchanged by cellphone. We only use Channel 19 for social exchanges between us.

"Did you hear about your old buddy, Brownie?"

I say, "No, what are you talking about?"

I know right away he is referring to my longtime friend of almost fifty years, Bob Brown. Jeff's voice comes back over the radio: "Well, yesterday afternoon when I was on my boat, there was a lot of commotion over by the State Pier where the *Hannah Boden* ties up." The *Hannah Boden* is Bob's ninety-five-foot offshore steel fishing vessel.

I know Jeff doesn't have a direct view of the *Hannah Boden* from his dock in East Gloucester. I answer back, "How do you know that? You can't see the State Pier from where you tie up."

He replies, "Well, I'll tell you this much. I saw a helicopter lift off and head toward Boston. After I finished baiting up, as I was going to my truck, someone told me that Bob was the one in the helicopter. He had fallen from the top of the access ladder and landed between his boat and the pier pilings. The guy saw him on the stretcher as they put him in the chopper and said he looked terrible."

Numbly, I reply, "I can't believe it."

The radio goes silent. I start to think of Bob and myself and how I got to be where I am at this moment. He was, let's see, a class behind me in high school and less than a year younger than I. What made him fall off the ladder? This could have been me. I have been fairly careful not to run a fisherman's body on McDonald's hamburgers, but diet is not so much discussed in these days. Stress, another silent adversary, is mentioned here and there. Bob certainly had his share of that, much of which he brought on himself by his actions.

The memories…all those years…How could I ever forget any of it— the old-timers, the fun, the tranquil beauty, the hard work, the fury of the Atlantic Ocean, the sadness and, once again, a possible tragedy.

# Chapter 2

# Bob Brown

**M**y relationship with Bob Brown goes back to 1951, when I was on the Marblehead Junior High School football team as the starting fullback and linebacker. I barely knew Bob. I was a ninth grader. He was a year behind and the backup for my position. By the middle of the 1951 football season, he had beaten me out as the starter, and I was relegated to playing only defense.

Bob had a running style that got his opponents going in one direction. He then executed a deft fake, leaving his potential tacklers wrapping their arms around air (and shaking their heads). This was a forerunner of things to come later in life.

During the summer of 1952, Bob started showing up at Fisherman's Beach in Little Harbor where we all moored our boats. He had a small wooden skiff with a one-cylinder engine in it that ran less than rarely. He usually rowed around to a handful of lobster traps he had acquired; I had my dory and string of traps, and we soon became good friends. Bob took to the life of growing up around the beach just as my old friend Dave Hildreth and I had. The next year, he had a sturdy skiff, built and powered with a ten-horsepower Johnson outboard motor. His industry was obvious.

The years in high school seemed to go by in a blur. I graduated from Marblehead High in 1955. In March of that year, I bought a twenty-eight-foot boat in Manchester. A month or so later, Bob bought the *White Horse*, the same size and style as my boat, from Little Harbor lobsterman Henry Briggs. Henry was modernizing to a larger boat with a pilothouse.

# The Rich History of a Small Fishing Port

The summer of 1955, Bob and I spent a great deal of time together. We bought a bait net for pogies. In the afternoons, we set it just southeast of Coney (pronounced Cunney) Island Ledge overnight. Leaving the Cove before daylight the next morning, each in our own lobster boat, we anchored one near the net. Then, in the other boat, we hauled the net. Usually, our catch provided enough pogies so we could each go our separate ways, hauling our individual strings. A friendly rivalry developed over the size of our catches. Small bets were placed.

Evenings we often went on double dates. Life was great! Being eighteen years old, with a lobster boat during the day and with my pretty girlfriend evenings and my whole life ahead of me, there has never been anything again quite like that carefree existence. Other things, in a different way, have been terrific, but that song "I Wish I Was Eighteen Again" rings so true.

September came on schedule, and I was off to college. Here I quickly found there were many young men my age who were a great deal smarter than I was. Life no longer felt so relaxed. Bob still had his final year at Marblehead High.

Successive years in the late 1950s had a pattern for me. I worked on my lobster boat and traps during college vacations and put them to good use in the summers.

Bob finished high school in 1956 and soon fell in love with a beautiful girl, Linda Nielsen, the daughter of Aage Nielsen, one of the top naval yacht architects in the United States. The next year, they were married. Their first child, Peter, became my godson.

By 1960, I had finished college and my active military duty in the army. Bob had spent two years in the navy. We both found ourselves back at Little Harbor. The carefree days of the summer of 1955 were gone, never to return. This was especially true for Bob and Linda because they now had a second child, Andrea.

In 1961, I also married and asked Bob to be my best man. We both had lobster boats built that year by separate builders in Maine. I named my new boat *Mistress*, and Bob named his *Sea Fever*.

During the early winter of 1962, Bob and I fished line trawls no more than twelve miles from Marblehead. Our new boats were considered modern for the day, but small-boat electronics were unknown to us. Navigation was accomplished by the dead reckoning method. We both had well-adjusted compasses, watches and rpm (revolutions per minute) indicators on our engine instrument panels. We previously had run a measured mile off Marblehead and knew how fast our boats went at a certain rpm. Time and

Bob Brown on launching day of the first *Sea Fever*, fall 1961. *Brown Collection.*

rpms determined how far we went (reminiscent of a school math class). We had flashing depth finders, which showed how deep the water was. Landmarks on shore, for instance, "this water tower over that island," were used to tell us if we were on target. Some of the spots we fished were told to us by more experienced fishermen. Others we learned by ourselves, Bob and I exchanging ideas.

As spring approached, together, but each in our own boat, we ventured out to Stellwagen Bank, called Middle Bank by commercial fishermen. This was a little over twenty miles from Marblehead. It was the first time either of us had lobstered or fished out of the sight of land. Most older fishermen in Marblehead told us we would be sorry if we kept going out that far, but to us, going out over the horizon really got our blood moving.

As the 1960s wore on, I decided to leave full-time lobstering and fishing and get a "real job." My fishing efforts were confined to weekends. I found work ashore interesting but not the same. Daydreams of catching something and thoughts like, "I wish I were out" were constant. I satisfied my need as best I could with a small string of lobster traps and weekend winter line trawling. After 1963, for eleven years, that was my pattern.

Bob Brown started to build quite a reputation for himself in the *Sea Fever*. He lobstered off Marblehead during the spring, summer and fall, and in the winter, he went line trawling. He "went out" in much rougher weather, and much farther, than the average man, and with his work ethic and aggressiveness, he became known as a "high liner." His nickname became "Suicide Brown."

Everyone talks about the biggest fish, the biggest catch and so forth, but the following is the way it was.

By 1965, Bob was tying up the *Sea Fever* in Gloucester for the winter tub trawling season and driving home each night to Marblehead. He had a Gloucester man named Joe Mitchell as his crew. Joe was big and powerful, with many fishing relatives in town. One twenty-six-hour day in early April 1965, they caught ten thousand pounds of haddock on Middle Bank with ten tubs of baited trawls. The way Bob rigged his gear, this was a total of four thousand hooks. Baiting, hauling and, of course, dressing the fish was all done by hand.

The *Sea Fever* left Gloucester for that trip about two hours before daylight the first morning and pulled into Madruga's Fresh Fish Wharf, next to the Gloucester House, at daylight the next day. The waterline on the boat, including the bow, was invisible. The price received was nine cents per pound. There were a lot of fish at that time, so even with the low price, the paycheck was a good one.

Looking back, the 1960s were pivotal and transitional times for small-boat fishing. Several significant things happened to facilitate change. Electronics started to become available and affordable. Loran, particularly, helped the adventurous. It gave a skipper an accurate and repeatable precise location when steaming out of sight of land. Previously, Bob and I had not left our marker buoys on the trawls' ends for fear we would never find them again. Better recorders made it possible to tell hard from soft bottom. We could also discern fish for the first time. By the late 1960s, small-boat radar gradually became a reality, and wire lobster traps were first built. In the boat department, fiberglass construction started. This was to eventually drive most wooden boat builders out of business.

Our high school years were now well behind us. Little did we realize all that lay ahead.

# Chapter 3

# Ed Hawkes

**M**y father taught me to row at age five. At that time, he built a six-foot pram out of plywood, which was perfect for the baby steps of a future mariner. At age six, he taught me to sail in a larger craft. This boat was one of a class of about ten that he and a group of his friends had built in the mid-1930s. These boats were built primarily to sail in winter, or frostbite, as it is known. These men started the second winter competition in the United States, the first being a few years before in Larchmont, New York. The men in Marblehead each built their sailing prams from the same drawing, or one design. They held their winter races on the weekends in the shelter of Brown's Island. This small fleet was called the Cocktail Fleet, each being named after an alcoholic drink. I learned to sail in the *Mint Julep*.

By the time I was seven, I felt confident sailing around Little Harbor, but I had outgrown the six-footer. That winter, my father built a ten-foot pram for me, as it was obvious to him that I had a young, but eager, passion for rowing. I had already explored Little Harbor and its working fleet of twelve to fifteen dories and powered lobster boats. My interest grew, especially when a lobsterman aboard his boat greeted me as I rowed past. They were a wonderful and friendly group of men.

The summer of 1946 comes into focus. That year, I was nine years old. My parents were either naïve or had enough confidence in me to let me expand my rowing boundaries. I was now able to row anywhere in Marblehead Harbor and out to Peaches Point. One morning, under the

My father teaching me how to sail in the *Mint Julep*.

influence of a slightly older boy, he and I ventured all the way to Salem Willows. Just as we got there, thick coastal fog set in. It didn't bother me, but apparently my mother's cry of my name was heard from Peaches Point to Naugus Head. This came as she frantically drove in and out of the estates along the shore, looking and calling for me. We arrived back in

Many hours were spent rowing around Little Harbor.

Little Harbor by mid-afternoon, nonplussed. This incident resulted in a restricted territory for a while.

The powered fleet in Little Harbor consisted of boats twenty-two to twenty-eight feet. They had spray hoods, which covered the forward half of each boat. This afforded some protection from wind and spray, but not much. The boat engines were either marine or, in the case of older boats, automotive. The latter still had the stick shift and a separate means to engage and disengage the clutch.

Traps on these boats were hauled by a brass winch on the end of a shaft powered by belts off the front of the engine. Separate clutches to start and stop the winch were unknown. Therefore, the winch turned constantly and slowed down or sped up with the engine.

The exception to this fleet was a "modern" boat in the Cove called *Bob*. It was built in 1945 by Albert Cloutman for his son, Bob, who was just back from World War II. The *Bob* was a breakthrough and forerunner of design to come. It had a trunk cabin and pilothouse but was considered too big by the old-time fishermen, though it was only thirty feet long.

Marblehead lobstermen could fish only single traps by state law. Upon reaching one of his buoys, a lobsterman gaffed it, pulling in an amount of

A typical lobster boat of the 1940s with a spray hood. *Bates Collection.*

slack line, put the line over a rail-side davit lock at eye level and took it down to the turning winch. Two turns of rope were taken around the winch and a strain put on this line. The strain took away most of the effort needed to bring the trap to the surface and up to the rail. With his arms moving as he handled the winch and the special motion needed to boat the trap, an experienced lobsterman made this look as easy and graceful as Ted Williams hitting a home run.

However, a constantly moving winch could be dangerous, especially if what was known as a "round turn" occurred. Here, the line rode under itself and kept wrapping around the winch. This resulted in the trap coming up, with the lobsterman having lost control of the situation. One of three things could then happen:

If he realized the problem soon enough, he could pull the end of the line he had in his hand as hard and as fast as he could, his goal being to pull the increasing ball of line off the end of the winch.

He could stop the engine. This, of course, stopped the winch.

Worst of all, if neither the first or second option had worked, the trap continued coming up, hitting the davit block and breaking something—either the line or part of the lobsterman.

Accidents were not unheard of.

The men who ran these boats were a diverse group. They were divided into two loose categories. One group was men like Bob Cloutman, Ed Hawkes, Ed's younger brother, John, and Dan Peach. These men were generally younger and had just returned from World War II. They had seen and learned a great deal and, in many cases, had been fired at in anger. The second group was, for the most part, older and had lobstered and fished most of their working lives. These men included Henry Briggs, Ralph Conner, Grover Cleveland Luscomb, Ern Cronk, Emerson "Azor" Goodwin, Gerald Smith and others. Both groups had ancestors who went back to the early roots of Marblehead.

In October 1945, Ed Hawkes had returned to Marblehead after four years in the Royal Canadian Air Force. He had spent his boyhood years in the 1920s and '30s around Little Harbor and knew it intimately. Like other veterans, he had to restart his life. After what he had seen and done in the war, he found returning home to be somewhat "flat." He told me that he could have had a job flying for Northeast Airlines, but he considered it like driving a bus compared to a racecar. When you have had 3600 horsepower at your fingertips in a Mosquito Bomber in wartime combat, civilian life offered no comparable experience.

Immediately after Ed returned home, he ran Gerald Smith's powerboat while Gerald was recuperating from a serious infection. Ed then decided to go lobstering on his own. During the winter of 1946, he built a string of one hundred wooden lobster traps. With very limited funds, he borrowed Gerald's eighteen-foot dory. This dory was named *Sluggo*, which was Gerald's nickname for his seven-year-old son. Sluggo was a popular comic book character of the day. Ed's borrowed dory was a type known as a Chamberlain or Marblehead Gunning dory. The class of dory had been designed, built and improved over the years by William Chamberlain. He had a boat-building shop off Orne Street on Wadden Court from the late nineteenth to well into the early twentieth century. These dories were, and still are, considered the premier all-around dory. In 1996, with my future wife, we visited the historic Seattle Boat Museum. I immediately noticed a Chamberlain dory among the many classic boats there. The description of the dory on the plaque was correct. I paid a small fee, and we went for a row. This boat, in a museum three thousand miles from its origin, was a true tribute to Mr. Chamberlain.

During the summer of 1946, even with my temporary boundary restrictions, I began to be aware of Ed Hawkes. When he was fishing the

Old-timers in the 1940s. Left to right: Ern Cronk, Ralph Conner, Grover Cleveland Luscomb, Herb Dixey, Henry Briggs, Albert Cloutman and Gerald Smith. *Conner Collection.*

*Sluggo*, he rowed lobsterman-style between traps. This meant using rowlocks that were special, raised oarlocks high enough above the dory rail to accommodate a standing rower. The individual faced toward the bow. This way, he could see where he was going, and upon coming to one of his buoys, he could gaff it and start pulling the trap up by hand. For a long row, say to Cat Island, it was normal to sit on one of the more forward thwarts and row conventionally. A dory fisherman like Ed in the 1940s hauled about one hundred traps a day. Different men fished different areas, but a typical string for an individual would run from Fort Sewall to beyond Peaches Point. Then he might row across to Coney Island Ledge, where he had another string of traps. After that, it was on to Cat Island for the final portion of his day's work. If a man started hauling about dawn for this size string, he probably would finish by late morning. Often, by this time, a light, onshore fair wind would be starting. Ed's day frequently ended near Cat Island. He had a small, portable sail called a leg o' mutton, which he could easily raise, ending his day by sailing back to Little Harbor. Ed recently told me, "This would be with a smile on my face." I could tell from the way he said it that these were great memories for him.

Ed was at the low end of the lobstermen's hierarchy, but he was determined not to stay there. As the summer wore on, he became an almost magical figure for me. He was extremely good-looking. With his shirt off and rowing along, his biceps would bulge bigger than those of Charles Atlas. In short, he looked like he had come out of central casting in Hollywood. Often I went rowing with my contemporary and friend Dave Hildreth. We would say to each other that when we grew up, we wanted to be just like Ed.

I have heard and read about the thoughts and feelings of World War II veterans during that special year of 1946. They were home after a long absence and had the relief and satisfaction that comes from accomplishing a very hard and risky job. Somewhere in there, they came to the realization that they had experienced things they would never know again. Men who never confront danger cannot appreciate the aftermath. Ed must have had thoughts of his war experiences as he rowed from trap to trap in the waters he knew so well from his youth. As things you like never seem to start soon enough and end too quickly, the lobster season of 1946 was over by about Thanksgiving. It was time for Ed to move on.

Albert Cloutman had retired as the foreman of Graves Boatyard of Little Harbor. He and his son Bob constructed a boat shop next to their homes on Calthrop Road. Ultimately, many thirty-foot lobster boats, dories and small yachts were built in this shop for North Shore fishermen and sailors.

Ed gave the father-and-son team their first order for the winter of 1946–47. Albert and Bob built him a thirty-foot, V-bottom, or hard chine, lobster boat. It had a trunk cabin but no windshield or pilothouse and a Chrysler Crown marine engine. The total cost, ready to step into, was $3,500.

Back then, the launching of a new wooden vessel was a grand occasion to celebrate. It was also the time to showcase the great skill and dedication of these exceptional craftsmen. A new wooden boat is the closest an object can be to something animate. If it is a commercial vessel, its new owner is just about always in a personal economic depression from its construction costs, but it represents a new beginning and a path to financial improvement.

Such was the case on an early March day in 1947. Ed's new vessel sat on a cradle well below the high-tide mark at Fisherman's Beach. Rocks had been placed on the cradle to hold it down until the incoming tide would float it off.

*Lizzie H* at the top of Fisherman's Beach prior to launching. Ed's father, Winslow, is in the foreground. *Hawkes Collection.*

According to a story in the *Marblehead Messenger*, Ed's party upheld the tradition of a gala launching event. A large crowd of fellow fishermen, friends and onlookers was in attendance. Chowder was served. Absent from the newspaper article, but mentioned by Ed, was the fact that there was "plenty of liquid refreshment." Everyone's spirits rose with the tide. Ed's mother, Elizabeth, christened the new vessel *Lizzie H* in her honor. As the boat floated from the cradle that day, Ed's hopes were with her. In one year, he had gone from having one of the smallest boats in Little Harbor to one of the largest. Along with the *Bob*, the *Lizzie H* was now the queen of the fleet.

Ed utilized the *Lizzie H* to the fullest as the 1947 season went on. He lobstered and also made occasional two-day cod, hand lining trips southeast of the Isle of Shoals, New Hampshire, spending the night in the protected harbor there. The next winter, Ed went line trawling three to ten miles off Marblehead for ground fish. In addition, he rigged the *Lizzie H* for fish dragging with appropriate net and doors. Dragging was undertaken to either get bait for lobster traps or, at certain times, get fish for sale. It was common in those days to drag in the soft, muddy bottom, more or less between the Outer Pigs and Egg Rock. This area was inside the three-mile limit for legal dragging but was commonly chanced by local, smaller boats hoping to avoid detection.

*Lizzie H* underway after launching. *Hawkes Collection.*

One day, with limited visibility, Ed was engaged in such a practice. Suddenly, he was aware that the state game warden's boat was coming alongside him with several occupants. Sensing an obvious violation, one officer in particular was making quite a spectacle of himself, including waving a pistol in Ed's general direction. Known for having a temper, Ed didn't try to talk his way out of this predicament. He did, however, tell the showman words to this effect: "I just got back from where there were a lot of guns, and some of them were fired at me. Now either you put yours away or it's going to find its way to a delicate part of your anatomy." Apparently, Ed was very effective at expressing himself, and the gun disappeared, but a substantial fine resulted, paid shortly thereafter at Lynn District Court. Ed said it was worth it.

Frequently, lobstermen set floating bait nets for pogies. These supplemented their bait needs, which were largely filled by a truck delivering filleted redfish from Gloucester. The bait truck generally came Monday, Wednesday and Friday in the afternoon and made deliveries at Commercial Street, State Street, Fort Beach, Little Harbor and Studie Smith's steps in Doliber's Cove. The bait nets were set overnight, especially if there was a shortage of redfish. They were then hauled in the afternoon after finishing the traps. Often, two men teamed up to haul the net together. I well remember being ten years old and hanging around afternoons at the beach with Dave. If we thought a bait net haul might be imminent, we made ourselves as obvious as possible. When men like Ed Hawkes or Bob Cloutman asked us if we wanted to go out and haul the net with them, nothing was more exciting. They often let us steer the boat to its location, which was usually just southeast of Coney Island Ledge. The net was hauled by hand, and we were allowed to help take the pogies out. Total exhilaration!

By 1948, Dave and I had really become students and worshippers of the Little Harbor fishermen. We followed their every move in good weather and bad. In winter and on stormy days, we were allowed inside their shanties, where trawls were baited, traps were built and stories were told. By listening, a great deal could be learned. It was before the days of synthetic rope. The tarred sisal rope used for line trawls and lobster warps had a certain distinctive smell, almost pleasant, that you don't experience anymore. That's one of the many things I miss about those days.

That fall, there was one day that stands out in my mind. Dave and I were in the sixth grade at the Gerry School, where our room had a good view of the main harbor. This particular day, there were gale-force northeast winds of about thirty-five knots. However, there was not a cloud in the sky, a typical dry northeaster. When I got to school that morning, I plainly remember the sun shining on the white caps rolling down Marblehead Harbor.

Dave, living right on the edge of the Cove, had a much better view of our idols. That morning, as usual, we compared notes. I remember saying to him, "I bet no one is out lobstering this morning."

*Lizzie H*, 1957, now owned by John Hawkes. *Peach Collection.*

Dave said excitedly, "Ed's out!"

I couldn't believe it. I found out later that he did go out that day, according to Ed, "to see if the *Lizzie H* is any good."

During grammar school, we went home for lunch. Upon arrival, I ran up to my parents' bedroom window, which had a good view of the bay. Just then, I saw a cloud of spray coming across Marblehead Harbor from the direction of Marblehead Rock. It was the *Lizzie H*! Ed was returning from what we call "the westard," a general area anywhere south and west of Tinker's Island, where he had been hauling pots. Ed's torso was plainly visible above the trunk cabin. He was dressed in black rubber oilskins and wearing what was known as a Portuguese round rain hat. From my position, I could see him, his red face glistening from salt water. As the boat rounded the northeast end of Priests' Island, she was bucking and tossing violently, and spray was flying everywhere. In a few seconds, the boat was heading downwind into the safety of Little Harbor. Even at my young age, I knew I had seen something special—a vision I have never forgotten. Ed's lobstering and fishing life went on, and he developed a reputation as one of, if not the, top fishermen in Marblehead. In 1954, he sold the *Lizzie H* to his brother John for $2,000. His commercial fishing days were done.

*Chapter 4*

# Stewart Smith

One summer evening in early June 1947, I was a ten-year-old boy sitting on a stone wall watching Mr. Smith launch his boat from the beach by my parents' house. He made his living primarily from lobster fishing but supplemented his income with odd jobs in the neighborhood.

Stewart Smith was born in 1895 in the family homestead at 32 Beacon Street, Marblehead. This was home for Stewart and his brothers and sisters, as well as for several previous generations of Smiths.

One of his sisters, Sadie, ran a small store that was part of the house. Here she sold homemade ice cream until nearly the end of World War II. When her freezer gave up, and with no extra money to buy a new one, Sadie fell back on another primary product: homemade fudge. She also sold candy bars and soda or "tonic," as we called it. Extra pennies, nickels and dimes that my sister and I saved would find their way into Sadie's store. Every child of that era in the old part of town had the same enjoyable experience. I remember a commercial sign on the corner of the house next to the store's entrance: "Hires Root Beer made with real root juices." The implied benefit of "root juices" was never revealed.

After his marriage, Stewart lived with his wife, Helen, in part of the second story over Sadie's store. They never had any children. Helen worked the better part of seven days a week running her small variety store at the entrance to Fisherman's Beach. Sadie's and Helen's were typical of the many tiny stores that dotted the streets of old Marblehead. Each small enterprise had a personality unique to its owner.

Studie and his brother Jake on the beach at Doliber's Cove, circa 1916. *Marblehead Historical Commission.*

If I could pick one moment in time that started me on the path of being a commercial fisherman and all the adventures that followed, it would be that June evening watching Mr. Smith. He was waiting for the tide to float his lobster boat off its winter storage cradle, having moved it down the beach on rollers and planks during the previous afternoon at low tide.

That evening, Stewart engaged me in conversation and, among other things, asked me if I would like to go out lobstering that summer. My excitement level immediately rose, and I, of course, said yes.

About a month later, at 4:15 a.m., I was standing by the steps across the street from his house with my little lunch bag my mother had packed for me. The time to meet was 4:30, but I wasn't going to be late. The steps led down to the Cove where he moored his punt.

This was a long time ago, but I remember that morning vividly. In the darkness, I could make out someone walking toward me from the opposite direction of Stewart's house. It turned out to be Watson Curtis, who lived around the corner with his parents. Watson was already an established lobsterman, nineteen years old, very aggressive and hardworking. From a ten-year-old's perspective, he seemed like a young superman. I noticed he had his lunch bag in one hand and a long-necked quart of milk in the other.

Watson gave me a cheerful "hello" and said, "You must be going out with Stu." He wished me a good day and continued on his way to Little Harbor and his own lobster boat.

Stewart came out of his house shortly. We got into his punt, and he rowed us out to his boat in Doliber's Cove a few hundred yards from Grace Oliver's Beach. I could see the first sign of dawn in the eastern sky, the first of thousands of sunrises I would witness in my fishing career. I didn't know it at the time, but a lifelong fishing addiction seed was being planted. It would bear fruit for years to come.

We got on Studie's boat, and as he prepared to start the engine, I heard a lobster boat come out from behind the east side of Brown's Island and stop at the mouth of Doliber's Cove. The morning was very quiet. Then there was the sound of a trap being hauled. It was still too dark to see who it was. Studie told me, "That's Henry Briggs; he likes to get an early start." Early start—we could barely see, and he had probably already hauled three or four traps.

Studie's boat was nothing special; as a matter of fact, it was at the bottom of the spectrum technologically speaking. The boat itself was a former World War I navy launch, about twenty-six feet. It was very heavily constructed of wood and fastened with copper rivets, considered to give excellent strength and durability. This was necessary because maintenance was not one of Studie's strong suits.

The engine was a used Chevrolet car engine with the original transmission, which meant that when you started the transmission with its stick shift, the clutch had to be engaged with a specially adapted lever for

Stu Smith's lobster boat ready for spring launching.

a boat. One hand handled the clutch lever and the other hand the stick shift, a far cry from modern, single-handled marine controls. There was a small cockpit behind the box covering the engine. A brass winch stuck out from the back of the box. Lobster pots were hauled by the turning winch. Power was supplied by a flat belt connecting the other end of the winch shaft and the front of the Chevrolet engine. Boards covered some of the cockpit floor. No attempt had been made to fit them together, and it was easy to step between them into the dank bilge below. Studie got water out of the boat by bailing the bilge with a large tin can into a two-gallon bucket and pouring the bucket over the side. Bilge water was always black, a combination of the fresh drippings from a newly hauled trap, bait juice from the bushel baskets of fermenting redfish, oil and grease from the engine and the remains of dead crabs that commonly found their way into the bilge.

Steering was accomplished by means of an upright mounted tiller, really just a stick that had rope tied to it that ran to either side of the boat and back through pulleys to the rudder. This was before the days of synthetic rope, and the sisal rope he used would expand or shrink, depending on the amount of dampness it absorbed. Almost daily adjustments had to be made depending on the weather conditions.

Caught lobsters were stored in a wooden barrel that sat in the middle of the boat, just forward of the engine box. There was a small belt-driven pump next to the engine that supplied water to the barrel.

Studie hauled from the port side. There was a space on the starboard side between the engine box and starboard rail large enough to walk through. Studie told me to stand in that space so I would be out of the way. If I got tired, I was to sit down on the remaining thwart from navy days, which ran completely across the boat just forward of the lobster barrel. This seat also gave the boat strength.

I spent my first day lobstering standing or sitting as I was instructed. Studie showed me how to plug the lobster claws to prevent being bitten. He spent idle time in the winter whittling these wooden pegs.

Starting at the mouth of Doliber's Cove and working through the ledges and islands to the east of Marblehead, we passed along Studie's string and by noon had hauled his one hundred single-buoy traps. Now we were near the Dry Breakers southeast of Bakers Island, and we headed back to Doliber's Cove. Studie rowed us in. I went home, and he took his lobsters in his wheelbarrow to Barber's Lobster Pool at Little Harbor. I think of this significant day often.

Studie may have gotten a low grade on boat maintenance, but he was considered an A-plus person. He was a very gentle soul. In the years that followed, I went out with him many times. I loved his tales of things he did when he was young. He gave me a small punt that I used in 1949 to set my first two traps, which he also gave me. The first few times I went out by myself in May 1949, he rowed along in his punt to make sure I was all right and issued safety tips to me. On Mother's Day, I caught my first legal lobster, which I gave to my mum as a present. Studie made me a wooden twine needle and then taught me how to knit heads. Heads were the netting that guided lobsters into the traps. All lobstermen made their own traps and fastened their handmade heads into them. I used to spend a good deal of time at his shanty on the hill above his house. Here, I would help him work on buoys or traps and listen to more stories. I'm sure, looking back, that I was the son he never had. Our friendship endured for the rest of his life.

I last saw Studie in his bedroom over Sadie's now closed store. It was 1985. He was bedridden and in very poor health. With complications from diabetes, he had to have one foot amputated above the ankle. We engaged in small talk. He asked me how fishing was, simple, basic fishermen talk. I told him goodbye and said I would be back soon. He died two days later.

There was a service at Waterside Cemetery at Studie's grave. I was standing next to Watson Curtis. Watson had many of the same memories I had, since Studie had also helped him on his way. We looked at each other after the service, not knowing what to say. It was a calm, peaceful day. Watson finally found words as he looked off into space. He said, "It's a beautiful day to haul pots, and I know Stu would like to be out there doing that!" This spoke eloquently of the bond between Watson, Studie, myself and all commercial fishermen—it was remembering the traps, nets and lines you have hauled with always the hope to haul some more.

*Chapter 5*

# Little Harbor

**I**'ve gone in and out of Little Harbor hundreds of times over the years, but even now, I don't really take it for granted. The familiar setting is home to me, but I realize it has a history as rich as its physical setting.

Gerry Island forms the eastern side of the main channel. It is named for Marblehead's honored citizen Elbridge Gerry, one of the fifty-six signers of the Declaration of Independence. Elbridge owned the island from 1797 to 1806, but the Gerry family had had possession since 1750. I guess I'd thought of him a few times out of the thousands I'd viewed this landmark but more probably realized who he was because the grammar school I attended was the Elbridge Gerry School. One reason I might have lost sight of our noted revolutionist was the fact that to those of us who considered ourselves fishermen, more often the area was referred to as Priests' Island.

The western end of the island was accessible at low tide from Gas House Beach. A raised bed of shells and rock deposited in the area had formed a bar. This was the result of the merger of the incoming tide from the Atlantic side of the island with the flow from Little Harbor. The debris carried by each was deposited as their meeting stopped the water's momentum. In colonial times, one of Marblehead's first ministers, Reverend Samuel Cheever, lived on the island. Each day at low tide, he led the local cows across to graze on his land.

There were two houses on the island in the late '30s and early '40s. The most westerly, made of stucco, was smaller than the imposing structure at the other end. That house was an impressive Victorian. It was built in the

Little Harbor and Gerry Island showing a Victorian house. *Marblehead Historical Commission.*

1880s, with the slate roof and gingerbread trim so typical of the era. At the very top was a cupola, internally fitted with seats affording a magnificent view of the exceptional sunrises over the Atlantic. A shift in position revealed the natural beauty of Little Harbor itself. The house was painted yellow with green shutters, but it had no indoor plumbing. Water pipes had never been extended to that part of the island, so its inhabitants had to transport their supplies via the bar at low tide or by boat otherwise.

During the 1870s and early 1880s, the island, sort of a white elephant, was owned by James J.H. Gregory. He was better known for his seed production than his politics, not with the eminence of Elbridge Gerry, but he was a clever fellow who became a renowned botanist. Gregory died in 1886, leaving the island to Michael J. Masterson of Peabody, "with the dwelling house therein." Masterson was a clergyman from Longford, Ireland, who in turn died in 1910, leaving "all real and personal property" to his brother Patrick Masterson and to Patrick Higgins—both priests. The will was dated March 15, 1910. Their use of the island and their presence was frequent enough to cause the land to be unofficially called "Priests' Island."

The other side of the channel was defined by Brown's Island. This mass was more familiar to me, since both homes my parents had owned as I was growing up, numbers 9 and, later, 10 Harding Lane, were waterfront properties. At high tide, the only land separating them from open ocean was Brown's Island. At low tide, mussel-encrusted flats allowed walkers access. Boats could only enter Little Harbor from this direction when the tide was in. Unknown to most of those who lived in our neighborhood was the fact that the island was actually two separate sections. The easternmost had been willed by Mary Appleton in 1887 to Benjamin Crowninshield. This section, less than an acre in size, was quite low toward the middle of the island, but it rose from the beach to eastward, through a meadow to the high rocky edge. Poison ivy was prevalent and the spoiler of many memorable picnics. The area was passed on by Ben to his son, Francis Boardman Crowninshield, in December 1918.

The other section was known as Orne's or the Great Island. Similar in size to Charles', it had a very high elevation. Although much of it was rocky, the "summit" was accessible by a small path leading from the beach. Between the two pieces was a small salt marsh that, over the years, eroded in depth to make a natural separation of the two parts. In later years, during northeast storms, the ocean actually came between the two. It had been sold to Francis a few months earlier, May 9, 1918, by the heirs of Samuel H. Brown. The Brown family had held title to their share of the island since 1797, when it was conveyed by Mary Orne to John Brown. Needless to say, ownership for well over one hundred years found many Browns with some portion of the land. The release of the deed shows 9/16 of the area owned by Carrie A. Brown (his wife); 1/16 by Carrie A. Brown and the four children of the late Samuel Brown; and 1/16 each by Henry W. Brown, Mary E. Brown, Robert C. Brown, Frank Durkee and Henrietta N. Durkee. The last 1/16 was held in the Samuel Brown estate.

Francis Boardman Crowninshield, born in 1869, married Louise Evelina duPont in 1900. They were both descended from extremely affluent families. Keno, as Francis was called, was the great-great-grandson of George Crowninshield (1734–1815), whose wife, Mary, was the sister of Elias Hasket "King" Derby of Salem. At about the same time, in what might have seemed like a continuation of their competition for shipping domination, King Derby married the beautiful Elizabeth Crowninshield, sister of George. The matrimonial unions did nothing to unite the two families. King Derby became America's first millionaire.

The Crowninshields were outshone by the Derbys at every turn. The best to which they could aspire would be the captaincy of a Derby vessel—but no ownership. George Jr., unwilling to settle for such degradation, had his sons trained in the necessary navigational skills to enter the lucrative shipping industry. In 1801, his *America III*, commanded by his son John, sailed for Sumatra. Within two years, the family had a monopoly on the cheap pepper, as well as the coffee, they found there. They were, however, still referred to as the "Codfish Aristocracy." Over the next few years, with the death of King Derby, the Crowninshields' shipping and real estate deals gave them preeminence in Salem.

Louise Crowninshield's ancestor, Pierre duPont, and his family fled France in 1799. His son Irenee knew how to make dynamite and was able to produce enough in Delaware to make a fortune selling to the United States government during the War of 1812. The Civil War only increased their worth. Henry, son of the founder, now a general under Lincoln, was appointed to take control of southern Delaware. He did just that, keeping most of the land for himself. As a result, Henry Algeron duPont, Louise's father, was extremely rich. His sister, Evelina duPont (also very rich), had purchased the northeastern end of Peaches Point, building what she referred to as a "small cottage."

In 1871, Francis Crowninshield bought a large tract of land on the point and erected his Seaside Farm a year later. It wasn't until 1899 that he met Louise, who was visiting her aunt. Certainly, he was smitten. The wedding took place in June 1900. During their fifty-year marriage, Louise gave huge

Crowninshield's Seaside Farm. *Peach Collection.*

A summer social scene on Cleopatra's Barge. *Peach Collection.*

sums of money to both the town of Marblehead and to Boca Grande, the Florida island where they wintered. Story had it that one summer she spent $300,000 at a quaint shop in Maine where they were cruising in their yacht. Her special love was finding priceless antiques, which she donated to the Jeremiah Lee Mansion in town, a historic ship owner's home on Washington Street.

Keno died in 1950. Louise had planted the Great Island with pines, leaving the eastern half open except for the daffodils her niece had planted. She subsequently donated the property to the Trustees of Reservations. She had always allowed anyone to use the area pretty much as they wished.

Diagonally across from the island, toward Little Harbor, the entire town side from my parents' home and one other residence to the beach in the Cove was owned by the James Graves Boatyard. This two-acre parcel of land consisted of drab gray storage sheds, a mast loft and shops for painters, riggers and machinists. There were long mill shops for the building of boats and a railway for hauling them out for winter storage. This was a true working boatyard, one of the biggest on the eastern seaboard. Our Cove had other small yards, such as the Bates Boatyard and Henry Baay's, started in the late '30s and '40s, but they were not in the category of Graves.

Bates's Boatyard was a favorite of fishermen. Repairs were inexpensive and easily expedited. Mandon Bates's prices for boat storage and other services lured most of the Little Harbor fishermen his way. An early list of receivables, handwritten by his wife, Virginia, showed Henry Briggs, Herbie Dixie, G.C. (Grover Cleveland) Luscomb and Ralph Conner all with a $10.00 storage fee. Robert Hurlburt and Lincoln Davis, both residents of Peaches Point and certainly in a different class economically, were charged $35.00 and $70.28, respectively. More than likely, Davis had had work done by the yard, such as a new coat of bottom paint and/or sanding the topsides for refinishing. The fishermen did repairs and painting themselves. Having spent several seasons preparing and setting a fish trap in the early' 30s, Mandon realized all too well the hardship of landing enough fish to support a family and the necessity of keeping one's gear in first-rate condition frugally.

I remember one day, standing in the open land near Dave Hildreth's house on Fountain Inn Lane. This area afforded a perfect view of the town end of the Cove, a flat area behind Gas House Beach. There was a large barge, perhaps one hundred feet long, being towed into Henry Baay's by a

Boatyard truck, 1935. *Bates Collection.*

MARINE RAILWAY                                    STORAGE AND REPAIRS

# BATES BOAT YARD

MARBLEHEAD, MASS., *February* 19*44*

OWNER *Mr. Robert Walcott*

OFF ORNE STREET                                    TELEPHONE 425

*1944*
*Feb 1  Storage Oct 1, '43 to Feb 1, '44      15—*

NO CLAIMS ALLOWED AFTER 10 DAYS FROM DATE OF BILLING

*Above*: Boat storage was inexpensive during the Depression. *Bates Collection.*

*Below*: Bates Boatyard sheds. *Bates Collection.*

small tugboat. Henry was a Dutchman who, rumor had it, had come to the United States to escape Nazi domination of the Netherlands. He was from a long line of boat builders and obviously from a country that knew about land reclamation. This barge and another almost as large were lined up end to end, the railway between the two. Their length formed a continuation of waterfront for his yard. They were filled with rocks and soil, adding substantial frontage at high tide and topped off by skids for moving boats around. After World War II, Henry purchased some of the yachts that had been painted gray and used as U.S. Coast Guard patrol boats, refurbishing them for civilian service. Two of them, the *Hollandia* and the *Troubador*, were moored in the main harbor and chartered out.

About 1950, Henry moved his entire operation to the main harbor. Dick Price took over. His tenure was short-lived, as Ted Hood acquired the area in 1954.

A couple of other notables from Little Harbor were two Harvard-educated men, both with a background in naval architecture. W. Starling Burgess, born in 1878, was building model boats and gliders while he was still in high school. His father was a successful boat designer who had designed some winning yachts in defense of the America's Cup. Starling (Burgess's mother's family name) worked with him for some time, the two men producing six winners from about 1885 to the late 1920s. In the early 1900s, Starling opened a small boatyard in Marblehead over by the Gas House at the west end of the Cove and built boats for about six years, but his obsession with aviation seemed to supersede his yachting inclinations. His aeronautical endeavors necessitated the construction of two large buildings, one uptown at Commercial Street and the other in Little Harbor. In February 1910, he chose the frozen Chebaco Lake in Hamilton for his first "flight." This design was a biplane with a Curtiss twenty-five-horsepower engine. At the demonstration, hardly impressive, the *Flying Fish* went about thirty feet high and one hundred yards. Nonetheless, his boat carpenters were skilled enough to turn out airframes of such high quality that they were licensed by the Wright brothers. At the world's second aero show in Boston, one of the famous brothers commented, "Everything in assembly of parts of the biplane gives evidence of skilled workmanship, strength, and speed." Through a series of ups and downs, Burgess entered the next Boston aero show. Receiving success with his improved designs, he was franchised by the Wrights to build their planes early in 1911. Sales to the army and navy increased in 1913 and '14, at which time he dissolved his association with the Wrights, teaming up with and, in 1916, selling out to Curtiss Aeroplane and Motor Corporation.

Toward the end of 1917, Burgess was notified he had been commissioned a lieutenant commander in the U.S. Navy, posted to Washington. His knowledge and design of aircraft had certainly improved in seven years. Sadly, all company records were destroyed during a fire in 1918 when the false armistice for World War I was declared and a mysterious conflagration erupted in the Burgess Company.

My father was always an ardent yachtsman. His first sailboat, the *Sylvia*, went down in the 1938 hurricane. While I was young, he chartered various vessels for cruising the coast of Maine, but when I was fourteen, in 1951, he bought a forty-eight-foot schooner, the *Landfall*, which had been built at the Bunce Boatyard in Huntington, Long Island. She had a brass plate in the cabin below, dated 1931, and inscribed with the designer's name: "W. Starling Burgess." Small world!

The last nautical landmark in the Little Harbor loop was William Brown's boat shop. Bill and his brother Sam were the Brown's Island "Browns," two of the four children of the late Samuel Brown. Adjacent to Fort Sewall, Bill's shop was the workplace for the construction of many of Sam's designs. Sam had graduated from Harvard in 1910 and had gone on to learn design at MIT (Massachusetts Institute of Technology) in 1911–12. He taught "steam" (steam combustion and marine engines). Many of his plans are preserved at the Peabody Essex Museum in Salem, Massachusetts. Both brothers were interested in dory racing, a competitive sport in the 1920s and '30s. They worked together on a class called the Yankee Dory and on other small-class boats. Situated on the edge of the tidal channel coming into the Cove, the boathouse had beautiful ocean views to the eastard. This channel allowed traffic to Hood's and Baay's from the main harbor but was inaccessible to Little Harbor at low tide.

Directly behind Brown's boat shop was Fort Sewall, one of Marblehead's well-known landmarks. The fort forms the outermost part of the main harbor but also curves around to border the shore that connects to Gas House Beach. During the War of 1812, British prisoners were brought to the area and confined at the fort. That seemed to me a dismal fate for the English seamen. On April 3, 1814, the frigate *Constitution* (Old Ironsides) was spotted being chased by two British ships. Many members of the crew were from Marblehead. About three miles out, the commander inquired if any of the Marblehead seamen felt competent to pilot the ship into the harbor. From a score of volunteers, Samuel H. Green was selected, successfully bringing her in to the cheers of the townspeople who were rimming the shore. The British, frightened by the cannons strategically

Burgess Airplane Factory. *Marblehead Historical Commission.*

aimed from Fort Sewall to protect the harbor, had to give up their quest, and the *Constitution* was saved.

My mind continued to wander and settled on my favorite part of Little Harbor, the one with the most memories. This was the beach and the shanties where all of us fishermen kept our skiffs and gathered for camaraderie and warmth after a hard day on the water. We were a close-knit group, joined by our common interest of the sea and the life it supported and by our work ethic, which needed to exist for us to be successful at our trade. Marblehead's fishing history had originated at our beach, Fisherman's Beach, a very small area, open to the northeast winds. Bob Brown had known the beach as well as I did. I thought of our early days together when we were still hoping we could do as well as the old-timers and were so anxious to prove ourselves.

# Chapter 6

# Fisherman's Beach

isherman's Beach is accessible by a short road, a sharp right at the bottom of Orne Street hill or, in my case, by a row around Graves Boatyard in my pram—not that I didn't make the trek down Beacon Street as well. The land approach was my route of choice, mostly for expediting the trip. When approaching from my house, I had to pass four other houses, take a left and I was there. The first sighting of the ocean quickened my senses. Everything about the place was interesting to me. I no longer smelled the tang of the salt water—I guess I was just so used to it—but the sights! At a young age, I mastered the use of binoculars, surprised at how sharp the images had become since I got my glasses in the sixth grade. From my house, I was able to pick out the various lobster boats seeking the crustaceans most people considered a delicacy. But at the beach—that was the real thing.

Sometimes I stopped at Helen's store for a Milky Way, relinquishing five cents of my carefully guarded allowance. Jack Roads had left Helen Smith the store and the whole house with two full apartments on the second floor. She was quite the entrepreneur, landlady and cook for many of the boatyard employees who enjoyed her "hot" lunches and supplier of necessities, such as laundry detergent and candy bars for the neighborhood kids. She even took in washing for summer visitors renting the two small houses on Brown's Island.

Fueled by my sugar rush, I'm sitting on the long bench at Fisherman's Beach, my bike beside me, checking to see who's "out" and who's "in." I swivel my head to see the panorama—Brown's on my far left, the boatyard

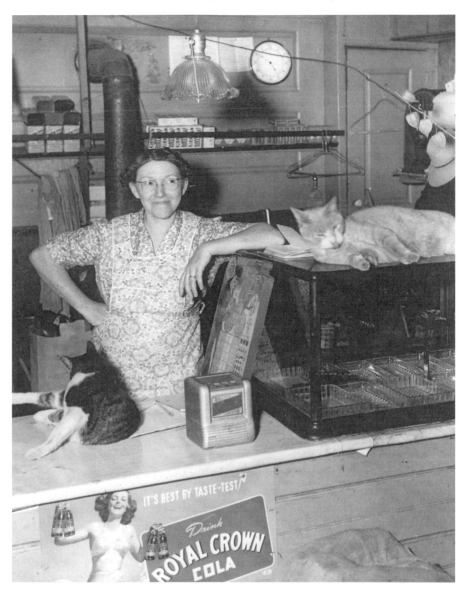

Helen Smith in her variety store. *Marblehead Historical Commission.*

on the near left, Priests' across the way, Fort Sewall at two o'clock, the far end of Gas House Beach, obscured by Dave's house, the old Percival Estate, on my far right. Dave Hildreth has been my friend since our kindergarten days at the Gerry School, and he and I are pretty interested in the goings-on in the Cove. You might say it is our focal point.

Ern Cronk.

We know all the fishermen—who moors his boat where but, more importantly, which skiff belongs to which man. These small punts are attached to running lines fastened to metal rings on the wall in front of me. The beach itself is only about seventy-five feet wide, but from Barber's Lobster Pool on my left to the rocks in front of Dave's, every few feet has one of these lines. They extend from the wall to a mooring in the Cove. The line is one continuous piece of rope, spliced together to form a loop. This loop extends about ten to twelve yards beyond the low-tide mark so that the skiff or punt is always afloat. The rope goes through another ring or pulley at the mooring site that is attached to a two-inch-thick by six-inch-wide by three-foot-long piece of wood. A lighter, steadying piece across makes it look like a cross, stabilizing the buoy board so the rope won't twist. The chain from the wooden cross is attached to a cement block or anchor sunk into the muddy bottom.

I saw that Henry Briggs and John Hawkes were "in," their skiffs back out on the lines. In fact, at three o'clock, usually everybody is in. The unwritten law of the Cove, especially in the fall, is that the last guy remaining ashore doesn't go home until he makes sure all the boats are on their moorings. In those days of no telephone communication or two-way radio, it was common practice to let at least one guy know in what area you planned to be lobstering. If you didn't show up at a reasonable hour, they'd have a starting point of where to search.

Case in point: one afternoon in 1948, a light cruiser, the *Rochester*, anchored off Halfway Rock. What seemed like a beautiful day had enticed Dave to row his pram the two and a half miles out for a closer look. As storm clouds developed in the afternoon, a frantic Mrs. Hildreth came running down the driveway. Thunderheads had darkened the sky. She had no sooner explained her fear for Dave than Watson Curtis hustled to his skiff to look for the boy.

Little Harbor, 1947. Ern Cronk's gray spray hood boat is in the center, and Lizzie H is behind. *Hildreth Collection.*

His engine running, he was just taking his chain off the mooring bitt when an unconcerned Dave rounded the tip of Priests' Island—and that's the way it was. Any able-bodied fisherman was ready at a moment's notice to help any one of his compatriots.

I turned to check the shanties. I could see Dan Peach through his window, working on some gear. The guts of Fisherman's Beach were the shanties. These small wooden structures formed a cluster of buildings about seventy-five yards from the wall. Crudely built, they were perfectly adequate for the no-nonsense men who used them. Their exteriors were stark as the ocean on a January day, but the insides were warm and inviting. There were seven in all, forming what I thought knowingly was a geometric shape called a trapezoid. Each man owned a share of the tract of land, the whole piece being only one-quarter of an acre. If a man wasn't lobstering that day, there was a good chance he could be found in his shanty. Dan and Gerald Smith had the front two, the ones with the ocean view. Gerald's, the smaller of the two, had been converted from a chicken coop into a workable space. It was overshadowed in size by Dan's but no less functional. A man named Colonel Bell, who had a wooden leg and lobstered in a small Friendship sloop, was purported to have built it.

Gerald Smith's shanty (left), with scallop shells on front. Dan Peach's larger shanty is to the right. Graves Boatyard is in the background. 1930s. *Peach Collection.*

The area containing the back five splayed out. Built from odds and ends of lumber and tarpaper, they were a motley grouping, all very individual. Behind Dan's shanty was a storage space owned by Henry Briggs and his brother-in-law, Rene Barber, who had started the Lobster Pool. Behind them, separated by a small dirt path, were slightly larger buildings owned by John and Ed Hawkes, Henry Briggs, Ralph Conner and Herbie Dixie. The only maverick was Grover Cleveland "Clevie" Luscomb, whose shanty was perhaps two hundred yards back, accessed from Beacon Street. These fishermen used these workspaces for patching traps, mending fish nets, knitting heads and painting buoys. Wooden lobster buoys would shortly become a thing of the past when irate recreational boaters claimed they were wreaking havoc with their propellers and the Division of Marine Fisheries required that all buoys be made of synthetic material. These small shanties all started as work sites. They later developed into a "home away from home," a place for socializing and storytelling. Dan Peach actually lived in his shanty for several years. It was impeccably maintained, with a tiny garden in the front. Lincoln "Link" Hawkes, cousin of John and Ed, was the best cook of the lot. He was extremely proud of his chowder recipe and often invited the neighbors and fishermen to one of his songfests, complete with a "band" and dinner. Link was a master on the accordion, often accompanied by Isa Smith, who lived nearby on Beacon Street. Dave became an excellent banjo player and joined the group during his college years in the late '50s. These small buildings were really the proverbial "tarpaper shacks," but no matter how humble, they and their occupants were the heart and soul of Fisherman's Beach.

Life at the shanties was, for the most part, an extremely pleasant part of the fishermen's lives. Many of them had "real" homes and retired to their familial bliss by late afternoon. The Hawkeses enjoyed a good time, but Ed had married in 1953, and his free time was curtailed. John and his cousin Link, however, were capable of occasionally overdoing their partying. One night in the mid-1950s, the two men had overindulged. A serious fire erupted. Having fallen asleep on their bunks, they awoke just in time to summon help. The landlords, at that time, were Watson, Mandon, Ralph, Azor Goodwin, Thea Barber and Dan. They decreed, "No more drinking in the shanties." Annoyed by this restriction, the ever-resourceful Link showed up a few days later with a secondhand 1948 Ford van, purchased from the Charlestown Navy Yard. Nicknamed "the rolling shanty," the vehicle was outfitted with a bunk and a workbench. Link used it during the day for transportation to his various odd jobs designing and constructing. It was parked at the beach at night, where he was legally able to partake as desired.

A Saturday afternoon at the shanty. Left to right: Ralph Conner, Ern Cronk, Gerald Smith, John Hawkes, Louie Amirault and Link Hawkes.

Link Hawkes extending a greeting from the Rolling Shanty. *Peach Collection.*

There was a screech of brakes as Dave came through the stone pillars from his house. He skidded to a stop. We both rowed at about the same pace, but I have to admit he was a pretty good biker. "Let's go over to the island [we dropped the "Brown's" when we were together] this afternoon. The tide is almost dead low, a good time to make one of our circumnavigations." Dave used big words. This tour we carefully kept from our parents, who luckily were oblivious to the steepness and difficulty of maneuvering the rocky crevices along our path. We loved stopping at the tide pools, exposing their catch of starfish, sea urchins and crabs at low tide. We prided ourselves on timing the incoming water to ensure we would be able to return to the mainland before the two sweeping bodies of water met and deepened, stranding the innocent on the island for another four or five hours.

Before we left, we gathered a small stack of sand collars from the mud flats. We didn't really know what they were but used to take them home and dry them in the sun. It turned out that our collection was the eggs of moon snails, cemented together with a gelatinous substance secreted by the parent. We must have assassinated millions over the years.

It was four o'clock, and the boatyard workers were starting to leave. With the end of World War II, the yard had terminated the night shift and was once again working on recreational yachts instead of military vessels.

By now, the bait truck had also arrived. At least three days a week, the delivery truck would stop by, filling the wooden barrels with enough salted redfish for at least two days of lobstering. In 1949, when Dave and I were twelve, the cost was about ninety cents per bushel. However, in this postwar period, times were changing. A young upstart, a strong and knowledgeable guy named Watson Curtis, the same one who stepped up for the rescue of Dave, had just bought a used truck, a 1949 green Studebaker with fancy lights on the top. Enviously, the old-timers termed him "Wonder Boy." Interestingly, Ralph Conner soon matched the boy wonder with his own purchase of a Studebaker, a sort of pinky orangey tone, which Dave and I referred to as "pukey." Soon the fishermen started picking up their own bait in Gloucester at their convenience. Now, Ralph, who had generously constructed two wheelbarrows, complete with pneumatic tires, for the transportation of bait from the barrels to the skiffs and was able to transport three to five traps at a time from the beach to the storage area behind the shanties, was using his truck on the newly renovated launching ramp. The old ramp, constructed of concrete in the 1930s, had been extended to at least the half-tide mark, enabling vehicles to back down to a punt, hauled in and waiting on its line, to be loaded with fuel and supplies for the larger fishing vessel. The launching ramp was one of only two with public access in Marblehead. To the right side of the ramp is a walled-off seating area with two more benches—not as long as "our" bench. This small area is usually crowded with lobster traps waiting to be set and skiffs in need of new bottom paint or hauled out because of anticipated bad weather. To the left of the ramp is the beach itself, laden with sand, small rocks and beach glass. Near the bottom of the ramp and to the right of the ramp are larger rocks, seaweed laden, rising up to meet the long extension of the Percival/Hildreth sea wall.

Dave and I took off, satisfied that all was well. I was free to ride the neighborhood or cross to the island until I heard the familiar cowbell, rung heartily by my mother, signaling the dinner hour. When the fishermen talked about meals, they referred to lunch as "dinner" and dinner as "supper," but at my house, the evening meal was dinner.

The summer season in New England arrives stubbornly, with some gentle teases in May and early June, but isn't thoroughly installed until close to the Fourth of July. By the end of June, with more daylight, many of the men would reconnoiter on the bench after supper for socialization and discussion. In these pre-television times, the days seemed longer. The evenings were spent in a more leisurely fashion, and with a hard day's work behind them, which had often been spent in solitude, the chance for companionship was a welcome relief.

Dave and I had already decided to check out the happenings at the bench after our meal. We liked to arrive when there were a few occupants, so sometimes I would go to Dave's yard, where we would casually play catch, discreetly checking for activity. This night, there was no sea breeze. A sea breeze can bring a chill in the evening to what has otherwise been a glorious day. The warmth of the night invited the men, and we weren't disappointed. Mandon Bates was already there. Soon, his friend John Higginson arrived. John wasn't part of the inner group of seamen but a machinist at Haskell and Hall in Salem, but he was best friends with Mandon. Although John had no kids of his own, he was very welcoming to us boys. He would wait until Dan and usually Clevie and Ralph arrived. Another regular on the bench was Ern Cronk, a retired older lobsterman who seemed to share our sweet teeth. John would then take ice cream orders. He made it quite clear he needed some helpers for carrying the booty, and Dave and I, perched on the very end of the bench, were glad to oblige. He would whisk us off in his 1936 four-door Dodge, alias "the shitbox," to Muggsy Harris's on Washington Street. The passenger side of the "box" had no floorboards; in fact, the street below was actually visible to anyone brave enough to sit beside the driver. We boys were safely installed in the back. In those days, Orne Street was two-way, so a sharp left up by Old Burial Hill and we were off. Muggsy was a balding, heavy-set guy wearing a large white apron tied up under his armpits, the ever-present cigarette in his mouth. He seemed to have the uncanny ability to let the ash on the end grow to a length defying gravity before he flicked it to the floor, seconds before it would have hit the half pint of chocolate ice cream he was stuffing into its container— and stuff it he did. The ice cream was mounded to twice the height of the cardboard, the cover crammed on and a napkin wrapped around the gap between the bottom and top. I kind of think when Dave and I were a bit short, John subsidized our purchases.

We would arrive back at the beach to a rousing discussion of postwar Europe or the latest death in town, discovered by one of the men who had left home early that morning, long before paper delivery. We two young boys loved the adult talk. There seemed to be no secrets, but more importantly, we felt like we belonged. We still were reticent, not wanting to push our luck. The place for little kids was at the end of the bench. We knew it and were both quiet and unobtrusive but learned a lot about local events, experiences in World Wars I and II, town and national politics—but, most importantly, about boats.

The fishermen seemed to find a certain contentment with one another (most of the time). They had their own homes, but their workplace was a comfort zone, where the passion and danger of their profession could be digested silently. While their wives and families might worry, wanting to discuss their fears, the fishermen preferred the distance, or denial, if you will, of the hazards and hardships. Very little discussion at home and less at the beach solved the problem or at least internalized it, instilling in them a certain confidence that they could conquer the sea.

# Chapter 7

# Ye Olde Cunner Kings

Davido Hildreth's family lived at 4 Fountain Inn Lane during the first years I knew him. In 1948, they bought 1 Beacon Street, the house where Laurence Percival had summered until his death in 1943. Converted to a year-round home, it afforded the Hildreths a commanding view of Little Harbor and the horizon. The property still had the remains of a small house at the corner of Beacon and Orne Streets that abutted the entrance to Fishermen's Beach. Percy had had all except one room of the house demolished. Complete with a large fireplace, the structure made for a glorified shanty. Ed Hawkes had been given the use of it during his school years in the 1930s, and now it was ours.

The summer of 1948, we used the location as our special space. We tried a few cigarettes, pretending to like them, but mostly we snooped on the fishermen, plotting our future. We wanted a way to fill our pockets beyond the twenty-five-cent weekly allowance we received from our parents.

Once a week, I was lobstering with Studie Smith, and Dave was doing the same with Grover Cleveland Luscomb. Both men fished cunner pots for bait, so we had seen the procedure firsthand. We pondered the idea of building some and selling our catch to the lobstermen. Youthful enthusiasm abounded as we discussed this can't-miss scheme.

Bait was the catalyst that made lobstering work, but supply was a constant problem. A truck brought redfish, pogies were caught in nets and cunners were a third source. Caught in specially built traps, this perch-type fish was heavily relied on by certain lobstermen. Cunners were prevalent around the rocky bottom, growing to a length of eight to ten inches.

*Left*: David Hildreth, age eleven. *Hildreth Collection*.

*Right*: Hugh Bishop, age eleven.

We started production with the basic wooden frame of a donated lobster trap. We stripped the lathes off, leaving those on the bottom, which we covered with newspaper. Cement was mixed, poured and smoothed over the paper. Lastly, the whole trap was covered with half-inch square-meshed, galvanized wire purchased from Chadwick's Hardware Store at the corner of State and Washington Streets. We fastened it down with bent-over nails and constructed a removable door for one side, held in place by wooden tabs.

The trapped cunners could be swept off the cement bottom by a gloved hand into a bushel basket placed under the trap. The key to the size of the catch was regulated by the entrance or funnel, fashioned from the same wire. These ten-inch-long openings were cone-shaped, narrowing from six inches on the outer end to three inches. One funnel was set in the middle of an end and the second in a partition of wire inside the trap. Smashed crabs or cooked lobster bodies were the attraction. The best catches were after a short set time of three to five hours. Lobstermen hauled their cunner traps first thing in the morning and again at the end of the day's work.

Dave and I earnestly started building what we envisioned would be quite a string. The fishermen, interested in our progress, gave us a few more old lobster traps. We returned to Chadwick's on our bikes and purchased an additional roll of wire. Word spread of our endeavor. Watson Curtis drifted into the shanty, observed our efforts and nicknamed us "ye olde cunner kings." Various other lobstermen stopped by with remarks such as, "I can use three bushels anytime you have any extra," or "Put me down on your list." The going rate was fifty cents per bushel. We had our multiplication tables down cold and figured we would have a bright future.

We finished the first trap in four and a half days. Rene Barber gave us some fresh lobster bodies for bait. Tying rope and a buoy on it, Dave rowed it out to the mouth of the Cove, where he dropped it over. His boat that year was a small square punt, no more than six feet long. I had a ten-foot pram my father had built for me. Dave and I agreed my boat should not be used, since it had a varnished yacht-like transom. Late that afternoon, we went out for our first haul. Production of the second trap was well underway.

Quite honestly, setting the cunner trap out was much easier than hauling it back. The cement bottom created strong resistance. Trying not to show the effort he was expending, Dave finally got it aboard. He had shipped a fair amount of water. Although a swamping was narrowly averted, we tried to act nonchalant. Deep down, we realized his punt was too small for the job. The catch was a dozen cunners. After two more perilous hauls the next day, we had enough fish to cover the bottom of a basket. Reality struck home. Rowing into the Cove, Ed Hawkes, aboard his *Lizzie H*, could see our body language. Feeling sorry for us and remembering some of his youthful endeavors, he gave us twenty-five cents for our efforts. The excitement was gone.

The next day, we retired the cunner trap. Ye olde cunner kings were finished.

*Chapter 8*

# Graves Boatyard

he Graves family members were no strangers to ocean trades. From Benjamin to Samuel, the alphabetical list of Marblehead Graves captains is prolific. Ebenezer, born in 1770, went on to become a selectman, but a subsequent Ebenezer died in Galveston, Texas, at the age of forty-eight. Samuel, born in 1804, crossed the Atlantic seventy-eight times and the Pacific six. His barque, *Elvira*, may have been maimed by an unintentional strike from the *Newark* off Cape May, but she was tight and probably was only able to return to New England because she was skippered by a captain with way more expertise than most.

James "Al" Graves had gravitated toward land. Born in 1860, he found rowing a dory more interesting than piloting a schooner. He and his contemporaries were responding to a generational change. Still interested in making a living from the sea, they were combining vocation and avocation to create a more balanced, less dangerous lifestyle.

Dories were no longer used only by the men of the Grand Banks schooners. During the 1800s, lobstermen were hauling their gear rowing dories. Needless to say, it was very strenuous exercise. Toward the end of the nineteenth century, these crafts were used as well by naval architects, boat builders and others with marine-related jobs. They also became a lure for sportsmen who enjoyed being on the ocean. For rich and poor alike, rowing for pleasure and rowing competitively were popular pastimes.

A dory is usually a flat-bottomed boat with double ends. Adaptation developed over the years to include some with rounded bilges and small transoms in the stern. Dories may be smooth sided, but when the planks overlap, it is commonly referred to as "lapstraking."

The dory races were about to start.

Al Graves was one of the strongest men in town and stood head and shoulders above his contemporaries. He and his friend Phil Woodfin, owner of a Marblehead moving company, are reputed to have had lifting contests, with the winner hoisting one thousand pounds on his back. Al was victorious and became known as the strongest man in town. Having been a rower for some time, the young Graves was not unaccustomed to making a day of rowing out around the Boston Lightship and back, a twenty-mile trip from Marblehead Rock. Another favorite destination was Manchester Harbor. He sometimes continued past Gloucester, as far north as the coast of Maine. A night on the beach was possible, but it was common practice to make a round-trip trek to Gloucester in the course of a day, another twenty-mile trip. Like most athletes, he wanted to go faster and felt he had the competence to build a better boat.

Al had tried his hand at farming, but after he met Ester Hudson Roads, who worked for the Roberts Box Shop in Marblehead, he went to work for the shoe box company as a teamster, transporting the goods by horse and wagon to the shoe factories in Lynn, a city just beyond Swampscott. The young couple was married in 1895, moving into a barn near the beach on Harding Lane. Al converted the barn into a home next door to the second house my parents owned in Barnegat. (The term "Barnegat" refers to our particular section of Marblehead. It encompasses part of Orne Street, including Old Burial Hill and Fountain Park, most of Beacon Street, Norman Street as far as Redd's Pond and possibly part of Pond Street. The nearer you live to the ocean, the less area you seem to include toward town. The derivation of the word is unclear, but one plausible explanation is that it came from a coastal town in New Jersey, where there was a gang of pirates who built fires on shore as false beacons to lure vessels toward their wreckage. A subsequent looting of cargo took place. Allegedly, they did the same thing in early times in Marblehead.)

Al started construction on his dory in a small building a short distance away, on the beach at the end of Cradleskid Lane. His new design proved faster in the local competitions, and soon he was building similar models for the other racers. His friend and neighbor from Peaches Point, Bowdoin Crowninshield, asked Al to build dories for him, one of which he took to Europe, resulting in very successful racing in Germany. Impressed by Al's designs, Bowdoin became interested in becoming involved in helping build larger yachts.

Born in 1867, Bowdoin Bradlee Crowninshield, Harvard educated, was a great-grand-nephew of George C. Crowninshield Jr. of Salem and brother-in-law of Louise duPont Crowninshield. B.B., as he was called, had a yacht brokerage firm in Boston but had plenty of time to enjoy the "good life." In fact, some people felt he had too much leisure time, criticizing his antics and his marriages.

Crowninshield had become a well-known naval architect, starting his own business in 1897. Because of his early sailing ties to Marblehead and the area around Little Harbor and respecting Al's expertise, he remained partial to Al Graves as a builder. The two established a strong alliance in the yachting trade, with B.B. designing twelve of the twenty-three vessels built by Graves between 1904 and 1920.

One of his early designs was a sleek-looking knockabout, *Miss Modesty*, built by the boatyard in 1903. This was the start of the expansion of the boatyard business. Although the boat was only eighteen feet at the waterline

Graves Boatyard, circa 1909. *Peach Collection.*

Designed by B.B. Crowninshield, the *Thomas W. Lawson* was the only seven-masted schooner built in the United States.

(LWL), she was thirty feet, ten inches overall (LOA). LOA (length overall) means the length of a ship's hull, longer than LWL, because ships usually slant upward and outward from the waterline at both bow and stern. Hardly modest, she was fast enough to win the Boston Yacht Club–sponsored eighteen-foot knockabout championship that summer.

One of Crowninshield's most beloved designs was the *Fame*. She was a forty-foot schooner built to fit his specifications as "the largest boat one man could handle all by himself." Proving his point, he sailed it alone from East Boothbay, Maine, to Marblehead. He moored it off Peaches Point and was a familiar sight sailing by himself off the back side of Brown's Island. He sold it when he left for World War I to drive an ambulance at Verdun.

He concentrated on commercial vessels for several years. The culmination of that early period was the design of the seven-masted schooner the *Thomas W. Lawson*. It was one of the largest working schooners ever built.

The men who designed and built boats in the Little Harbor area include three generations of Cloutmans, three of Graveses, two brothers named Brown and one each of Crowninshield and Chamberlain. Their lives and work were very individual but often intertwined.

Will Chamberlain was three years older than B.B. and also a sporting type, enjoying rowing, gunning and sailing. He started building and racing dories in the 1880s and was very good at both. The name Chamberlain is pretty much synonymous with "dory" or "dory skiff." The skiffs were fourteen feet, built in large quantities. These were used as instructional boats, teaching children to row, and as tenders for large yachts as a means of reaching shore when the large vessels were cruising. He also designed surf dories for the Metropolitan Police Beach patrol at Lynn and Swampscott beaches in the early 1900s, and his dories were also available at Devereux Beach, Marblehead, for rescue purposes. He was known for his V sterns, used on double-enders. This design and the flat bottoms of the dories made them easy to launch from a sandy beach, such as the long expanse in Lynn. Even with heavy surf, they could be handled effectively.

The eighteen-foot gunning dories were sleek and moved quickly and quietly through the water. Lightweight, they were perfect for hunters who wanted to cover mileage and make a silent approach. There was one lobsterman who used such a boat for lobstering, but as Ed Hawkes put it, it was like using a Rolls-Royce to transport gravel.

Chamberlain's shop on Orne Street was a busy place. It was a two stones' throw from Gas House Beach, making launching relatively easy. Many a dory entered the Cove from that venue. Albert Cloutman, a young boat builder apprentice, was working for Will part time. Will's declining eyesight and increasing workload necessitated assistance. Albert also worked for W. Starling Burgess during World War I, building airplanes until the fire in 1918. Albert, son of the renowned Henry Cloutman, was about twenty-five years old. He had learned extensively from his father, as Henry had been instrumental in starting the boatyard with Al Graves in 1895. Al and Henry were actually related, as were many old Marblehead families. Born in 1851, he was the third key member of the early boatyard crew of Graves and Crowninshield. This was the golden era of the small boat shop.

Chamberlain's famous early designs were the Beachcomber and Alpha Dories. The former was named for the Beachcomber Dory Club of Little Harbor, of which Will was a member. The Alpha was the Salem Dory Club's answer to the Beachcomber, a slight modification in design.

Both of these were easily stored just back from the beach, their sails removed and taken home to dry. They were both derived from the Swampscott or beach dory, a bit longer and sometimes decked over, with a long boom that accommodated a mainsail longer along the foot than the luff

Beachcomber Dory Club, Fort Sewall Beach. *Peach Collection.*

(the angle that goes from the end of the boom to the top of the mast). The sail would actually extend out beyond the stern of the craft.

The Corinthian Yacht Club (CYC) had started midsummer races for small boats in 1904. The days of informal rowing dory races were superseded. At the CYC event, there were two classes of sailing dories. They were both twenty feet, eleven inches long. Chamberlain, sailing his boats *Alberta* and *Scamp*, was a champion in 1895, 1909 and 1910. Al Graves had joined the club in 1902, and Sam Brown, from across the Cove, was the measurer in 1907, checking sail area and other set requirements. By 1912, the regatta had grown immeasurably. Known as Marblehead Race Week, there were over one thousand men in 184 boats at the start, a total of thirty classes. In that year, fifteen-year-old Albert Cloutman was a shining star in the dory classes. It was the beginning of an amazing winning record, which continued with an accumulation of silver cups in 1913, '14, '16, '19, '20, '21 and '22. His boats, named *Freak I, Freak II* and *Freak III*, were well known on the North Shore. The impending birth of his son Bob marked the end of his astounding racing career, as another Cloutman joined the boat-building family.

About this time, Albert—who had worked for Chamberlain part time— and Will had an argument, and Cloutman quit. Albert lived just down Orne

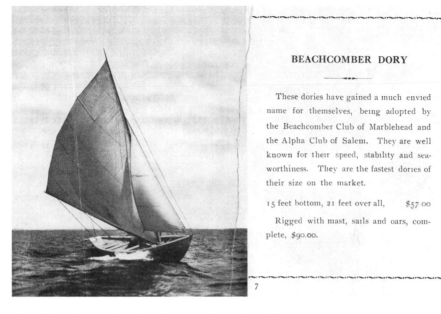

### BEACHCOMBER DORY

These dories have gained a much envied name for themselves, being adopted by the Beachcomber Club of Marblehead and the Alpha Club of Salem. They are well known for their speed, stability and seaworthiness. They are the fastest dories of their size on the market.

15 feet bottom, 21 feet over all,     $57.00

Rigged with mast, sails and oars, complete, $90.00.

*Above*: Chamberlain Dory, Beachcomber Dory. *Peach Collection.*

*Below*: Alpha Dory. *Peach Collection.*

Street from the boat shop. Having gotten a wheelbarrow from his house, he loaded his things and started home. Al Graves happened by and hired him on the spot, and Albert never skipped a beat, wheeling along up Orne Street, past Old Burial Hill and turning in to the Graves Boatyard. He became a full-time employee in 1922, and by March 1930, he had been promoted to general manager. Five months later, Al Graves died at his New Hampshire summer home. His son, E. Selman Graves, who had joined the business in 1919, took over. That same year, the company acquired a second location on the main harbor at Front Street.

Albert supervised the construction and repair of all types of fine yachts, many by America's top designers. Between 1926 and 1940, Graves built fifty yachts ranging in length from twenty-eight to sixty-six feet (LOA). John Alden had become one of the yard's top designers, but L. Francis Herreshoff and the firm of Eldredge-McInnis of Boston were also contributors.

Originally, Al had stored the boats handled by the yard in the open cradles on the beach. They were covered by tarpaulins, hardly enough protection for a storm as fierce as that of February 1898. Unless you've grown up as I did, exposed to the northeast, it's hard to imagine the fury of a real nor'easter, the power of the ocean and the destruction that follows in its path. The Atlantic would flood the entire lower area of Barnegat, encircling the boatyard land, filling the cellars of neighboring houses and depositing tons of rock, seaweed and pieces of timber in its wake. Inhabitants were virtually stranded until the tide subsided. If it were a particularly high tide, with very strong winds, the next low tide cycle would not recede to its normal low point. As the tide turned, the incoming surge would have a head start, and worse flooding would result.

The original railway for hauling and launching boats was powered by a live horse that walked around and around a capstan on which the cable was wound, hauling the boats. The horse was trained by his owner, Henry Cloutman, who gave commands by a whistle. This feat could only be performed on a high tide because of the shallowness of the Cove. Launching a boat was accomplished by lashing the cradle that held a boat to the railway and then removing the stop blocks. As the signal was given, the boat in its cradle would begin to slide down the railway. Speed increased, causing a huge splash as the cradled boat dove into the water. If all went well, the boat would float off the cradle, which would be underwater, still secured to the railway.

From 1905 to 1910, Al built the first sea walls around the yard. Unshaken by severe storm damage halfway through his project, he regrouped and

Fisherman's Beach, 1930. Lobster boats are stored in the foreground. Graves Boatyard is in the background. *Peach Collection.*

completed the work. He obtained the necessary fill from the town dump trucks that left their refuse. An unexpected result was an influx of rats, which thrive and survive to this day.

Graves Boatyard now had the capability and facilities to build, store and service boats of all sizes. A motor-driven railway made launchings safer and easier, as the yachts were lowered by cable in a controlled manner. Inside the safety of the sea walls, additional sheds had been erected. On the beach side, facing the shanties and the backyards of neighbors on Beacon Street, were shops for painters, riggers and machinists.

The boatyard had attracted highly skilled workers, some of the best in the trade, including a few imports from the great shipyards of Maine. The long mill shops provided a protected environment for boat building, and the large doors opened directly onto the railway for launching.

The final problem of shallow water was corrected by dredging a basin from the "Ring Bolt" at the ledge by Brown's Island to the float and railway. It was now possible to handle the larger and heavier yachts without waiting for high tide.

Amid all these capable men was one very capable woman, Al's sister-in-law, Edith Russell (Roads) Copeland. According to Al's daughter, "'Auntie,'

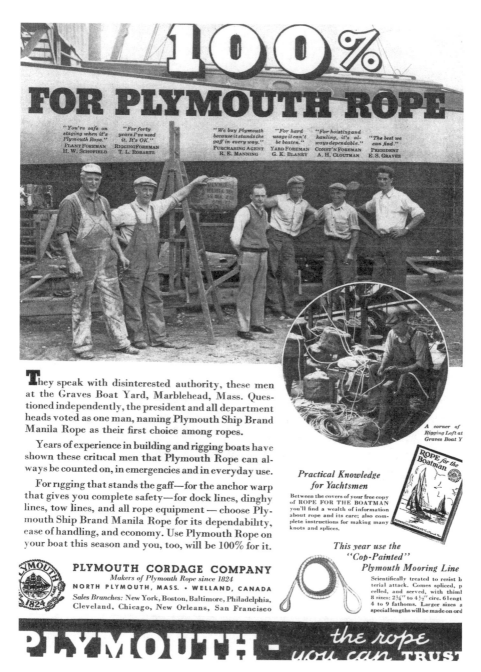
Graves employees featured in an ad for Plymouth Rope. *Peach Collection.*

Five members of the Graves family, 1970s. *Marblehead Historical Commission.*

as all who knew her called her, was clearly a genius at her job and was largely responsible for my father's business success in those early years. Working at a roll-top desk with nothing even resembling a typewriter or an adding machine, she did everything by hand. She was an invaluable asset who worked quietly, without fanfare."

A fire in the summer of 1927 completely destroyed the mill shop. Put rather simplistically, the new design streamlined production, allowing the lumber to go in one end and the finished product to come out the other.

The quiet beginnings in 1905 had mushroomed into a yacht yard employing over thirty full-time employees. At one time or another, almost every young boy or man in Marblehead with maritime interest had some contact with Graves. The experience and skill of these workers enabled the yard to build, maintain and store yachts up to seventy-five feet in length, both power and sail.

As has historically been proven true, the small operator was becoming eclipsed by the larger company. In 1929, the business was incorporated with the firm name of James E. Graves, Inc. Al died with a record of which to be proud. In this little part of Marblehead, he had created a first-

Graves Boatyard, 1980s. *Peach Collection.*

rate boatyard, known far and wide as one of the best in the country. One-design racing classes such as triangles and 210s originated at the boatyard. Such famous yachts as Charles Hovey's *Easterner* and Ross Anderson's *Nefertiti*, 12-meter candidates for the defense of the America's Cup, both bore the name of Graves of Marblehead as the builder.

# Chapter 9

# Bricks Were Two Cents Apiece

**I**t was the fall of 1953, the last week of October. I hauled my small string of lobster traps after school in my dory previously bought from John Hawkes.

I had three very close friends in those days. One was my pal from infancy, Dave Hildreth. The other two were boys I had met at the Gerry School when I entered kindergarten. Their last name was Foss, brothers who lived on Meadow Lane, next to Green Street playground. Donald was David's and my classmate. His brother, Charlie, was a year older. By the second grade, we had all become close friends. In the front yard of my parents' homes, first at 9 Harding Lane and, after 1947, at 10 Harding Lane, we played numerous sandlot softball, baseball and football games. My sister, Brenda, often joined us, and I think that's what made her into such a good, lifelong athlete. Donald and I were about the same ability athletically and were always on the same team. Charlie was superior and was paired up with Dave, who, if I can be objective, was a little less accomplished than Donald and I in baseball and football. If Dave wasn't around, Brenda was Charlie's teammate.

The winter of 1947–48, my father and mother and a neighbor named Jim Sutherland were the driving force behind building a skating rink in our front yard at 10 Harding Lane. That winter, there was a record snowfall of 121 inches. Black Joe's Pond and Redd's Pond, let alone Neily's (long since buried under the "progress" of real estate development), were covered with several feet of snow and were unavailable for our developing skills. Pee Wee Hockey was unknown.

We shoveled and flooded the rink with a hose brought out from the kitchen sink. After a warm spell, when the ice turned to slush and dogs walked on it, Jim Sutherland spent hours smoothing the softened slush with a cement trowel to make it ready for the next freeze and subsequent flooding.

That winter, Donald, Charlie, Dave and I skated on our little rink when no pond ice was available. Neighborhood girls and boys would come by and partake. One of them was Ned Perkins. Ned was a poor skater but was good as goalie. Donald, Dave, Ned and I all became starters for the high school hockey team our senior year. Brenda was one of the early hockey cheerleaders. Everyone was jealous of our team because we had the girls.

Every Friday night in the fall of 1952 and 1953, the Fosses, Dave and I drove over to Lynn Arena and paid seventy-five cents for two hours of public skating. Charlie, being a year older, had a driving license. Here we would sort of get our legs and skating skills honed for the upcoming Marblehead High School hockey season. Our other objective was to look at the pretty girls from somewhere like Saugus or Lynn. They never seemed to get turned on by my kicking up ice chips as I made a flashy turn just ahead of them. Then, of course, there was the occasional "older woman" of about twenty-one or so, in tights and a very accomplished skater. We exchanged smart-assed comments with each other that certainly were not based on experience.

The last Friday night in October, Charlie drove us back to Marblehead after our skating session, where we all had impressed nobody but ourselves. I knew that Dave had bought a small cider press from Link Hawkes for eight dollars and had scraped up some fallen apples from a small, abandoned orchard on Pond Street. On the drive home, he suggested we try some of his newly bottled cider. Every little venture at our age was going to be very profitable. Dave was sure this was no exception. When we arrived at Dave's family home, we all went into the cellar, where Dave showed off his new product, which was bottled in former Martins' Dairy milk bottles. He had gotten some cork stoppers that were way too large for the bottle tops but, with his ingenuity, had whittled down each one so that they sort of fit the bottles.

Then we drank some of the stuff. It wasn't destined to be a bestseller. It may have been the first time I ever drank something that affected me more than water. I'd heard that hard cider does that, or it may have been my imagination. In any event, I made the announcement that I had a great idea to make money by saving it.

I was planning to build fifty new oak lobster traps that coming winter. Each trap would require four bricks to weigh it down. Used bricks were two

# ICE HOCKEY

H. BISHOP
*R.D., Co-Captain*

E. PERKINS    R. ELLIOT
*Goalies*

D. FOSS
*L.D.*

Front row, left to right: W. Hodgkins, D. Hildreth, H. Bishop, D. Foss, E. Perkins, P. Gray, R. Phillips, J. Barnes, H. Hazen. Back row: Mr. Robarts, P. Dinsmore, P. Noyes, W. Winslow, G. Breed, D. Grant, T. Fitzgerald.

D. HILDRETH
*R.W.*

W. HODGKINS
*C., Co-Captain*
46

P. GRAY
*L.W.*

The Marblehead High School hockey team, 1955.

cents apiece. I knew from having been there the previous summer that there was a large supply near the Cove on the northwest side of Misery Island. There, a house had burned to the ground a year or so before. With the bravado of Dave's cider, I said I was going to row there the next morning and make four dollars! Dave gave me one of his looks.

The next morning, about 6:30 a.m., just as the sun was coming up, I was in my dory heading out of Little Harbor for Misery. I had my mother's garden wheelbarrow stowed in the stern of the dory. I didn't tell her I was borrowing it. Dave had a Chamberlain dory of which I was always jealous because it rowed so much easier than mine. I noticed as I left that it was missing from its mooring. He was unpredictable, and I wondered what he was up to.

It was one of those beautiful Indian summer mornings. The temperature was near thirty-two degrees at daylight. There was no wind and not a cloud in the sky, a "weather breeder," as it's called—a great day to be alive. I rowed across Salem Sound and enjoyed every stroke of the oars. By a little after 8:00 a.m., I had reached the west corner of Misery Island, a distance of about three miles. I looked ahead, as you do every once in a while when rowing, and who did I see but Dave rowing toward me from the direction of Manchester.

Greetings ensued. He had left Little Harbor well before daylight and had already been to the head of Manchester Harbor and seen Mandon Bates, who in those days worked at Manchester Marine Yacht Yard. He lived on Beacon Street about halfway between where Dave and I lived and was a familiar figure around Fisherman's Beach. As Mandon drove into Manchester Marine that morning to go to work, he spotted the figure of Dave and his dory rowing up the harbor and exclaimed, "'Deep Sea Dave,' what are you doing here?" That was Dave for you.

Dave told me he thought I had been all talk the night before about rowing to Misery for the bricks, but if I wasn't, he was going to one-up me. He saw my mother's wheelbarrow and said, "Come on, I'll row back to Misery and help you." We went side by side to the little beach at the head of Misery Cove. The tide was coming in as we went up in the woods to the abandoned homesite. The bricks were plentiful. We started taking wheelbarrow loads to my dory. I could get about fifty bricks to a load. The price was right, and Dave decided he could use some at the bargain rate. I'm sure I got a little greedy. As the tide came in, we edged my dory up on the beach, and by late morning, we had way more than we needed and had definitely overloaded the dory.

Ralph Conner finishing a lobster trap. *Conner Collection.*

About noon, we shoved off for Marblehead. There's no sad ending to this story. To me it's just how we grew up and what we did fifty or more years ago. It was still a very nice day. A light sea breeze was setting in, the forerunner of a southeast storm due that night. My dory was way down on its lines. Dave only had to dabble his oars to keep up with me and my full, hard strokes.

We went along like this until about 2:00 p.m., when we were abeam of the nun northwest of Eagle Island. Dave was bored stiff. To make things interesting, he said, "I bet I can let you row toward Little Harbor [about a mile and a half away at that point] for ten minutes and I will row east around Eagle Island and beat you to the Cove." I said, "You're on!" About an hour and a quarter later, with both of us rowing as hard as we could, we reached the mouth of Little Harbor neck and neck. The wind was picking up from the southeast, and as I came into Little Harbor, I was pretty proud of myself. I had rowed Dave to a tie and had more than five dollars worth of bricks aboard!

Ralph Conner, a wise, experienced and very accomplished lobsterman, now in his fifties, was on his boat unloading his catch for the day. As I glided by him in my semi-sunken state, he asked where I had been and what I had been doing. After I explained, he said, "You must be crazy!" I could offer no argument to his statement.

*Chapter 10*

# I Want to Be Like Those Guys

The summer of 1953 came and went. The Wednesday after Labor Day was upon me, and it was back to school. It had been a great season of lobstering with my sixty traps, fished with my Grand Banks–style dory bought from John Hawkes. I had given up on the Lawson engine by August. It had a mind of its own and decided it would only run about 25 percent of the time. I showed it who was in charge by removing it and dumping it over the side one day! With my early instruction, I knew I could rely on myself to row.

I was also maintaining my father's forty-seven-foot schooner yacht. She was moored in the center of Marblehead Harbor. Like so many others, my father and mother had lived through the Depression years and didn't have any extra money to throw around. In the late 1930s, my father got a job as a salesman for a then-small company, Sylvania Lighting Products. He received sales positions of increasing pay and responsibility and often reminded me that he sold the very first fluorescent light bulb. After World War II, he was in a position to do well in the expanding economy.

From the 1930s to the 1950s, his yachting knowledge increased commensurately. He went from having zero knowledge about boats and sailing to becoming a very competent sailor. His new boat, the *Landfall*, was his pride and joy, the pinnacle of his yachting career. He didn't have the money to hire a paid professional captain, so I was pressed into service. I was excited at the prospect of the responsibility of shining brass fittings, maintaining the endless varnish and all the other work that went into keeping a yacht in "Bristol fashion." These pastimes consumed a good deal of my time.

Both of my parents were socially conscious. My father joined the Boston Yacht Club and, about 1952, also the Eastern Yacht Club. I never felt comfortable when they dragged me to either place, particularly the latter. The Eastern was a very elite place. I felt provincial and out of place. Having a background from Marblehead public schools, I knew few of the kids my age who hung out there. Almost all of them were attending private schools. I had nothing in common with them and did not relate. It got to the point during my high school years that when my parents wanted me to go to dinner with them at the Eastern, I found one excuse after another to avoid the occasion. If I wasn't going out with my girlfriend, I much preferred to go down to the long bench at Little Harbor with the older local lobstermen and neighbors. It was a comfortable and welcoming environment.

The two maritime positions were perfect. I had my dory and traps and also the responsibility for my father's yacht. When I was sixteen, my father gave me the green light to take the *Landfall* alone under power into the Marblehead Transportation Company wharf for fuel, ice and fresh water. I remember how nervous I was that first time. My landing at the floating wharf was a little less than perfect, but the experience elevated my confidence.

About the middle of that summer, my father had a heart attack and was bedridden for an extended period, as was the practice at that time. He had made a previous commitment to take business friends out for an afternoon sail two weeks hence. As the date approached, he told me to captain the boat.

The day arrived. I rowed out from the Boston Yacht Club dock early that morning to prepare the *Landfall* for the sail. My father's friends came out from the Eastern about noon and settled aboard. Of the six men, only two had any boating experience.

My father, unlike most of the other large boat owners, prided himself on sailing *Landfall* off the mooring and out of the harbor without using engine power. Quite frequently, he would sail back in the harbor and also make the mooring under sail. Marblehead Harbor wasn't as crowded as it is today, but there were only a few men who would try this with a large vessel. There was little room for error, and any mistake would lead to, at the very least, an embarrassing collision or a ripping of considerable hardware from a yacht moored nearby.

That particular day, the cockiness typical of a young man rose up in me, and I decided that, since this was to be my first time taking *Landfall* out for a sail alone, I was going to make it memorable. I did just what my father had shown me many times before.

The wind was light southeast with the bow aimed at the shoreline of the Neck. I hoisted the mainsail and immediately sheeted it in tightly. This kept the boat directly into the wind. The large sail aft acted as a weather vane. Then, with the help of one of my father's friends, I hoisted the foresail. One man could hoist the foresail alone, using both the throat peak halyards, but it was much easier with two. I then made sure the foresail sheet was slack so the sail was loose in the wind.

Before hoisting had started, I had brought the yacht tender in along the starboard side and made it fast to the mooring buoy. I had also secured the mooring pennant on the mooring bit in a manner that made it very easy to cast off.

The *Landfall* had a single head rig, or jib. I hoisted it and made sure that sheet was also slack. I had previously picked out one of the men who had some nautical knowledge and had him with me near the bow. I showed him how I wanted him to hold the jib when I gave him the order. I walked back to the helm and said to the man forward, "Let the mooring line go and backwind the jib on the starboard side and hold it there." The breeze on the sail slowly pushed the bow to port, and soon the *Landfall* was pointing toward the mouth of the harbor. With a sigh of relief, I slacked off the mainsheet. I also asked one of the other men who were standing around dumbfounded to make the foresail and jib sheets fast and then told the man forward to "Let the jib go."

Now we were starting to move quietly but smoothly toward the entrance of the harbor. She was now under full sail. My heartbeat was starting to slow down. After a few minutes, we cleared the last of the moored boats.

It was one of those moments in time everyone should have. Passing Lighthouse Point, I think my chest puffed out a little. I know my armpits were wet. I later wondered if my father had seen me leave the harbor, a view visible from my parents' bedroom.

Not wanting to damage my euphoria or push my luck, I lowered the sails well outside Marblehead Harbor upon our return. I proceeded sedately to the mooring under engine power. It is a day I love to remember.

In 1953, the pull of the salt water was magnetizing me. I liked to do things alone. I brought in forty of my sixty traps as September came and went. This left me with about twenty, which I hauled on weekends and afternoons after school, weather permitting.

October was a beautiful month. The weather was placid, with no major storms. I had my traps placed where I wanted and caught lobsters regularly.

*Landfall.*

The first week in November was to show me one of the worst northeast storms I have ever seen. Mother Nature has a way of evening things out, a payment for the peace of October. I came home from school on Friday, November 5, to a gale-force east-northeast wind. The forecast in those days was always given on the radio as "Eastport to Block Island," such and such. I went into Helen Smith's small variety store at the entrance to the beach. There, fishermen gathered to listen to WHDH and the report that followed the news every half hour. This station provided as good a marine report as was available. No one except Helen was there, but she said the report was "terrible." I walked out to the head of the beach. It was low tide, and the dozen or so full-time lobstermen were making obvious preparations for what they anticipated.

The common procedure prior to such storms was that all lobsters stored in floating cars (holding containers) were brought ashore and sold to buyers. Buyers in the fall were in Salem, Lynn or Boston. There were no substantial buyers in Marblehead except in the summer season. An extra anchor with a great deal of scope was set out from each boat. The individual lobsterman then crawled up to the bow of his boat and pulled his extra anchor line to the extent possible, making it fast to his boat's mooring bit. This made the anchor take some of the strain off the short mooring chain and block. Also, in the event the mooring chain parted, it provided a fallback provision so the boat could ride out the storm on its anchor alone.

That afternoon, I distinctly remember Ralph Conner on the bow of his spray-hood boat, *Junior*, which was named for his son. He had already pulled his anchor line as taut as possible and was wrapping chafing gear around the anchor warp where it went through the bow chalk. Burlap strips were wrapped around the line and lashed tightly with manila twine to prevent the anchor line from wearing through as it worked in the chalk.

Other men were in various stages of storm preparation. The last step was for everyone to pull his punt well above the high-tide mark. This was already underway by a couple of fishermen, using their pickup trucks for power. I rowed out and put out the extra anchor on my dory, which was moored

Helen's store at the entrance to Fisherman's Beach. The store was torn down in 1964. *Marblehead Historical Commission.*

behind Ring Bolt and visible from my house. John Hawkes's open lobster boat, *Green Hornet*, was moored next to mine.

That evening, my Marblehead High teammates and I went to Lynn Arena for our public skating enjoyment. I waited at the end of my driveway for a ride from Charlie and Donald Foss. The trees were moaning and the wind was shrieking. I came home that evening and slept fitfully, with the noise of the wind and the bursts of gusts against the house disturbing my normal night's sleep.

The next morning, I arose at first light. The tide was halfway in. I don't think I have ever seen a more ferocious sea, including the blizzard of '78. Fortunately, the tides were on a low cycle. All that day it blew east-northeast, fifty-plus knots, a stalled low off the Long Island area and a high over eastern Canada. We didn't have the satellites and weather wisdom we have now, but that's what it was.

That day, at high tide, the lobstermen huddled near what is now the entrance to Marblehead Lobster Company. They all wore the black oilskins of the day. The Portegee hats were common, but some wore the top-of-the-line rubber sou'wester headgear. These cost $1.75 at Nelsons in Gloucester and were considered very expensive but the best.

High tide was late morning, so I went down to hang around the fringe and listen. There, about ten to twelve men looked out periodically at their

Grover Cleveland Luscomb outside his shanty. *Peach Collection*.

surging boats and knew in their minds that they were suffering huge economic setbacks because most of their traps were being destroyed. I remember a gallows humor comment from Ralph Conner that I can quote verbatim: "I wonder if the town will be hiring snow shovelers this winter?" (hand-shoveling snowbanks into trucks was still common). This drew a good laugh. As the tide receded, several men went into Gerald Smith's shanty to ease their concern and enjoyed some liquid refreshment. Some instinct told me that because of my young age, I was not wanted in there, but knowing those men, they would have made allowances for me if I had gone with them. It blew hard that afternoon and most of Saturday night.

I arose Sunday morning and looked out of my bedroom window. The wind had died down to a light northeast breeze. There was a tremendous sea and surf. My dory was there, half filled with water but still wallowing in the rolling swells coming over Ring Bolt. I looked again. John Hawkes's *Green Hornet* was gone; what an empty feeling. It turned out that she had been swamped by the breaking seas at high tide in the middle of the night and was ground beyond repair on the bottom.

By Tuesday, everything was over. I came home from school and rowed out in my dory to look for my gear. I found four of the six traps I had set off the mouth of the Cove. Then I rowed to Cat Island. I didn't find any there. The sun was low over the Marblehead shore as I started to row back from the island. Instead of going directly home, I circled out toward Lighthouse Point, hoping to see one of my yellow and white buoys. None was there either.

It was half dark by the time I got to the first black can off the point. I could see a lobster boat coming from the westward and knew by the profile and sound of the distinctive, wet exhaust that it was Ralph Conner in the *Junior*. He came alongside and threw me a towline of pot warp. "I'll take you into the Cove," he yelled.

I replied, "I lost most of my pots."

According to Ralph, he had found only 60 of 180. He said nothing else. The tone of his voice was dismal. I was a kid with plenty of parental backup. He was the breadwinner for his family and basically out of business for the rest of the season.

He towed me into the Cove and let me go. I rowed the last seventy-five yards to my mooring, securing my dory. It was almost totally dark, as still as a church mouse, the stars twinkling overhead. I could see flashlights on Ralph's boat and a couple of others as the men put away what few lobsters they had salvaged.

I remember saying to myself, "I want to be like those guys!"

# Chapter 11

# Henry Thomas Briggs

**H**enry Briggs was a man I always admired. Henry was born in 1896 at 64 Orne Street, Marblehead, where he lived his whole life, with the exception of his military service during World War I. He was the son of Charles and Nellie Briggs and had a twin brother named Charles.

As a young man of about ten to eleven years old, in the summertime, Henry started to go lobster fishing with his father. Eagle Island was about the outer limit of lobster fishing east of Marblehead by men fishing from Little Harbor.

Henry rowed the dory for his father in the early 1900s. One of his favorite memories was being put ashore on Coney Island Ledge at low tide wearing his hip boots, with a farm basket in each hand. One was empty, and the other had bait. Coney Island Ledge had extensive tidal pools in its confines, where his father had set traps. They were from ankle to waist deep. While his father hauled gear in deeper water off the ledge, Henry waded from pool to pool. Lobsters were put in the empty basket. Henry then dragged the re-baited traps to slightly different locations. It was, Henry used to say, "good lobstering and a good memory."

About 1912–13, Henry's father acquired his first small, powered twenty-two-foot boat, named the *Nellie B*. The heavy, Gloucester-type dory was taken over by Henry. Henry had not gone past the eighth grade in school, but he was an avid reader and continually read books from Abbott Library. Henry and a contemporary neighborhood boy named Frank "Hyfer" Newton

The Briggs homestead, first house on left. The Crowninshield house is in the background. *Briggs Collection.*

engaged in reading competitions. Both boys became very knowledgeable, despite their lack of formal education.

On April 7, 1917, the United States declared war on Germany. On April 8, 1917, Henry and his brother rose early and put on their three-piece suits and ties. Shortly, in front of 64 Orne Street, Hyfer from 22 Beacon Street arrived. He was dressed like Henry and Charles, and all wore fedoras. The three young men then set out to walk to Lynn, almost eight miles away, to sign up for military service. As they walked through downtown Marblehead and beyond, the group grew. By the time they reached Swampscott, it was a crowd of one hundred men. This story speaks for itself.

Henry went to Europe in the not-too-distant future as a member the Twenty-sixth Yankee Division. It was traumatic for him—a life-threatening time. Charles enlisted in the navy. On November 11, 1918, when news of the Armistice reached 64 Orne Street and the boys' mother, Nellie, it is said she cried for the first time since they had left for duty. She knew she was actually going to see her sons again.

After Henry returned from the war, he got his own small powerboat for lobstering and winter fishing. While the number varied in the 1920s, there was a solid core of about fifteen men of various ages making their

Name .,.Henry. J. Briggs.......... Age. 21..... Number.........

Home address (town or city) Marblehead:..... Street and No. 64. Orne:....

Regiment .101st..........................Company Battery. D.............

Date of mustering in..............,1917.. Department ......................

Branch of service...Artillery Field. Rank .,1st Class Private:.......

Names of nearest relatives (state relationship). Father & Mother.......
Charles O. and Nellie Briggs..........................

Address of nearest relatives....64 Orne St. Marblehead.

......................................................................................

Information to be received from and sent to.........................................

......................................................................................

RECORD:

Henry Briggs's World War I identification card. *Briggs Collection.*

living solely from the sea. Henry developed into a skilled and hardworking fisherman and became one of the top producers in Little Harbor.

When fishermen are on their way up, they want a bigger and better boat. Henry was no exception, and in 1932, he had a boat built by the Chaisson family in Swampscott. They were very competent and highly regarded builders. Henry's new craft was twenty-eight feet and, as his father's boat years before, was named *Nellie B.* Nellie must have been one powerful wife and mother to deserve the honor of two namesakes. This vessel was top of the line for that era. With it, Henry increased his efforts. He could fish more single lobster traps and extended his area beyond House Island off Manchester and out through the broken ground east of Baker's Island and the Dry Breakers.

Ed Hawkes was born in 1920. In the spring of 1933 and 1934, he sometimes played hooky from school and went gill net fishing with Henry. Gill nets were set in the winter and spring. The primary catch was codfish. The bottom of the net, which had lead weights attached to it, rested on the ocean floor. The net itself was about twelve feet high, the top edge floated up by a series of cork floats. The net or twine made a fence in the water that fish swam into, ensnarling their gills—thus the name.

The procedure when Ed was with Henry was to leave Little Harbor about mid afternoon with four boxes of nets—1,200 feet total. They proceeded along the shore to the southeast corner of Nahant and then into Revere Beach. Henry called this "going up to the flying horses," since Revere Beach was home in those days to a large amusement park that contained several merry-go-rounds. After setting the nets, they returned to the Cove.

Daylight the next morning would find the *Nellie B.* approaching Revere. They hauled by hand with the fish removed as the net was brought over the rail. A catch of 1,500 to 3,000 pounds was common.

In order to reset nets in those days, they had to be "cleared" or reboxed. The lead weights, in particular, were always dipping into the twine during the haul back. The clearing was done by taking the net out of the box and extending it over a reel, normally eight to ten feet high. Because of the space required, this had to be done on shore.

Henry would return to Little Harbor by late morning. The dressed codfish and nets were unloaded into a punt and rowed ashore. A man named Bill Thorner had a small trucking business and took the fish to Boston for Henry and other fishermen from Marblehead and Swampscott. Henry and his crew then reeled and reboxed the nets. If the weather report was favorable, they returned to Revere Beach and reset for the next night. Gill netting in this manner and at that location is now unheard of—a fading memory for all but a few old men.

One winter, in the 1930s, Henry and Rene (pronounced "Rainy") Barber, who married Henry's younger sister, Thea, went line trawling. Both men took pride in "battling the elements," as Henry said. Henry's *Nellie B.* was a stout vessel for inshore lobstering, but that winter, the two men pushed the boat to its limit. They fished four to six tubs of line trawl gear, a total of two

Gill nets being cleared. *Peach Collection.*

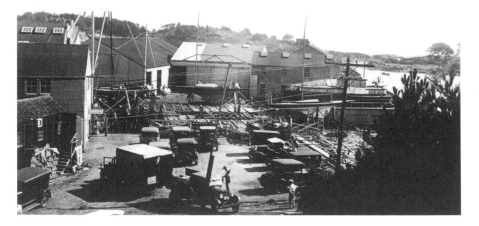

Early Fisherman's Beach. Thorner's fish-hauling truck is backed up to a pickup. *Peach Collection.*

to three miles in length, on Cape Ann Ridge and other grounds to the east and southeast of Marblehead. Cape Ann Ridge was twelve to fourteen miles to the eastward of Little Harbor.

The *Nellie B.* had a small trunk cabin forward, from which a canvas spray hood, about four feet in length, angled up toward the stern. Steering was accomplished with a tiller. The helmsman stood at the back edge of the spray hood, which came up to chin level. That was all the protection he had. In February of that winter, Henry and Rene made seventeen trips to the ridge.

Departure from Little Harbor was about one hour before first light. They took turns steering. The man not steering lay on his side under the spray hood and trunk cabin and, with a flashlight, kept an eye on a box compass on the cuddy floor next to him. If the vessel needed a course adjustment, he so advised the helmsman.

Upon arriving at the ridge, the tub trawls were set out by hand. After a waiting period, normally one to two hours, haul back proceeded. Everything was done by hand. By early afternoon, the *Nellie B.* was on her way back to Marblehead with fish. After unloading, trawl tubs were brought into Henry's shanty, a fire was started in the pot-bellied stove and baiting for the next trip took place. Their workday often ended after suppertime.

Seventeen days under the harsh weather conditions and in the small vessel with no heat, no decent shelter and no modern, comfortable, appropriate clothing was quite a feat. That winter fishing season, from January to early May, Henry and Rene landed over 250,000 pounds of ground fish, mostly cod and haddock, at the beach of Little Harbor.

The years went on for Henry, and in 1938, he married a woman named Helene "Alvina" Lepine, having been introduced to her by a friend and fellow fisherman from Salem. A daughter, Arlene, was born to them in 1942.

In 1936, Rene Barber started Barber's Lobster Pool, which he and his wife ran from Memorial Day to Labor Day selling lobsters, both retail and wholesale. Henry continued lobstering in the *Nellie B.* and developed a reputation as a man who knew what he was doing.

One story tells a great deal about Henry and why he was a "high liner." Henry, like any top fisherman, was very competitive and used to say, "I don't care how many you catch as long as I catch one more!"

Wire traps are now the norm, but they were unheard of until the early 1970s. In order to sink wooden traps, they had four bricks built into them, but when set for the first time, extra weight had to be added to them so the dried traps would sink. Beach stones, often taken from Fisherman's Beach and Priests' or Brown's Islands, were added to each trap for the initial season's set. After a couple of days, the stones were removed and tossed overboard.

Henry hauling, Peaches Point. *Briggs Collection.*

Henry gauging. *Briggs Collection*.

Henry off Peaches Point. The DuPont "summer cottage" is in the background. *Briggs Collection*.

The bottom, three to four hundred yards east of the entrance to Little Harbor, turns into mud, a spot where, each spring, Henry always had two or three traps that he hauled religiously. In the spring, lobsters are not caught on muddy bottom. Traps must be on rocky bottom to be productive. A perceptive person would wonder why Henry continually went to that particular spot. The real reason was that for years he saved the rocks in his boat, stopped on his way in at the same spot and carefully dumped his stones. Using landmarks, he gradually made himself a private piece of rocky bottom for catching spring lobsters.

I first spent time with Henry one fall day in 1948 when I was eleven. He came rowing through the Cove behind Brown's Island. I was in my pram in front of my parents' house and rowed out to meet him. Like all the lobstermen in Little Harbor, Henry was very friendly to me. As I rowed along with him, he said he was going around Peaches Point to get a trap that a previous northeast storm had moved in so close to the rocks that he couldn't haul it with his power boat. The *Nellie B.* was still going strong.

The wind that day was a stiff, west-northwest breeze, but Peaches Point afforded a lee. It is a nice memory for me. Henry talked that morning about how rowing along reminded him of days when he was my age, rowing and lobstering with his father.

When we reached his trap, I remember he hauled it and got three keeper lobsters. As he reminisced about his father that day, I remember he said to me, "You see what you can do with a small boat around the rocks!" That was a practice I was soon to start acting on and continue to follow to the present. That same little nook where Henry hauled that trap in 1948 has fattened my wallet many, many times.

As I grew through my teens, I often spent winter afternoons either stopping in or hanging around John Hawkes's shanty. John was Ed's younger brother. I remember well the workbench and large vice where gear was worked on. In the opposite corner was a good-sized pot-bellied stove fed with pieces of scrap wood often cut off ends of oak lathes from traps under construction. This place had a 100 percent nautical atmosphere, with equipment from past, or for present or expected future, endeavors. Oilskins, oars, coils of rope, lobster buoys and balls of twine were among the articles always present. There was generally a chair or overturned trawl tub where visitors could sit.

On a little shelf behind the workbench, there was a gray radio that could receive, among other things, marine calling channels and station WOU, which was the band used by vessels through a marine operator to talk to people on shore. The radio went on with the light switch for the shanty and was thus constantly going. Except in the summer months, the callers were mostly commercial fishing skippers calling home or to a fish buyer advising of their catch or arrival time from offshore trips. Four times a day, at 5:20 and 11:20 a.m. and p.m., the marine weather was broadcast. If bad weather was due, Little Harbor fishermen gathered around and, after the broadcast, offered their own opinions of what was to happen weather-wise. The information one could get was usually worth what it cost. All in all, the shanty gave me the feeling that I was in a safe and enjoyable place, especially if a gale was screaming overhead.

The shanty was a social center, and boatyard workers, fellow fishermen and John's many friends were constantly coming and going. Every once in a while, a group of friendly Swampscott fishermen would show up, especially if a two- or three-day easterly storm was underway. Before he built his abode on Norman Street, John's cousin, Link Hawkes, was a fixture, using the shanty as a base for his job as a jack-of-all-trades.

Alcoholic beverages were not unheard of, particularly as the afternoon happy hour approached. Dave often joined me, and if the situation became animated and festive, we would try to melt into the hanging oilskins and listen to the stories and observe the goings-on.

The men involved were generally full of life, and looking back, Dave and I received all sorts of lessons. It was in this setting that I learned from Henry Briggs's own words many of the anecdotes that made so much sense. The following story, which I heard many times over those years, came out under special circumstances.

If Henry had come in from lobster fishing on a cold winter afternoon, he would be one of the many visitors enjoying the conviviality before he walked up the hill to his home. John or Link might offer him some liquid refreshment to ease his cold and tired body. Henry was now in his mid- to late fifties.

After a drink or two, Henry would start saying, "I survived forty-four battles in World War I." Sometimes with an innocent question from Dave or myself, he would go into more detail. He had been in charge of a two-horse team (he named his horses Pete and Repeat) that took ammunition on a wagon, or caisson, up to the front lines. This procedure time and again put Henry in great danger. He occasionally mentioned shells bursting just over his head or men being killed right next to him. For reasons unknown, Henry survived in spite of being in, as he put it, "forty-four battles." I never heard him refer to World War I at any other time during my years of exposure to him. According to his family, nightmares of his war experience plagued him for the rest of his life. The single facet of his life that stands out in my mind was how positive he was. I never heard him speak ill of anyone.

Just before Henry died in 1977, his daughter, Arlene, for the first time ever, heard him talk about the horrors he had seen in the war. Literally, those were his last words. Thousands of Americans died in that war. So many years have gone by that it is lost in the wake of recent events. Anyone who doesn't take a moment once in a while to thank the people like Henry for what they did is missing an obligation.

Henry and Alvina took over Barber's Lobster Pool after Rene's premature death and for many years ran it as a seasonal business. The seven-day retail market was staffed by his family from Memorial Day to early October. Besides doing his share (or more) at the Lobster Pool, Henry continued to lobster. He was an early starter (as was I). At 4:30 a.m. every summer morning, Henry's energetic stride was visible, descending the hill from his house and passing under the streetlight at the entrance to the beach. After checking the pumps and lobsters at the pool, he set out alone to haul enough traps to make a showing. Back by noon, he helped at the pool. After an afternoon nap, he would return to assist with the retail rush. Following supper, he spent his evening doing the bookwork.

The hours that Henry spent meticulously recording the day's catches and payouts kept his business expenses and payroll in order and also left us a record that now, almost fifty years later, is a stark contrast not only in prices but also in items expensed. In 1951, sales were $15,060.37 and expenses were $17,249.20, a ratio that would often be repeated by future owners over the next half century. Labor for Link Hawkes's repairs was $10.00, and a bushel of ice cost $0.30. Amazingly, the entry for the cost of gloves was $25.00, probably explained by the amount of lobster meat they were selling. The charge was $2.90 wholesale and dropped to $2.75 at the end of August. It all had to be handpicked. Dave Hildreth, a fourteen-year-old, made $14.00, and Ern Cronk, almost ready for retirement, grossed $1,473.00. That year, Mrs. Crowninshield spent $208.14. On October 4, which was the end of both the Crowninshields' summer season as well as Henry's, she bought twenty pounds of meat for $60.00.

In 1953, once again, the company lost money. They had spent $2.75 for a listing in the Marblehead Directory. Eddie Harbick, who later became my crew, grossed $3,210.60. Studie Smith was plodding along with $794.80. Dave had progressed to $150.35. The phone bill averaged $20.00 per month, and three hundred bricks cost $10.50.

*Cleopatra's Barge. Peach Collection.*

The following year, bait was seven dollars per drum. Henry was "out" all but one day in July and eighteen out of thirty-one days in August. He also caught over half as much as other men on most any given day.

By 1955, ice was up a nickel. Dave had found his stride and increased to $609.75. Winslow chips, made in a sprawling wooden structure up by Green Street, cost $0.10 per bag, and boat gas was $0.24 per gallon. Grover Cleveland Luscomb landed $1,890.63. Henry spent $180.89 with Link Hawkes. A new stove had cost $37.45, but Mrs. Crowninshield must have been off cruising in *Cleopatra's Barge*, because her bill was only $105.21.

Henry did this for many years, working well into his seventies, seven days a week during the summer. Most of those later years he made a profit, and during that time, he accomplished much.

In 1949, an unfortunate accident took place on the *Nellie B*. There was a gasoline explosion and fire on July 31 near the Brimble's Spindle. The morning was thick with fog, and Henry, unable to subdue the flames, hung onto the stern of the boat in the water for forty-five minutes until recreational fishermen heard his cries for help. The flames were put out by Henry and a Beverly lobsterman who happened along. Henry was all right, but the *Nellie B.* and her proud history were finished.

A few days later, Henry purchased a suitable boat to keep fishing. He named this boat after his daughter, Arlene. It was used by Henry until August 31, 1954, when it broke loose in Hurricane Carol and was smashed to pieces against the wall of Graves Boatyard.

He then bought an old-style, twenty-eight-foot spray-hood-type boat from Ern Cronk, who had lobster fished out of Little Harbor for fifty years but recently retired.

The following spring, he bought a new thirty-two-foot open hull from a Nova Scotia wooden boat builder. This was trucked to Little Harbor, where it was cradled in the parking lot. Link Hawkes installed an engine and constructed a pilothouse. Also named *Arlene*, this was to be Henry's last boat.

Sadness was to come to the Briggs family on July 7, 1967, when Henry's wife suffered a severe stroke while in the back room of Barber's Lobster Pool. She was discovered by Arlene. The doctor told Arlene that her mother wouldn't last through the night and then, the next day, changed that to

Henry Briggs's grave.

"wouldn't last through the week." She died thirty-two years later in 2001. Her later years were spent in a nursing home, but her care from Arlene was loving and generously given.

The Lobster Pool passed out of the Briggs family after Alvina's stroke. Henry died in 1977. Alvina was well enough to attend his funeral but had great trouble talking. I went over to give her a hug. She said, with tears flowing, "Henry and I were a great team!"—a touching tribute from a wife to her deceased husband.

Recently, I was walking among the graves on Old Burial Hill. I happened on the Briggs family plot, not seventy-five yards from the back door of Henry's homestead at 64 Orne Street. I looked at Henry's simple bronze plaque. Then I looked out over the waters of the bay he knew so well and thought—Henry Briggs, a life well lived!

# Chapter 12

# Barber's Lobster Pool

Thea Briggs was excited. Henry's younger sister had worked as a nurse's aide at the local hospital, the Mary A. Alley, since graduating from high school. Today she had a day off, and she was going to the town landing. I have to admit when I think of Thea and the Mary Alley, it always gives me a little pang of annoyance. Why did my mother insist on birthing me in Boston, when everyone knows that to be a true Marbleheader there were only two methods: either being born at one's home in the town or checking into the Mary Alley. Oh well, there's no changing all that!

Calvin Coolidge's presidential yacht, the *Mayflower*, was anchored off the Corinthian Yacht Club at the mouth of Marblehead Harbor. The vessel was an impressive 273 feet in length with a beam (width) of 36. She had been used by the navy during the Spanish-American War but was decommissioned in 1904 to be used by the commander in chief. In 1905, President Theodore Roosevelt introduced the Russian and Japanese delegations on board, the start of negotiations for the peace treaty that ended the Russo-Japanese War. In the late 1920s, Coolidge had his summer White House on Little's Point in Swampscott. The *Mayflower* was officially his for his term in office, but the size of the yacht necessitated anchorage in a large harbor, and Marblehead was the closest to Swampscott. She arrived in August during Race Week.

Rene Barber had enlisted in the navy a number of years earlier and was a boatswain's mate on the *Mayflower*. In 1926, anxious to see the sights in town, he and others in the crew were taken by tender to the State Street Landing. Thea Briggs was certainly one of the best-looking young women watching

Calvin Coolidge's presidential yacht, *Mayflower*. *Taylor Collection*.

the arrival of the sailors. Rene noticed the dark-haired beauty immediately. She had a warm smile and was equally attracted to Rene in his spotless uniform. Rene had grown up in Keeseville, New York, but was always drawn to the ocean.

Thea also enjoyed all maritime activity, having been raised at 64 Orne Street, Marblehead, a few hundred yards from the Atlantic. Her father, an inlander from Danvers and a semipro baseball player, had left his roots to be with his wife, Nellie North, in her homestead. Charles Otis Briggs became a fisherman and fathered five children: Bill, who was brought up by his grandmother back home in Danvers; twins Henry and Charles; and two daughters, Mary and Thea. The North/Briggs household, although small in square footage, was huge in family inclusion.

After a brief courtship and correspondence, Rene and Thea were married and moved in with Thea's brother Henry and parents, Nellie and Charles. A short time later, they were joined by Father Barber, who also seemed happy to move closer to the ocean. Aunt Mary (North) and Uncle Chent (also North) were later residents after Charlie Jr. and Mary married and moved off with their spouses.

Life in the small home revolved around the kitchen table, where meals were eaten, bills were paid and lobster catch reports were kept up-to-date. Big brother Henry kept impeccable journals. Rene worked for Graves Boatyard for a while, but in a matter of months, having realized that Front Street was the hub of tourist trade, he had opened a small shop near Fort Sewall, on the main harbor. Henry caught the lobsters, and Rene sold them. Business was seasonal (Memorial Day to Labor Day),

Rene Barber. *Briggs Collection.*

but he and Thea were now able to move to the downstairs apartment in the house where Helen Smith was running her store. This location moved the Barbers even closer to the activity of Little Harbor and the shanties where the fishermen congregated to have some downtime. Although the men individually kept their daily catch as secretive as possible, they loved to relax, play cards together, sing along with an accordion or a banjo and often cook up a chowder to supplement their liquid diet.

The early years at the Briggs home had often been difficult. The assorted relatives all shared the outhouse, which was not so bad in summer but extremely uncomfortable in the dead of winter. Rene had been instrumental in building a new two-holer on the edge of the shanty/workshop in the backyard of the Briggs abode. Years later, when Henry's daughter Arlene planted a vegetable garden on the original site, she grew the largest tomatoes in the neighborhood.

The new apartment actually had indoor plumbing. With Helen Smith as their landlady, Rene and Thea always found coffee and Lindsey's turnovers waiting for their early morning appearance. They were two of the few to witness Helen's smile. She gave them out sparingly, whether through lack of time or lack of desire. Two things that were sure to annoy her were the person who bought her last loaf of bread and the kid who neglected either "please" or "thank you." I guess I was so intimidated by the woman that I became practically speechless in her presence. I was almost always greeted by the same lack of expression or comment.

Soon after the Barbers' move, Rene's brother Bill appeared from "the West." He was definitely duded up, complete with Stetson, high-heeled boots and rope. Nobody seemed to know where he had come from or what he had done. He enjoyed life at the Cove, forfeited the hat and dropped the rope for the most part, but he continued to substitute cowboy boots for the more sensible rubber ones. Bill had a truck, which he began to use to haul bait. Ed Hawkes, while still in high school, used to drive for Bill. He would pick up the bait in Boston, making the daily stops in Nahant, Swampscott and Marblehead, continuing along to Salem and Beverly. The bait from the Boston Fish Pier, mostly mackerel or redfish, was salted and packed in bushels. Each lobsterman had a large barrel called a drum. The drums were set out in proximity to the skiffs. For the guys at Little Harbor, they were over near the ramp. For Studie Smith, the barrel was at the top of the steps to Doliber's Cove, where he moored his boat. The bait delivery occurred about three times per week, with Sundays off, as many of the lobstermen abstained from fishing on the Sabbath.

Bill moved into Helen's second-floor apartment and became an integral part of the Briggs family. At this point, Rene and Henry were fishing trawls in the winter and hauling traps in the summer, but Rene was becoming more and more involved in the sale of lobsters. He decided to move his retail business down to Little Harbor.

In 1936, renting a small section of the boatyard adjacent to the Cove, he opened Barber's Lobster Pool. He ran this operation seasonally each year. With Henry's help, they supplied the general public, as well as the hotels and restaurants in town, for the busy tourist season.

One stormy August afternoon in 1939, some of the Swampscott fishermen came over from the fish house to visit. Visits were common on non-fishing days, both by the Marbleheaders and their arch rivals from the neighboring town. This particular day, Bill Barber had finished his deliveries and had resumed his western mode. Boots on, he strutted by the shanties. The Swampscott men were incredulous. *Who is that guy? What is a cowboy doing at the beach?* There had been much conversation among the fishermen at the beach about Bill—nobody really seemed to know his past, but out of deference to Henry and Rene, they kept the gossip to a minimum.

Corinthian Yacht Club and Marblehead hotel sales slips, 1937. *Briggs Collection.*

At that point, one of the Swampscott guys stepped out from the shanty, emboldened by the home-brew. A loud disagreement erupted. The Swampscotters (also known as Sculpins, a ridiculous spiny fish) suggested that Bill was a phony and couldn't rope a telephone booth, let alone a running steer. Bill left, returned with a rope and dared anyone to run across the beach and he would damn soon show them who was a phony. I think the guy who broke into a run was named Kennedy. He was going quite fast when Bill tossed the rope. Kennedy flipped off his feet and was unable to get up. He had a broken leg. After a few more gulps of painkiller, Kennedy was slipped into the back seat of a car, and off they went. He subsequently reappeared wearing a cast and the opinion that it was just a lucky toss. He declined to run again.

Rene went off to World War II, reenlisting after his naval tour. In 1943, he wrote from North Africa, expressing his sorrow at Henry's loss of traps in a recent storm. He also mentioned appreciation of the photos of his wife: "Thea sent me five snaps and two large pictures of herself. They were swell." I could understand why he thought that.

His letter to Henry and his wife, Alvina, written November 25,1943, stated, "Today is Thanksgiving and I shore have a lot to be thankful for. Well, Hess Chateau Richard is where we are living. It is not bad at all— better than you had last war. Well so long for this time. Love to all Rene." The postmark was stamped, "Passed—Naval Censor."

In the meantime, Alvina, Thea and Mary, with Henry's supervision, were running the Lobster Pool. From 1940 to 1945, they continued Rene's dream.

On April 18, 1945, Rene, a chief boatswain, was honorably discharged from the navy. Five days later, the USS *PE-56*, the ship on which he had been serving, was hit by a mine or sub off Portland, Maine. Of the sixty-two crew members, only thirteen survived, clinging to life in the cold waters of Casco Bay. Sadly, Rene remembered the party his friends had given him the night before he left for Marblehead.

The mysterious blast, termed New England's worst disaster of the war, inexplicably exploded the boat three miles offshore while it was practicing maneuvers. The two-hundred-foot craft was hit amidships, tearing the vessel apart. The forward half sunk within minutes, the stern a short time later. Of the few survivors, some thought they had seen a submarine; others thought they had hit a mine or depth charge.

Rene was safely back in Marblehead. For the next eight years, he would be spared. He had served his country well.

# Chapter 13

# The War Years

During World War I, the Burgess factory was extremely busy with its production of government warplanes. The Graves Boatyard provided storage space for the engines and helped in the manufacture of V-type wings for the experimental tail-less Burgess-Dunne models. However, that era was entirely different from what was to follow when our very coast was threatened by enemy ships. During World War II, Graves was a first-string player. In 1938, Albert Cloutman signed an agreement with Selman Graves making him superintendent of the yard. He was paid $60.00 per week plus overtime of $1.20 per hour and 10 percent of the net profits. According to Bob's modest wife, Betty, "The Cloutmans thought they were rich."

Within three years, all production work would be for the military. Prior to the war, the boatyard had started testing a fast-moving, inverted V-bottom boat designed by William Albert Hickman. Born in New Brunswick, Canada, in 1877, Hickman was a highly intellectual character from a wealthy shipbuilding family. He had earned an engineering degree from Harvard in 1899, and although he had written a bestselling novel, he was drawn to boat designing. His first effort was a fast, seaworthy motorboat that produced a record speed—14.3 miles per hour with a seven-horsepower motor. Flat-bottomed and singularly unattractive, she became known as *Viper*. After a series of adjustments, including the reverse V-bottom, he refined her into the fastest craft around. *Viper V* (a gradual upgrade from *Vipers II, III* and *IV*) had two outward-turning bows, which forced the aerated water along through the tunnel in the middle of the bottom. The pressurized water mix reduced surface friction and generated lift, the principle of planing. There were no side spray and wake to cause drag to the craft. He further improved his design by a surface-piercing propeller system, which eliminated further unnecessary resistance. His hull type, a rather unattractive boxy-looking vessel, became know as a sea sled. The straight outboard keels on both port and starboard and its perfectly parallel sides were responsible for its moniker.

Hickman tried to market his efficient hull, but his sales skills did not seem to equal his architectural prowess. Although he had approached both the United States Navy and the British Admiralty during World War I, his only real success was two fifty-four-foot sea sled torpedo boats used as aircraft carriers to launch bombers in the Zuider Zee in the Netherlands. The boat worked well in the shallow waters of this North Sea inlet. These sleds could reach speeds of fifty-five miles per hour carrying a Caproni bomber on board. With the aircraft's engines also racing, they could go even faster and were able to launch.

In the late '30s and early '40s, Albert Hickman became a familiar figure in our neighborhood. Graves had decided to test and build his sea sleds. There were three sizes: thirty-five feet, forty feet and seventy-eight feet. Wartime had once again aroused the belief that his sled design could be of benefit to the United States Navy.

In the spring of 1944, Dave Hildreth had come to my house to spend the night, the first time our parents let us have an overnight. The next morning, we felt pretty grown up and couldn't wait to get outside to help

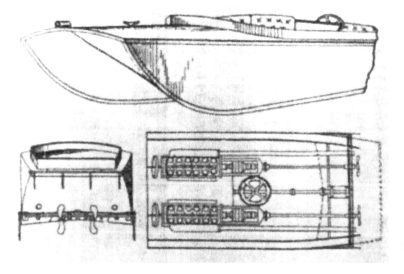

Hickman
Sea Sled
drawing.

my parents with their spring cleanup. This entailed raking the leaves from the property and throwing the debris over the wall to the beach below for burning. Dave and I were in charge of tossing twigs and branches onto our pile. We could hardly wait for my dad to start the fire. We ran to the wall with our latest collection of debris and looked in shock as a speeding sea sled appeared from behind Brown's Island, heading directly for Priests'. "Dad," I screamed, "what are they doing?" The boat, veering sharply to port, quickly reversed, disappearing again behind Brown's. We watched in shock as the sled reappeared, this time screaming onto Priests' with so much momentum that it planed well up onto the rocks. Having attained a speed in excess of thirty knots, it roared up the ledge and came to a halt, high and dry, almost to the grassy field by the old Victorian. We jumped to the beach and tightroped the wall around the boatyard, where three or four small work boats were already manned and headed out to search for the missing boatyard workers. It being low tide, we raced along over Molly's Rocks and onto the causeway leading to Priests' Island. We were the first ones there. I still remember touching the boat and wondering what had happened to the men. How could this have taken place? Within minutes, the police arrived and roped off the area, telling us to leave. As I think back on it now, I feel it had to have been the hard chine (angle where the bottom of the boat meets the side) that caught on a high-speed test turn, violently throwing the men overboard.

Hickman's ideas were sound, but his inability to work well with others and his attempt to patent every single change he made hampered him along the way. The final test of the seventy-eight-foot sled built at Little Harbor was fraught with bad news. On the way to the test area, it ran aground and subsequently ran over a can buoy in the Potomac River. Hickman's chances of a lucrative contract with the government were very limited. It seemed he was his own worst enemy.

A letter written in 1960 to the "Maine Coast Fisherman" by Lincoln Hawkes, in his inimitable way, provides an enlightening view of the testing:

> *In answer to some inquiries on the larger sea-sled type of vessels, I have a very definite personal opinion based on many hours in the engine room of the last and fastest of them all.*
>
> *I worked with the machine shop crew during her construction and was the engineer during trials and subsequent delivery to the navy at Norfolk. There were three thousand horsepower in 55 ft. of boat and the hardest job below during high speed test runs was trying to keep from getting your ribs stove in as anyone who had the dubious privilege of riding her would agree.*

*She was designed and built as a prototype, high speed air sea rescue vessel and was supposed to effect rescue operations up to 80 miles offshore and return at speeds far in excess of more conventional type hulls.*

*She was also supposed to maintain her course and speed as weather conditions worsened long after other boats would be forced to reduce speed. This in effect she did do. We cruised at 40 and made high speed runs in excess of 60 m.p.h. (for some reason she was timed at miles per hour instead of knots).*

*Her main disadvantage was that if caught offshore in a whole gale she could not be hove to. Cutting engine speeds to 1000 r.p.m. or less would result in loss of steerage way and render her as helpless as an old halibut box caught in a tide rip. You could not jog out a spell of bad weather in her. She might survive the awful slatting but the crew would come ashore in a basket.*

*Lincoln Hawkes, Marblehead, Mass.*

*(NB DESPITE CAREFUL PERUSAL OF THE MCF 1959 AND 1960 I DID NOT SEE ANY MENTION OF SEA SLEDS EXCEPT FOR ONE LETTER TO THE EDITOR)*

Meanwhile, both uptown and downtown yards were turning out assembly-line crafts: sixty-four thirty-eight-foot picket boats for the coast guard; forty four-foot tugs and thirty thirty-foot sea sleds for the army; and one thirty-six-foot and one seventy-eight-foot sea sled for the army air corps.

In 1941, the Marblehead police chief had asked Selman Graves to name six men to be sworn in as special patrolmen for the Graves yard. Security was tight. Along with Albert Cloutman and Selman were Cliff Stetson, who lived at the top of Cradleskid Lane (the entrance to the boatyard); Lynton Wright; Yuol Nichols, from nearby Green Street; and Elliott Gantry. All were confirmed in December 1941.

The clock that Laurence Percival had donated to the fishermen was still keeping perfect time, mounted high on Dan Peach's shanty. It stood keeping watch on the beach, as Percy's house had kept watch majestically over Little Harbor. The boatyard was working three full shifts, and Helen's store was doing a land office business as the men came and went. She offered hot lunches, relished by the men after a morning in the drafty sheds. In a very tiny area to the left of the small counter and crowded shelves, she set up chairs and tables covered with colorful oilcloth. The coal stove warmed many a weary worker as he ate a hearty meal or took his coffee break with a delicious homemade donut or pastry made by Lindsey's, an uptown bakery on Anderson Street. Lindsey's billed itself as "wholesale bakers of biscuit specialties." The ad describing this "old-time product" stated:

> *When the first Marblehead "Hard" Cracker was made, or who made it, is not known. But we do know that it had been a popular article of diet in old Marblehead for many years before the establishment of the Lindsey Bakery in 1852. In the old days, before the invention of modern machinery, each cracker was rolled out, cut, docked and even thrown into the oven by hand. The fire was of faggots only, a sort of bonfire in the center of the oven, and the embers were drawn out upon the hearth before the crackers were put in. Up to fifty years ago each town or city had its own cracker bakery. Lindsey's Bakery, however, is still producing Marblehead Crackers at the old stand, perhaps because its aim has ever been to realize the boast of the true Marbleheader, that they are "the best crackers on earth."*

These tooth-breakers could only be softened by placing them in a steaming bowl of Helen's chowder. Lindsey's raspberry and apple turnovers, laced with a sweet cream sauce, were also in great demand. A shift change could deplete Helen's supply in about five minutes.

Her bread and rolls, however, came from Boardman's, a versatile shop situated behind the old yellow Town House on Washington Street (known as Market Square). They supplied baked beans and brown bread on Saturday afternoons and a full line of cakes and pastries.

A few of the neighborhood women were also helping out at the yard, especially in the accounting office, under a plan called "mother's hours." Volunteer work at the Red Cross, folding bandages and knitting gloves and socks was highly enrolled.

As we ran down Orne Street hill heading for Harding Lane, we glanced in at the Cove. The morning shift had broken for lunch, and many of the workers had headed for Helen's store to supplement their brown bags with a candy bar or a Hires root beer. In the '40s, the era before the school lunch program, Dave and I, together with our sisters, Alice and Brenda, walked home every weekday noon to meals alternating between the Hildreths' house and my parents' home. Meals were served indoors in the cool months but often outside, weather permitting. At that time, it never occurred to us that this arrangement might have been any sort of interruption into our mothers' routines. We figured it was so we could all have a good time together.

My mother considered herself quite a nutritionist. One of her major campaigns was selling us on the value of the twenty-eight vegetables she was capable of preparing. Alice, who was quite small and fairly cautious, lived in fear of the broccoli menu. I can still hear my mother suggesting strongly, "Just try one bite, Alice." Alice slowly put the fork to her mouth, the small green floret poised delicately on the tines. She inserted the fork, made a horrible gagging sound and lost her entire lunch. Dave, Brenda and I found this fairly hilarious. My mother, seemingly unembarrassed by Alice's upset, mopped off her face and blouse, removing the wasted vitamins from her place mat.

Dairy products were also a large part of my mother's body-building regimen. When we went to the Hildreths' for lunch, Brenda and I secretly joked about the "Hildreth-size" glass. Milk was served in what we called a juice glass, leaving us feeling a bit deprived, but Mrs. Hildreth was pregnant with her fourth child, so I guess she was practicing the needed frugality of a large family.

These noonday repasts lasted until Dave and I were in the sixth grade and Brenda and Alice were in the fourth. The school then began selling milk in the classroom, and we brown-bagged it. School lunch was never the same for me.

John Gardner, designer, builder and longtime journalist, worked the second shift at the boatyard from mid-December 1941 through March 24, 1943. He was planking the twenty-eight-foot McInnis-designed U.S. Coast Guard picket boats. His crew shaped the white cedar planks and installed two strakes per eight-hour shift. These boats were to patrol the coast.

Albert Cloutman handled the first shift. All sixty-four of the picket boats were completed in a little over a year—a pretty amazing feat, considering the intricacy of the planking. Albert's son, Bob, had joined the Graves workforce. He was a valuable employee, working on the picket boats until he enlisted in the navy in 1943. Many local fishermen were also in the boatyard's employ. Dan Peach went to Graves as a part-timer in 1943, after active duty overseas. His specialty was working on transoms (the rounded end of the stern). Ralph Conner and his brother, Albert, were both skilled craftsmen and experienced woodworkers. A man named Dan Grant, a well-known coworker, actually made violins in his spare time. Ted Homan was in charge of lumber stock and preparation, a very demanding job. Tremaine Robarts, the father of my hockey coach, was a regular, and Charlie Stacy ran the *Selmilede*, the boatyard towboat. The *Selmilede* was named for Selman, Mildred and Edith Graves, Al's three offspring.

The workers were also converting private yachts for coastal patrol work. They needed suitable deck houses, heating systems and protective ice sheathing for the hulls. The final preparation was a coat of gray paint. Most of these "yachts" were forty-five to fifty-five feet in length. They were

Selmilede. *Marblehead Historical Commission.*

skippered by men like my father who were too old for active duty. In June 1939, Congress had passed Title 14 of the U.S. Code, establishing the United States Coast Guard Reserve and subsequently a "temporary reserve," a group who worked without pay but received fuel reimbursement on private yachts. Their purpose was for coastal patrol and harbor security. The Marblehead contingent covered the area from Newcomb's Ledge whistle buoy to Pig Rocks Bell to the southwest, and northeast to the Eastern Point whistle off Gloucester. The men and boats were armed. There were machine guns on the bows. They were positioned as a deterrent to approaching enemy subs. During World War II, these coast guard units, active on both the East and West Coasts, sank twelve German and two Japanese subs and two German surface vessels.

There were strict rules for the waterfront houses. Our neighborhood was certainly made even more aware than most of the dangers surrounding us. All houses that had windows that could be spotted from the ocean were required to use heavy shades called blackout shades. The shore division of the coast guard auxiliary, armed and uniformed, was known as the coast guard patrol. Our good friend and neighbor at 5 Harding Lane, Jim Sutherland, was one of these men. They walked our area and the beaches, checking for

Yacht prepared for coastal patrol duty. *Bates Collection.*

any forbidden sliver of light that could be visible to an approaching enemy vessel, as well as for the enemy himself. As further backup, there were air raid wardens. Rupert Jacques, an older, white-haired man who lived on Beacon Street at Doliber's Cove, served our neighborhood. There were periodic exercises. Air raid warnings, similar to school fire drills, where every shade in the house had to be down with windows secured, took place every couple of months. I remember our mother being reprimanded by Mr. Jacques, looking very official with his armband and insignia, because he had sighted a slit of light under one of our curtains.

# The Rich History of a Small Fishing Port

The headquarters for the patrols was at the Kingsley estate, a home on the harbor at Front Street that had been commandeered for service. Each patrol of two men, ready for duty, would be driven by Jeep to the entrance of Little Harbor and dropped off at a hut that had been erected at the previous site of Percy's shanty. The structure also provided shelter in times of inclement weather. Even the headlights of people's cars had to be painted with a special black paint, although driving was very limited because of gas rationing.

Proof that our waters were truly being invaded was evidenced in the summer of 1942. As I stood on the beach in front my house, I witnessed a one-time sight looking to sea toward Half Way Rock. It had been a foggy morning, but by 11:00 a.m., the fog had burned off rapidly. With the now improved visibility, I saw several naval and coast guard vessels between Cat Island and the "Rock." They ranged in length from fifty to two hundred feet. In the haze beyond them, a couple of larger vessels could be seen slowly circling. They looked like destroyers. The word around town was that a local lobsterman had come across a German submarine earlier that morning, lying on the surface. With no means of communication on board, he had immediately returned to port and notified authorities, and thus the activity. I never did hear if anything resulted from the search effort I saw.

The following year, an empty six-man life raft washed up on Devereux Beach in Marblehead. At about the same time, strewn along the sand by my house were soggy boxes of provisions that were either from the raft or from a ship itself, probably a merchant vessel sunk by the Germans. During the war, there were ships leaving East Coast ports transporting food and fuel to Europe, as well as tankers transporting coal and other goods from cities like Norfolk to northern New England destinations. Needless to say, we were very much in the war effort.

The lobstermen who had not joined the armed forces were still fishing but were required to have very large identification numbers on their boats, easily readable by the coast guard. These numbers were one and a half to two feet in height.

I still vividly remember August 15, 1945, known better as V-J day. Everybody was out in the streets, cheering and waving flags, celebrating victory over Japan. I was allowed to honk the horn of our old Cadillac, while my sister, never wanting to be outdone, was permitted the privilege with the Sutherlands' '38 Dodge. We marched up and down Harding Lane, banging pots and pans with spoons, and later got in the car and rode uptown, feeling totally emancipated.

*Chapter 14*

# Dan Peach

S ome people talk a great deal and don't have much to say. Others say little but have a way of making much more of an impact; Dan Peach was one of those.

One afternoon in the mid-1950s, I was sitting on the bench at Fisherman's Beach after a day on the water. Among others, Dan was there. I made some comment about something my father wanted me to do. Having been influenced by a contemporary who called his father "my old man," I used that term in reference to my dad. This wasn't my habit, but at age eighteen, I knew everything there was to know. Dan immediately said, "He's not 'your old man,' he's your father. Don't ever let me hear you call him that again." Who Dan was and what he meant to me is demonstrated by the fact that I never used that term subsequently. It was proper advice at the perfect time. As years went by, I learned more about Dan. He was the type of Marbleheader common in the first half of the twentieth century. An ordinary man in most respects, Dan and his compatriots positively affected my value system as our paths crossed.

Dan Peach was born on January 1, 1900, a descendant of one of Marblehead's oldest families. His father was a mason and a caretaker for a Peaches Point estate. Dan spent his whole life living in Barnegat and much of his time around Fisherman's Beach. By the time he attended Essex Agricultural School, where he graduated in 1918, he had become known as a loner. During that time, he almost died from the influenza epidemic. This prevented him from volunteering for World War I and left a wound

Dan Peach (left) and Mandon Bates hauling a fish trap. *Peach Collection.*

in his soul that would take over twenty years to heal. He spent a considerable amount of his younger working life in the '20s and '30s catching lobsters and fish. He and Mandon Bates ran a fish trap off the southwest side of Tinker's Island for several years in the late '40s. They caught mostly mackerel and sold it to fish dealers in Gloucester.

He also pursued other interests. He was a skilled woodworker and boat builder, creating skiffs and dories in the large shanty he maintained at Little Harbor. He worked as an employee at Graves Boatyard from time to time and could handle the most skilled tasks required in wooden vessel construction. As an avocation, he maintained a large piece of property in Henniker, New Hampshire. Here, his agricultural training helped him raise a 165-tree apple orchard, which he harvested on weekends from August to October. He sold apples to retailers for many years, including Marblehead Community Store and Louie's Supermarket on Washington Street. A sailor with several modest-sized sailing vessels, Dan enjoyed the serenity of sailing.

In the late 1920s, he had a job as a boat man working for the Eastern Yacht Club. The summer White House of President Calvin Coolidge was in Swampscott. The presidential yacht, *Mayflower*, was anchored at the mouth of Marblehead Harbor at this time. Mrs. Coolidge and her children spent time at the Eastern Yacht Club. She wanted the children to learn how to sail. Dan was an obvious choice but took the job only after he told the Secret Service agents assigned to them to stay clear of the sailing. History has it that the children were well taught, and Mrs. Coolidge was amused at Dan's handling of the Secret Service.

In 1942, Dan satisfied the hole in his soul. At age forty-two, he volunteered for active duty. After basic training, he found himself on the front lines in the North African Campaign. There is a story relating to that time that is impossible to verify but too good not to tell.

During the late '30s, Dan had a job for a year or more as a gardener for an estate in Beverly Farms. It seems that someone had heard of Dan and his good reputation years before teaching the Coolidge children how to sail. This person found Dan a side job teaching General Patton's daughter how to sail off Manchester. Some type of dispute arose. The lessons stopped. Patton apparently didn't like people who bucked him in any way. His reputation as an authoritative man is well documented.

One day while in the army in North Africa, General Patton passed by Dan's unit. At forty-two, Dan was no kid and not easily intimidated. In the course of this event, Private Peach and General Patton came face to face. The private always knows the general. In this case, there was a very rare occurrence. The general recognized the private. Their eyes met, nothing was said and Patton moved on. Knowing Patton's reputation and Dan personally, I would caption the scene, "Strong minds duel to a standstill."

Dan died in 1994. I was talking to Ed Hawkes about him later. I didn't know until then that Ed, as a boy, had learned much from Dan in the 1930s. They went line trawling and lobstering together. Dan liked seal shooting and duck hunting and often included Ed in his travels, giving him early training in these endeavors. Ed spent a lot of time hanging around the shanties with Dan and the others, just as I would a generation later. I loved to compare stories about what we both did and learned in comparable situations, even though our experiences were twenty years apart. From a perspective of seventy or more years, Ed said, "Certainly for me growing up, Dan was the ultimate example of resolve, honesty, good humor and conservatism. We had good times, and he taught me a lot, quietly." I didn't have the exposure to Dan that Ed did, but he taught me too.

Ed related another quick story about Dan. Ed was away from Marblehead for four and a half years during World War II. He had received correspondence from home that Dan had enlisted in the army during that time. Ed quickly found Dan and asked him where he had been. Dan replied, "Africa." That one word was all he ever said.

# Chapter 15

# Gunning Here and Abroad

I still see Ed often. He was so instrumental in my early interest in lobstering. I now realize that his life was patterned after the generation before him in much the same way that mine was. In referring to the old-timers who had helped him, he often mentioned gunning (duck shooting), as well as lobstering.

Fishing and hunting are man's salvation, his basis for survival. Ed was attracted to both. His interest in gunning started when he received his first BB gun at the age of ten. That same day, his mother stepped out on the back porch just as he squeezed the trigger and a chickadee fell to the ground. She said nothing, simply extended her palm forward in silence. Ed never saw the gun again, nor did he expect to. He had been told many times never to point a gun at anyone. Target practice excepted, he was not to shoot at anything unless he intended to eat it.

In 1934, when he was fourteen, with his parents' knowledge, he bought an Eastern Arms ten-gauge single-barrel shotgun from a school chum named Antoine Lausier for three dollars. Ed's first stop was at Horace Cloon's Hardware store at the corner of State and Washington Streets. Horace had a brother, Sam, who owned the hardware store at 92 Washington Street. Apparently, there was little goodwill between the two. If one put a wheelbarrow or a lawnmower outside on display, about fifteen minutes later there would be one out next door. Horace sold shotgun shells by the piece as well as by the box. Twelve-gauge were five cents apiece. Ed never went gunning with fewer than five. He once said, "I don't recall the price of ten-

Early duck shooters, Fort Beach, circa 1900. The left cupola is on Old Burial Hill, and the right cupola is on Fountain Park.

gauge, because I only fired one." That was at his first outing on Peaches Point late in the fall. The summer people had hibernated south, so he wandered past the Crowninshields' and down into the ledges in front of the DuPont house. He had no decoys for luring his prey, so he was pleasantly surprised to see a pair of shell ducks (mergansers) round the point, headed straight for him. He was again surprised when he fired and the trailing duck fell, since he had been aiming for the leading one. The biggest shock of all was that he had landed in the water, a startling jolt in late November when the Atlantic Ocean is a chilling forty-six to fifty degrees.

The heavy "duck loads" had caused an excessive recoil from the lightweight gun. The high-velocity shells and the slippery rockweed were too much for the young Hawkes. Ed dragged himself back up onto the rocks, knowing that the easterly wind would blow the duck toward his perch. His older brother Win, the more rugged of the three siblings, used to swim out to retrieve the ducks, even in winter, but Ed quickly learned that was not for him.

He took the cleaned and plucked bird home and asked his mother to cook it, which she did. He was informed that should he shoot anymore, he had better cook them at the shanty because they were not welcome at home. Ducks are fish eaters and quite gamey. Ed, disgruntled, took the gun back to Antoine.

Live decoys had been outlawed by the government in the 1920s. In their place were three general types of man-made wooden ducks: working, decorative and miniature. Shore birds, which were also legal game, were made in the same three varieties. Working decoys, of course, were just that and meant to shoot over. Decorative were for display only. They had every feather burned or carved and then painted. If one was not aware, he might wait some time for the decoy to move. They were very lifelike.

Material depended on the section of the country where they were made, varying from old light and telephone poles to discarded cork-filled life jackets. In New England, the cork pieces were placed together and fastened with long tapered hardwood dowels fitted with wooden heads. Eastern white pine, basswood and cedar were common, but tupelo was frequently used in the South. Pine heads were common. In the '30s, one could buy a dozen decoys for ten to twelve dollars from a full-time carver, mostly solid with a minimum of detail in the painting.

Antoine and Ed must have made up, because Ed bought another gun from him, this time a LeFevre, an expensive trap and skeet gun for shooting clay pigeons. Ed's was one of the inexpensive models, but choked full and full, it was ideal for duck shooting.

Before he had a chance to try the gun, Lincoln Davis showed up at his house to ask if Ed wanted to go gunning with him in Ipswich Bay. Linc was a boater and a sportsman. He lived on the exclusive area of Peaches Point and happened to be Louise Crowninshield's nephew. They set out to shoot a few coot (scoters). The method they used was called flight shooting, where the shooter took aim from an anchored dory with decoys set downwind from the boat. The first move was to guess where the birds would fly, depending on wind direction. Southwest generally produced the steadiest shooting and the most birds. The interesting thing was that not only would the birds come within gunshot but often they would make two or three circuits of the boat with time for reloading and firing again—hence the saying "crazy as a coot." It was challenging shooting because of one's range estimation and the motion of the craft.

Ed recounted the trip:

> *The first time I fired the LeFevre, I was instantly aware of very heavy recoil, far in excess of the old ten-gauge. When I opened it to reload, both shells had been fired, even though I had pulled only the front, or right*

*barrel trigger. I thought I must have been clumsy and pulled both, so I slid in two more shells. More birds—I fired one barrel and knew instantly both had fired again. From then on, I only loaded one barrel. It took us some time to gather a bag of birds. Linc had done very little gunning and was at best no better than I, who was just getting started. I wondered subsequently if Linc asked me because I would row. Two pairs of oars were certainly better than one!*

Disassembly of the LeFevre showed the cause of malfunction to be a worn sear, part of the trigger assembly. Ed returned the gun to Antoine and this time suggested he try selling newspapers rather than guns.

Through some stroke of luck or genuine fondness, Charlie Turnbull, the Hawkeses' uncle, gave the Hawkes boys, Winslow, Ed and John, three guns to share: a Winchester .22 WRF (Winchester Repeating Firearms) octagon-barrel, pump-action rifle for target or small-game shooting; a Savage model 99 lever-action .303-caliber rifle, which they used to shoot harbor seals for their five-dollar bounty and later on for deer hunting in New Hampshire; and a double-barrel twelve-gauge L.C. Smith. The third gun was a beauty, with engraving and a Circassian walnut stock. Choked full and full, it was probably made for live pigeon shooting, a popular sport in the 1920s before the advent of clay pigeons. The boys took good care of their new treasures, the only failure being a broken firing pin in the Smith. Mandon Bates turned one out on his lathe, which evidently was quite a feat because he said to Ed, "Please don't ask me to make another one."

The three boys slept in the attic, which was basically unheated in the winter. The ironic thing about that loft was that there was a fireplace, but the boys used it only as a backstop for target practice with the .22. All three of them could put out the flame of a lit candle. The attic was on the third floor, and the windows were always open, unless foul weather prevented it. Close to the harbor, the house resonated with the sound of foghorns blowing for the yacht club launches and the roar of boat engines. In the fall, just as day was breaking, the gabble and chatter of the squaw ducks would start. Named by Indian tribes, the birds were so called for either their garb of bright-colored feathers or their vocal ability. They sounded like packs of hounds hot on the trail of some game. In fact, the locals called them hounds. True to their word, remembering the maxim, "Never shoot anything you're not going to eat," the boys never gunned the squaws. They were extremely gamey.

Dan Peach, twenty years older than Ed, was certainly someone Ed admired. In the mid-1930s, while Ed was still in high school, the two spent considerable time together. Dan never talked about anyone, including himself. He might tell you what size birdshot he preferred shooting over decoys, but that was about it. This is not to say he had no sense of humor. He appreciated a joke and was not above activating one. One cold winter's day, with a crowd gathered in his shanty, he built a fire in his small barrel-like stove. Carefully avoiding observation, he poured a little gasoline in the stove and tossed a match in the bottom. The result was a good-sized bang. The lid hit the roof, starting a panicked exit for the door.

Acceptance by the fishermen had to be earned. One time, a rather pushy type who was going fishing, but not with Dan, took it upon himself to leave his shoes in Dan's shanty. Unable to put them on when he returned, he discovered they were nailed to the floor.

Once when Ed was gunning with Dan at the Dry Breakers, four ducks came in over the decoys. Both men fired. Dan dropped both of his, but Ed's kept on going. Dan said, "If you don't do any better than that, we're going to be here a long time filling two limits."

They reloaded quickly. A gunner had to be ready for the next bunch. Dan went to pick up his birds while Ed sat down on the rocks from where they had been shooting. Glancing in a puddle where the empties had landed, he noticed that the spent shells were the same color but the brass bases were different. Ed's had been high or long base; these were short. He picked one up, and the legend stamped on it read "12 GAUGE BLANK." Dan returned, all smiles, and Ed exclaimed, "You owe me two." Both men burst out laughing. Dan had thought Ed wouldn't notice. After that, the question "Can you spare a couple of shells?" became an inside joke between them.

The wind had started to blow so hard that they frantically picked up the decoys. The row, a few hundred yards to the powerboat in the lee of the Southern Gooseberry, was almost impossible for them. They discussed the possibility of spending the night on the Breakers, as it appeared they were making no headway. Rowing into the wind with two pairs of oars, they arrived at their craft, exhausted and relieved. The two expert oarsmen barely made it.

Dan became a skilled craftsman of decoys. Many of his are now on exhibit in the museum at Mystic, Connecticut. Ed has followed suit, making wonderful specimens. A fine carver, he feels it "most satisfying to see a flight of birds sharply alter course to come into your spread. It really does quicken one's pulse!"

When Ed was in high school, he played football, which happened to coincide with open season on ducks. He loved both sports and had trouble figuring out how to include them simultaneously in his life. He used to get up at 4:00 a.m. on Saturdays and row down to Coney Island or adjacent ledges, depending on the tide. He was gunning by dawn. Back by late morning, he would have a short nap, toast and scrambled eggs and then be off to play football for the afternoon. Marblehead had some pretty good teams in the late '30s, and extra fun and excitement could be found in postseason games with such teams as Curtis High School, Staten Island, New York; Miami Edison in Coral Gables, Florida; and the team from Port Arthur, Texas. Ed came home from Texas with a gap in his back teeth, the result of someone's boot. The dentist there used a tool like a marlinspike to lever out the remains, broken off flush with the surface. The dentist said, "You all hold on, now," which did not prevent Ed's eyes from watering. The age limit to play football at Port Arthur was twenty-one; Marblehead's was eighteen. The difference was obvious and almost insurmountable. The Massachusetts boys lost the game by a point—a tribute to their fortitude and skill.

Charles McInnis was the high school coach. He taught Pop Warner's unbalanced line formation and a lot of sleight-of-hand ball handling. The opposition found it difficult at times to discover who had the ball. For example, the quarterback would fake giving the ball to the fullback, who, with head down and bent over, would charge the line as hard as he could. The quarterback would turn away from the line with the ball on his hip and very slowly jog toward the end as though he was going to stop. As the dust was settling on the pileup in the line, the quarterback, having reached the end of the line of scrimmage, would run for the goal, usually with only the safety in the way. Sometimes there would not even be a safety, he having closed up toward the action. Of course, there was a limit to the frequency this strategy could be employed, but on the whole, it worked quite well. This type of coaching earned the Marblehead team the moniker "Marblehead Magicians."

Ed also sang in the choir at the Old North Church. Choir members were rewarded for their efforts, but not necessarily for their devotion, at the rate of twenty-five cents for practice on Friday night and fifteen cents for the main event. That amounted to forty cents per week for true believers, or the price of eight shotgun shells for the "sports."

Another effort at making a buck involved seal hunting. According to the state fish and game department, seals were a menace to local fish and lobster supplies, hence a five-dollar bounty per head. After World War II, it became illegal to hunt or take them, but in the mid-1930s, Ed and his brother

John did their best to cash in. The seals arrived in the fall and stayed until spring, when they went north to breed. They generally went to forage when the tide was up and moved into shoal water, where there were numerous ledges exposed, to sun themselves. Being stationary targets, they were most vulnerable at this time.

However, when in the water, a bobbing head didn't provide much of a target from a moving boat. If the seal's lungs were not full of air, it would sink when shot, posing a recovery problem. Having rowed a few miles, and full from their packed lunch, the boys devised a scheme to prevent them from going home empty-handed. In order to retrieve the seal, it first had to be found. Fatty and blubbery, the creature would exude oil through a puncture in its skin, and sure enough, it would find its way to the surface and form an oil slick. By rowing to windward, lowering a gig (pronounced jig) and slowly towing it on the bottom, it would hook the body, which could then be hauled to the surface. A gig was a cast lead, tapered cylinder with halibut hooks set in it. It worked very well. The seals varied greatly in size, from about sixty pounds to a few hundred. The large ones had to be towed and then rolled up on the rocks in order to get them in the dory.

Ed and his brother, John, thought nothing of rowing to House Island in Manchester, where they might get one seal, and then to the Dry Breakers, where often they could nab two. If they were still seal-less, they might continue on to Flying Point and then the Outer Pigs. Their entire course was seven or eight miles. They didn't sit around listening to the battery-operated radio very long after supper.

Dan and Ed used to keep track of each other when they were on the water. Usually, Dan would go fishing, tow his skiff and leave it in the lee of an island and retrieve it on his way home to try his luck with the seals. He had a Savage model 99 lever action .250-3000 (caliber of the bullet). He could drive tacks with it. He almost never missed. Quite often, he would correctly guess where the boys were and give them a tow home. Ed and John never turned him down.

Ed was thrilled to get his driver's license. Always on the lookout for ways to make extra money, he approached Laurence Percival. Percival was an anomaly in the neighborhood. He was the rare exception of a well-to-do abutter to the Cove. He, and his father before him, had done very well with their jewelry business on Washington Street in Boston. He bought the large stucco estate approached through two field stone pillars from Little Harbor. His long stone driveway was diagonally across from the shanties, but the house was extremely private. The property included Molly's Rocks on the far side and ran up to Fountain Park away from the ocean. He was no stranger to the beach. He would saunter down to chat with the local fishermen and occasionally enjoy a shot or two in one of the shanties. He was quick to contribute a bottle of Four Roses (his favorite), generous with his snippets of free time and well liked by the fishermen. He was also extremely familiar with the ocean. In bad weather, he watched from his living room for any problem in the Cove, which was entirely visible from his front window. He was often a first responder to a dragging lobster boat or a skiff adrift. Their mutual love of the ocean seemed to bind him with the locals more closely than their huge economic disparity might have separated them.

He seemed to be aware of the industry of Ed Hawkes and started using him as a driver. Percy (as he was known familiarly) had a Packard 180. In the summer and during vacations while still in school, Ed drove Percy to Boston, to the jewelry store at 373 Washington Street. The pay was ten dollars for the week, but the fringe benefits were many. Percy had a thirty-foot, V-bottom powerboat with a big Sterling engine, which he used to go to the Vineyard. There he had a camp on Chilmark. Ed was sometimes privy

The Laurence Percival house, with Grover Cleveland Luscomb's lobster boat in foreground. The umbrella is to ward off the summer sun. *Peach Collection.*

Laurence Percival suited up for yachting.

to the trip, meeting Laurence's old friend, a Vineyarder named Dr. Mayhew. The two men and the teenager used the blinds on the island for shooting. For a boy who had seldom left Marblehead, these occasions were very special.

Ed had also been interested in flying since he was twelve, and although there was little spare cash in the Hawkes family, he was able to squirrel some money away from his earnings at Little Harbor. As Ed assembled a cache, he would either buy model airplanes or, as he got older, get a flying lesson in a J-2 Cub at Beverly Airport or the runway at Plum Island. The lessons were at the most an hour, costing twelve dollars for a dual lesson or eight dollars for a solo. To replenish his cash supply, Ed always returned to "the beach."

He recalled, "One of my favorite tasks when I was about ten or eleven was stringing up cunners." The young boys hanging around the beach used a sewing device fashioned from a length of one-eighth-inch-diameter brass rod. One end was pounded flat, a small hole was bored and a long string was threaded through the eye. The other end of the metal was also flattened but shaped to a sharp point. That part was pushed through the fish, pulling the string with it, until enough cunners were threaded for a lobster trap. They were then tied off with a loop for hanging. Ed would get twenty-five cents per bushel for these strings, salted down. They were packed into butter firkins from Kennedy's Butter and Egg on Essex Street in Salem.

On weekends, Ed would often skip Sunday school looking for work. "There was always something doing at the beach," reminisced Ed. "I could make some money. Grapes were shipped by rail from the West Coast in open crates made of soft wood lathes that were eight feet long, two inches wide and about one-quarter-inch thick. They were unloaded at freight yards on Northern Avenue in Boston and salvaged by Marblehead fishermen." These lathes, together with cherry bows from the fields a short distance from the beach, were assembled into lobster traps. Added Ed, "In the early '30s, this was the method: the old-timers did all the work on their boats and gear themselves."

The devastation that Hitler was inflicting on Europe was a storm Ed wanted to see ended. That loathing and the excitement it instilled in him prompted him to go to Salem with his friend Buddy Clark to sign up for the U.S. Navy Air Force. The two twenty-year-olds were informed that two years of college education was mandatory. The boys, who had sought each other's support for enlistment, were crushed.

They were boyhood pals who had played together and, as they matured, spent time tenting at Brown's Island. There they had met Steve Clauson, who was renting one of the small cottages from Louise Crowninshield. Steve was a Brit who lived in East Boston and was an orderly in a Boston hospital. According to Ed, "He had a Latin-type wife and two rather sickly children." The sea air was supposed to be a panacea for ailments, and obviously Steve would make any sacrifice for his girls. The island had no amenities except its natural beauty. The Clauson family had to either carry their supplies across the mud flats by foot or row to the mainland at high tide for food and water. Helen's store in Little Harbor was the most accessible location. Steve's wife became a frequent shopper.

Steve befriended Ed and his pals. Both groups enjoyed the solitude at Brown's, but some diversion was welcome. Ed and the boys were enthralled with Steve's stories of the desperate straits of his home country. Steve felt compelled to take care of his family and consequently couldn't go back to England, but his talk of war inflamed the younger men. He told them of the movement in Canada to train recruits.

In the early 1940s, more than nine thousand Americans decided to enlist in either the RAF (Royal Air Force of England) or the RCAF (Royal Canadian Air Force) rather than wait for their own country to step up to Nazi aggression. Unable to coax Buddy into leaving the country, Ed struck out for Canada, his reasons being "the chance to fly full time, excitement and maybe help in wiping out the 'little ranting man.'" He flew from Boston to Montreal on Trans Canada Airlines for the fee of twenty-eight dollars for a one-way ticket. A bit in awe of the large city but spurred on by his strong convictions about flying and the expanding war, he found the RCAF recruiting station. They informed him that if he was really serious about this mission, they would provide him with a train ticket to Toronto. After some rudimentary physical and mental testing, Ed was sent to Manning Depot, the start of the most exciting years of his life. "Manning Pool," as it was

Early Graves Boatyard, showing houses on Brown's Island. *Peach Collection.*

called, was the site for the trainees to wait for their postings. It was a way station for new civies. The date was December 1, 1941. According to Ed:

> *There were various con games at Manning Depot, such as asking for six volunteers who could ride motorcycles. After stepping forward and saluting smartly, the recruits were given large shovels and told to go shovel snow off the roof. We were also asked if we would like to inspect some aircraft and, of course, everybody wanted to. They led us to Maple Leaf Stadium with all our kit, where we were informed we were going to guard some planes. They materialized as old clapped-out Anson Mack IIs stowed under the stadium. We were also stowed under the bleachers in what were originally dressing rooms, now converted into bunk houses. It was cold and uncomfortable.*

Ground school (GS) in Toronto was next. The recruits—American, Australian and Canadian—learned about navigation, weather and Morse code. Interestingly, Ed never used the dots and dashes, since all discourse was by talking (VHF radio). Pearl Harbor was bombed a mere six days after Ed arrived in Canada.

By early June 1942, Ed was ready for EFTS (elementary flying training school) in Goderich, Ontario. The DeHavilland Tiger Moth was a perfect training plane. It had a simple four-cylinder 140-horsepower Gypsy Major engine and was easy to maneuver. Explained Ed, "DeHavilland Tiger Moths were open-cockpit biplanes reminiscent of World War I and great fun to fly, being fully acrobatic. Night flying with a full moon was unbelievable." Ed's decision to stay with RCAF, even after the United States had declared war, was based on the fact that "it took too much effort to get where I was. I was not about to toss it in for anything." Most of the Americans seemed to share the same view; they were glad the United States had finally joined the effort, but they were so well accepted by the RCAF personnel that there was no point in transferring back. Everyone was just really anxious to get in the war. Ed felt that if he hadn't been good enough to join the United States Naval Air Service before the war, he was not good enough after it started. In Canada, he was treated the same as any Canadian. The subject of who you were or where you came from seldom surfaced. Ed felt proud to wear the Canadian shoulder patch.

The next posting at Centralia, Ontario, was at No. 9 SFTS (service flying training school). Ed arrived on August 6, 1942, and received his wings on November 19, 1942, just under a year after his arrival in Canada. He also received a new commission as a pilot officer (P/O). This is the equivalent of a second lieutenant in the USAF. A F/O (flying officer) would be the American first lieutenant. Ed was ready for action, but the RCAF had other ideas for him.

Ed's good friend and roommate at Centralia was a fellow American from Indiana named John Birky. On September 30, 1942, during a solo night-flying exercise, John crashed and burned. Ed had taken off directly after Birky and explained, "You had to wait for the control tower [for takeoff] to give you the signal. There was also a portable control tower on a truck at the end of the runway. If there was a difficulty, they aimed the red light at you." Having been given a green, Ed made a routine takeoff, thinking all was fine. However, he seemed to be unable to see the faint white light on the tail of the plane in front of him, which should have been Birky's. As he looked down, he spotted the flames and with them the demise of his friend. He knew it had to be John.

Up to this point, Ed's flying career had included plenty of hard work and a lot of acquired expertise, but the actual flying part had been a larger version of the fun and games a young boy dreams of. Unauthorized low flying was a practice in which most of these enlistees partook. They loved taunting the trees in the desolate forest or skimming the grasses of the Canadian marshes. They knew there was no punishment if they weren't caught except death. A horrible realization of mortality was now forced upon them.

Many of the fighter pilots seemed to share the thoughts of Clem Weidenfeller, a resident of Hawarden, Iowa, who kept a detailed diary of his Canadian tour. He asked his F/O if he would have any "fun" in coastal command. The officer looked at him incredulously as if to say, *So you're one of these mad Americans who want to get shot.* "Well," he said, "it depends on what you call 'fun.' I don't think I'd call it that. We had 80 percent casualties last year."

It was a sobering experience for Ed and many others, who came looking for excitement and revenge and met death square in the eye. The boy exited, and the man took over.

At Summerside, Prince Edward Island, Ed was sent to GRS (general reconnaissance school). However, the training was strictly navigational. For practice, they were given a course to figure out. Using the dead reckoning and allowing for drift, they might be told to go to North Sydney, Nova Scotia, the Magdalcne Islands and finally back to PEI. By this time, Ed was a skilled aviator, and the Canadians were desperate for trained pilots. Getting good instructors was absolutely key to their building a strong air force. Ed was chosen to be one of these trainers of future recruits. He was exceedingly grateful for the respect he had been shown, both as an American and as a flyer. His gratitude allowed nothing less than filling the slot. He realized its importance and was glad to pay back. Nevertheless, Ed, ever-anxious to get to the front, found his job as staff pilot to be an "experience in boredom." He lamented that he was "flying endless circles over the Gulf of St. Lawrence, not a hell of a lot of fun."

Finally, Group Captain Lewis, the station commanding officer (CO) at Summerside, called him in and said to him, "It has come to my attention that your bar bill exceeds your pay. We can't have that, can we?" Ed's reply was, "Well, a posting overseas would just automatically fix it." The CO promised he'd see what he could do, and three days later, on February 14, 1944, Ed was off to England. He sailed from Halifax, Nova Scotia, on the *Ile de France*, a French liner that had been appropriated by the Allies before the German occupation of France. She was a prewar luxury ship refitted for wartime transports. Ed was one of twenty-four fellow flyers confined to a two-person stateroom. There was barely room for all of them to fit in their hammocks. "You had to slide in sideways," said Ed. Most of the men suffered terrible seasickness during the five-day trip, but Ed, with his

Ed (far right) and fellow drinkers, Prince Edward Island. *Hawkes Collection.*

Ed (on the wing) and his navigator on a Mosquito bomber. *Hawkes Collection.*

fisherman's background, was one of the few whose experience with swells and surges allowed him to partake of the three gourmet meals served each day. They had the same chef who had prepared similar fare for the ship's wealthy patrons a few years earlier. They landed at Liverpool. Ed had finally arrived overseas.

There was more training. England was foggy, and lots of rain made visibility low. A course in instruments called BAT (beam approach training) involved pulling a hood over your head, enabling you to see only the instrument panel. Familiarity with all systems, including activating and deactivating them by touch as well as sight, was important. This was low visibility at its worst. Ed's navigator, David Anderson, was from Trinidad. The navigator sat to the right of and just behind the pilot. Many navigators in those days knew little about flying, and by the same token, the pilot needed his navigator. This created a close union.

The conversion course to the Mosquito Bomber in April 1945 was everything Ed had hoped for. Built of balsa, spruce, birch and plywood, the plane was known as the "Wooden Wonder." This construction eliminated the use of strategic materials necessary for the conventional type of aircraft. The twin engines, V-12 Rolls-Royce Merlin engines, were "really magical," marveled Ed. The total horsepower was 3600, and the plane held six hundred gallons of fuel (with the drop tanks), weighing a hefty twelve thousand pounds. Cruising speed was 240 knots, consuming fifty gallons per hour per engine. These planes were a very important part of the coastal command. Their extreme power and maneuverability made them ideal for a quick ascent, and the self-propelled rockets under the wings were fired electrically, enabling greater accuracy, capable of destroying a variety of targets, including merchant vessels and subs. Armament also included four .303-caliber machine guns and four 20-mm cannon. The planes were used as night fighters for attacking shipping vessels and for low-altitude bombing as well. Difficult to fly, these aircraft required experienced pilots who found them responsive and exciting. Ed loved flying the Mosquitoes, but the fact was that the war was almost over. "Disappointing," said Ed. "What if I had gone sooner?" The fact that the loss rate in the Mosquitoes was very high seemed irrelevant. For this brave man, it was "the experience of a lifetime."

"What if" was Ed's equivalent of Dan Peach's answer of "Africa," a short reply to the question, "Where were you during the war?" In true fisherman style, where the answer to the query "How did you do today?" is usually a noncommittal "Made a day's pay," these men kept to themselves, divulging nothing of the bad and incremental amounts of anything else.

# Chapter 16

# Finding Normalcy

**E**d loved flying, but there was nothing quite like rowing. In years past, with Ed at the oars, Harry Foss and George Coffin hauled their strings of lobster pots. Harry had a bright yellow Chamberlain dory, George an old leaky wreck. Ed never got paid for rowing, nor did he care which boat he was in.

He just enjoyed rowing—the tranquility he felt, being alone with his thoughts, a chance to unwind both physically and mentally. Gerald Smith's Chamberlain dory was on its running line. On the first day of his one and only leave from World War II, that brisk November day just before Thanksgiving, Ed headed for the Cove. Gerald was glad to loan Ed his dory for the morning. The steady stroke of the oars marked a cadence in his mind as he let some of the horrors of war release into the fresh northwest breeze. His muscles tightened as he pulled and relaxed, pull…relax. It was cathartic, an adjustment, a start to some semblance of normalcy. Ed felt he had plenty to be thankful for.

After three hours, he returned to the Cove and spotted his old friend Gerald in the shanty window. The two made plans to go gunning the following day. What could be better—more rowing, some shooting and a big turkey dinner with his family.

It was open season on ducks, but to get a waterfront pass, one had to be interviewed by the local police, who required more interrogation by the coast guard. There were many restrictions for coastal dwellers during the war. Ironically, the questioning took place at the Salem Custom House, next to another historic site, the Hawkes House. Designed by Samuel McIntire, it was built as a residence for King Derby in 1780 but was left unfinished when Derby decided on a different home. It was used as a warehouse but later purchased by Benjamin Hawkes in 1801. Hawkes, an early ancestor of Ed's, owned a shipyard near Derby Wharf.

The next day, in the dark early morning hours, "Smith" (which is what Ed called Gerald) and "Hawk" (which is what Gerald called Ed) were off in the Chamberlain. Smith customarily bought shotgun shells by the case (five hundred rounds), so ammo was not a problem. They were at Coney Island, with decoys set, just as a glimmer of daylight was starting to show. At times, they could hear the whistle of wings overhead, even though the birds were still invisible. The limit at that time was ten black ducks. By 8:00 a.m., they both had their quota and were back at the beach at Little Harbor. Smith took his home; Hawk hung his on the end of Percival's shanty.

The shanty consisted of a fireplace and some seat lockers, with green latticework parallel to the structure. It was all that remained of a house at the beach end of Laurence's property that he had torn down when he purchased the large home. Since this shanty was just across from the others, it, too, became a place for socializing. Ed had added a gun rack and kept some of his supplies there. Often on a nice summer's evening, Laurence would appear with his bottle of Four Roses. He enjoyed the beach and the camaraderie of the men.

The blacks Ed hung on the latticework disappeared rather quickly. Rene Pouchain, Percival's cook, appeared and asked if he could have a pair for Mister Laurence's dinner. Ed was quick to oblige. Then, one of Ed's numerous relatives showed up and asked if he could have some birds for Thanksgiving. Probably turkeys were scarce and/or expensive at that time. He prodded and squeezed every bird, walking off with four.

Freshwater ducks are basically non-fish eaters, vegetarians feeding on the grasses and weeds of freshwater ponds and marshes. Although they will eat tiny fish in the winter when they are frozen out of their habitat, their preference is wild celery or rice. As they migrate south, starting in November, they have to improvise.

Varieties of ducks are rather limited along the northeast coast of New England. Massachusetts Bay is fairly deep, bounded by land to the west. Large numbers of southbound migrants fly across it rather than around it, which keeps them well offshore. There were no eider or brant prior to World War II. Eiders started trickling down just after the war, quickly increasing in numbers. They loved to gag down whole mussels from the large beds in the

Marblehead mudflats. A few nested off town at the Dry Breakers and the Outer Pigs. Brant are even more recent arrivals and stay well into the spring, as late as the middle of May. Scoters are usually the first to arrive, with native blacks and mallards, mergansers, oldsquaws, buffleheads, goldeneyes, Canada geese and an occasional teal.

Hawk and Smith gunned together for fifty-five years. They tried just about every island in Salem Bay with the exception of the Gooseberrys, which were ill suited and where, for some reason, birds did not decoy well. Pope's Head, a small rock pile within a gunshot of the Northern Gooseberrys, however, was consistently a good choice. With the invention of small outboard motors, just after World War II, the men went as far as Great and Little Salt Rock, off Singing Beach in Manchester.

Ed and Gerald never forgot the one-time occurrence that took place at the inner end of the Dry Breakers bar. It was blowing hard southeast. Three goldeneyes came in over the decoys with no sign that they were going to stop. Gerald fired, and down came all three. "There," he said, "let's see you do that." They rowed out and picked up the birds and had no more than sat down when another small flight of goldeneyes appeared.

Perfect example of a Chamberlain gunning dory. *Hawkes Collection.*

As Ed recalls, "When they were about thirty yards off, I fired one barrel and was about to fire the other, when down came three." It had never happened before, nor has it since.

One day, late in the season, Ed was on the Outer Pigs. It was beautiful, with little wind, but nothing was flying. Noticing a pair of buffleheads, he shot one, missing the other. It was a him and a her, and he had shot the him. Back came the mate making little squeaking noises. She circled the ledge several times, always flying directly over her downed mate. It was about all Ed could take. He rowed out and retrieved the bird. The female came by one last time as he was hauling the dory up. He never shot another bufflehead.

After the war, the economy was stronger and people felt they could splurge a bit. This led to a tremendous increase in the use of retrievers for duck hunting. It added another dimension to hunting, including the training of the puppy. There were many good kennels with AKC (American Kennel Club) and other registered lines. This often ensured proof of ability of hard-won titles such as FTC (Field Trial Champion), AM (American) or INT (International).

There were, however, no guarantees. Ed learned to train his puppies to make blind retrieves by using only hand and whistle signals. A blind retrieve means the dog never sees the bird until he is sent for it. He is led out of sight while the bird is planted by a handler.

Ed had five Labradors over the years. One of the early ones, Helen Highwater, was a huge disappointment. No matter what Ed tried, she refused to have anything to do with the water. The other three he ran in field trials and used for hunting and companionship.

One day in the late fall of 1949, I stopped in at John Hawkes's shanty after school. Ed was there with his latest, handsome Labrador, Blackmann of Timbertown, shooting the breeze. There was a strong northeast wind, a typical stormy November day. Ed suggested we try getting a few birds. The tide was out, so we set out under the gangway and along the wall of the boatyard, sloshing across the mudflats to the lee of Ringbolt Ledge. Ringbolt is a rocky promontory, a perpendicular extension of Brown's, parallel to Priests' Island.

After a short explanation about the safety and the trigger, Ed crouched down behind the ledge, holding the dog. He had spotted a goldeneye on the other side of the rocks. He handed me the big shotgun. It was shockingly heavy. "You give it a try, Hugh."

My previous experience with guns had been limited to a little squirrel chasing with a BB gun or a try at some tin cans I lined up on our fence. I tried to control the shaking of my arms as I slowly raised the gun. I couldn't see a darn thing, since I had stopped wearing my glasses after a girl in my homeroom class referred to me as "four eyes." I shot blindly into the vast unknown. "I think I missed," I said dejectedly to Ed.

My shot had scared off any other ducks in the vicinity, so we went along the beach to the rocky area at the other end of Brown's. This time Ed told me to wait up in the woodsy area above the rocks and that he would go with the dog to try for a hit. I think he planned to show me how it should be done. It was a long twelve minutes with no shot, the blame being mine, since evidently, I had moved and once again scared the ducks.

A duck dives for fish and then surfaces to ingest it. Nobody (almost) shoots at a "sitting duck." The sport of gunning is based on hitting a duck in flight. It's the same idea as the "fish in a barrel" thing.

I guess that was enough for one day. We went back to the shanty, where the happy hour had already started. Boyd Martin, a food salesman and friend of both John and Ed, had stopped in for his afternoon snort. When Ed told him I had missed, Boyd retorted that kids are killed all the time like that. That was my first and last time gunning with Ed. I'm not sure if Boyd scared him or if he figured my future would be best spent on other endeavors.

*Chapter 17*

# Dave Abbott

The fall before Thanksgiving 1952, I was sixteen years old, lobstering and helping my father with the upkeep of our schooner. One bleak day in November, as I made my way into Graves Boatyard, where our family's vessel was stored for the winter, I noticed activity in the spar loft. A man named Dave Abbott was stripping varnish from a hatch belonging to the *Bounty*, a wonderful yacht, of which he was the longtime paid, professional captain. He asked me if I played football at the high school. I retorted with a negative. Besides lobstering, I was doing maintenance work on the *Landfall*.

It was pouring outside, but I knew enough about upkeep to realize that the maintenance of the *Bounty* was a year-round job, with enough work to carry a conscientious captain from season to season, rain or shine. Even to someone my age, the meticulous care of the *Bounty* was obvious. Her topsides were spotless, the brass perfectly shined and the varnish beyond reproach. This was especially amazing, and a tribute to Dave, since the boat had been taken by the U.S. Coast Guard during World War II and painted gray. Now restored to its previous dark green, it was probably the best cared-for yacht in the harbor, the queen of the fleet.

Dave was stripping varnish from a hatch, a job that in those years was done by hand. Without this continual upkeep, the finish would bubble and peel, leaving an unkempt appearance.

I knew Dave by sight and respected him, knowing that he had come to Marblehead from Nova Scotia. What I didn't realize was that Dave was a seasoned fisherman of the first order.

A few days later, as he left for the day, he stopped by the shanties to socialize. Maritime interest was a common bond between fisherman, boat owner and crew member. In his still-audible Canadian accent, he carefully divulged some stories. The give and take of the conversation between the Barnegat men and Dave was done effortlessly. He started talking about fishing out of Boston on a line trawl schooner. In the winters of 1917 and 1918, there were still several sail-only schooners out of the city. The crew left port in a large sailing vessel with several small dories stacked on deck, four to six on both port and starboard sides, between the foremast and the mainmast. Each of these small rowing vessels would be manned by two men. As soon as the captain reached the fishing grounds, the crew members would set out. The dories had high double ends, flared sides and broad bottoms, enabling them to be lifted by approaching waves instead of plowing through them.

These eighteen-foot dories each had a hole bored in the bottom, which allowed drainage when they were stacked on deck but could be plugged before the boats were lowered into the ocean. The mid portion of the boat, known as the waist, was partitioned off for the catch with pen boards. The sections toward the bow and stern had two sets of oarlocks for the men. Dave and his mate were the first in that day. As the schooner slid away to launch the next dory, the two men first set the high flier, a marker buoy. The tubs of trawl consisted of pieces of tarred cotton ground line that had gangings tied onto it every six feet (six feet equal one fathom), a total of fifty gangings per line, each with a tinned-steel codfish hook looped on the end. Ten of these lines strung together, each a total of fifty fathoms in length, was a "tub of trawl," and the "set" would be a two-tub set or a three-tub set (1,500 hooks). The whole length of ground line was secured by two anchors. Two lines led up from the gear to two buoys made from 100# nail kegs. The windward buoy was marked by a flag for visibility, numbered correspondingly with the dory. The other buoy, set downwind, was simply a keg with the same number. The hooks had been baited with chunks of fish on the schooner and coiled into three-foot-high barrels or tubs with rope straps for transporting them to the dories. If visibility were poor or if fog had set in, the oarsmen would count the number of strokes between the high flier and the end buoy. That would give them at least a rough estimate of the distance between the two ends of the set. Upon completion, if the wind was favorable, they could set their spritsail for a leisurely sail back to the schooner for their midday meal. That, of course, necessitated the schooner being downwind of the sets. A vessel to windward meant a hard row. The food break for the fishermen allowed time

Fishing schooner with dories stacked amidships.

for the fish to locate the hooks. While the enticing bits of bait lured the fish to the newly set trawls, the men were treated to a bountiful feast prepared by the full-time cook. The cook was a revered part of the crew who worked tirelessly baking and preparing sumptuous meals for his "boys."

As I listened to Dave, I tried to do the math in my head and figured a three-tub set had to be a good mile and a half of line. We were no strangers to line trawls at the beach. In the 1920s and '30s, Little Harbor lobstermen would trawl in the winter to supplement their summer income. More recently, Albert Hayes and Marty Sylvester, a couple of Swampscott transplants, had both set trawls between five and ten miles from the beach, so I was familiar with the procedure. They would bait in the shanties, setting for twenty-four hours before returning to haul. At that time, the hauling was still done by hand but out of boats much larger than dories. They had used landmarks and islands for geographical location and could do the simple math of engine speed and time to figure the distance from their start, but schooner men were out of sight of land. The mother ship would vary her route from set to set, the wind direction might change or the velocity. Fog could engulf the whole operation. Many of these desperate men never resolved the situation.

On returning to the trawl, Dave and his mate would have a plentiful catch, the usual mix of haddock and cod, with some cusk, pollock and catfish in their midst. Known for their fierce teeth, the catfish are feared by man and beast alike. One time, rowing back with their ground fish, the men saw the dory filling fast with water. Dave realized the problem. One of the catfish had grabbed the plug with its powerful teeth and removed it from the opening. He plunged his arm down through the catch stored in the pen. Luckily, his first effort met with success. Discovering the plug, which was attached by a line, he shoved it back into the hole. The two men bailed for a good half hour, arriving at the mother ship after dark. The skipper gave them hell. Ever fearful of the man in charge, the guys apologized, never telling him of their frightening dilemma.

The jobs of skipper and crew were then, as now, completely separate. On the ocean, the captain's power is absolute. What he says is final, no matter how strongly any crew member disagrees. He is completely divorced from the crew, both on the boat and off, making all navigational and fishing site decisions. There were no weather reports to warn of impending storms, but these experienced captains had been educated over the years by many trips as crew members themselves. They used the knowledge and values that they felt made for a lucrative and successful trip. As with any boss or manager, some were kinder than others, some more driven and some were downright obsessed with catching the most fish.

Dave told of the intuition of the skippers. On one trip, returning to Boston, the schooner, in a blinding snowstorm running before the wind, had sailed about two hundred miles. The skipper announced that within twenty minutes they should hear the horn of the Boston Lightship. The horn, called a diaphone, was a very powerful automatic sounder that was blown in times of fog and poor visibility. The lightship itself, painted red and white, was about ninety feet long. Located ten miles south of Marblehead and five miles east of Graves Light, it was anchored as a landmark, a navigational aid for those going into port. Sure enough, right on the dot, as predicted, they heard the blare of the horn. The vessel was in good hands.

Many men were lost on these trips. The dories themselves were often out of sight of the mother ship. Skippers and dory men alike feared losing contact with one another. If it started to breeze up while the dory men were hauling, they could be blown off course and caught in danger. The added weight of boots and oilskins made a man feel heavier and slower. If a dory swamped or capsized, it stranded the men, who often couldn't swim and, in the cold waters of the North Atlantic, had little chance of surviving. For just such emergencies, each dory was outfitted with what by today's standards would seem quite meager: a large glass water bottle containing one to two quarts of water, wrapped in cord to prevent breakage, and a leather box containing a compass, snipper, some hardtack and possibly tobacco with a metal container of matches. They also had a galvanized mouth-blown foghorn for use if they were lost or off course. This horn and the schooner's pump-handle horn were the usual means of communication between skipper and crew. In addition, someone on the schooners would continually hit a large brass winch with a ball hammer. The clanging was a welcome sound to a dory man who had lost his bearing. Dory mates became extremely close to one another, depending heavily on each other. They were generous men who often would lay down their own lives for their partner. Tough and brave, they understood the danger of their mission, but often their youth gave them an unfounded confidence.

In an effort to reach port with a full load of fish, some skippers would keep full sail on. This was usually, especially in winter, a mainsail, a staysail and two forward headsails. Summer winds would allow staysails over the main and foresails for more speed. Dave told of a trip when crew members went down on their knees begging the skipper to reduce sail. This had to have been extremely "rude" weather, as it took a lot to scare those hearty men. In fact, the ability to forget past dangers removed a certain amount of stress from their lives. Dave quoted his skipper's reply: "The only way any sail is going to come off this vessel is if the good Lord takes it off."

Evidently, the Lord decided to spare the canvas, and Dave returned to Boston a believer. Lowering one of the headsails was a double-edged sword, because while it would slow the progress of the vessel, it was an extremely dangerous job. It entailed

Bowsprits were called widowmakers.

149

crawling out onto the bowsprit and standing in a net of roping below it. A close-hauled boat's bowsprit could go under water as the crewman attempted to furl and lash the sail. Sensing this about to happen, he would wrap himself around the bowsprit. According to Dave, even the strongest of men could only take about three plunges under water before losing his grip. The wave would either wash him overboard or carry him back onto the vessel's deck. Dave witnessed, more than once, mates being washed the whole length of the boat before being grabbed by the helmsman.

Dory trawling was a proven method of fishing, but as time went by, they were out-caught by the men of the diesel-powered trawlers, which required fewer hands. Obviously, the smaller crew would receive a larger share than the dory men who caught the same amount of fish.

I wish now I had had the presence to ask more questions of Dave. His knowledge spanned an era in early fishing untried by my friends at Little Harbor. I thought of Studie Smith, who was really the only man I had lobstered with for any amount of time. I had always done what he asked, but I thought of him as one of the kindest, nicest people I had known. The thought of a captain jeopardizing his men to get more fish and for personal gain was a shocking piece of realism. But this wasn't the only time I'd hear of such horror. I did think to myself, however, that if I continued fishing, I hoped I could keep my priorities straight. My mother and father had both stressed the importance of respect for others. I hoped I would have that kind of maturity.

I was spellbound by the stories. The skill of those seamen and the peril they encountered had me fascinated. I wanted to know more, and I wanted to do more. I was hooked.

*Chapter 18*

# White Horse and Pat Noonan's Boat

**I**n 1995, at my fortieth high school reunion, an old friend and hockey teammate, Pete Gray, and I were reminiscing about what we would like to do once more if the opportunity presented itself. We had played hockey together during the winters from 1953 to 1955. I loved to both practice and play ice hockey games. All of our league games were played at Lynn Arena. My sister was on the newly formed hockey cheerleading squad. The other cheerless teams were jealous of our "girls." Large crowds usually attended these games, and like many things you don't appreciate at the time, those days are gone and not possible anymore.

Peter said he would like to play one more hockey game at Lynn Arena. I agreed that this would be at or near the top of my list. Upon reflection, I realized that my life had given me so many memorable days and experiences that it would be hard to pick out one that would stand above the rest.

I thought again about some of those special events when, on January 8, 1998, I was riding along Jeffreys Ledge in my fishing boat. As I approached the place where I was going to set my line trawls for the day, my mind wandered back to how I came to be in my line trawler that morning. Like many people's lives, especially a commercial fisherman's, it was a twisting path with several situations along the way where I had squeezed through tight places.

After that exciting winter of hockey in 1955, I was ready to graduate from high school as well as to a larger lobster boat. Early in March, I saw an ad in *Maine Coast Fisherman*, the recognized commercial paper of the day. There

I found a twenty-eight-foot lobster boat for sale nearby, in Manchester, Massachusetts. My father and I went to look at it where it was hauled out for the winter at Manchester Marine Yacht Yard. The owner, Pat Noonan, had the boat built in 1940. He was having a larger, more modern boat, about thirty-two feet long, built at Harvey Gamage Shipyard in South Bristol, Maine. His boat for sale was the traditional style of the day. It was open with a canvas spray hood covering the forward third of its length. The engine was a four-cylinder, gas Red Wing. Diesel-fueled engines for lobster boats were nonexistent. The boat equipment was Spartan—a brass winch and steel davit for hauling pots; a simple, belt-driven water pump to oxygenate caught lobsters; and an almost crude, chain-driven manual steering system. The boat appeared basically sound.

Since Pat was in Florida for the winter, I negotiated with his brother Jerry, who worked at the Manchester Post Office. The asking price was $1,500. After a minimum of negotiation, I bought it for $1,350 on March 20. A provision of the sale was that the boat had to be out of the boatyard by April 1.

With the two weekends available and each weekday after school, I got the bottom and topsides painted in time for the April 1 launch. I put the boat on a mooring in Manchester Harbor and painted the inside, as weather and time permitted. Soon, it was time to bring her to Marblehead. I named her *Send'er*, the same name as my dory, a legacy from John Hawkes.

*Send'er.*

Coming across Salem Sound from Manchester to Little Harbor, I felt like I owned the *Queen Mary*. I now had a boat equal in size to many full-time lobstermen!

I needed a mooring. Bob Cloutman had started a new venture, a boatyard at the John S. Martin Company coal wharf on Cliff Street. Bob had sold his lobster boat, *Bob*, to my close friends Charlie and Donald Foss the year before. His old mooring, one of the first two out from Fisherman's Beach, sat vacant. I talked with him for about two minutes, and for $25, I bought the berth and two chain-bridled

10 Harding Lane with *Send'er* and Stewart Smith's boat in Doliber's Cove.

granite blocks. That's all there was to it. There were no mooring permits in those days. It was a man's word and a handshake. That was the way we did business. Phil Clark, the manager of the Marblehead Transportation Company, was the harbormaster and settled what few problems there were. He was paid $100 per year.

By May, I started setting the first of my 110 lobster pots I had ready for the season. I received a nice dividend from my new boat later that summer. One day while hauling near the Inner Gooseberry, Pat Noonan came along. I had never met him before. He stopped, introduced himself, admired his old boat and wished me well. He was, and still is, a very friendly man. The dividend I referred to is the relationship I have maintained with him to this day. Whenever our paths have crossed, often in Gloucester, there is always a warm conversation. I value something like that because no matter how many dollars you have at your disposal, you can't buy such a thing for any price.

A month later, Bob Brown, by then a junior in high school, bought a similar size boat, which was sitting right in Little Harbor. It was the *White Horse*, the boat Henry Briggs had bought from Ern Cronk in September 1954, in an emergency transaction. Henry had lost his thirty-foot lobster boat at the height of Hurricane Carol on August 31, 1954. This storm

153

Two parts of one picture of Little Harbor, taken from Fort Sewall, circa 1900. *Marblehead Historical Commission.*

struck the North Shore completely unpredicted. It was a strong hurricane that came in off the Atlantic. With no satellite system, this type of thing was all too possible. Winds exceeded one hundred miles per hour that morning. Henry's boat, moored next to Bob Cloutman's, snapped its chain at the height of the storm, came in against the wall of Graves Boatyard and was

smashed beyond repair. He bought the *White Horse* from Ern, who was close to seventy years old and had retired the year before.

Ern is long gone, but I loved listening to his stories when I was a boy. He came to Marblehead about 1900 from Nova Scotia. He was twenty years old and immediately gravitated to Little Harbor. In the 1950s, Ern, while sitting in John Hawkes's shanty one winter day, told me the following. When he first arrived from "Novie," he started rowing for an older lobsterman. Soon, he had his own dory and string of traps. Sixty traps were about the most a good lobsterman handled in those days. There were a couple of skippers who had small Friendship-type sloops and fished line trawls within sight of Marblehead. This was just before the advent of one-cylinder gas engines (one "lungers"), so all the power to operate boats came from oars or sails. Ern and the other top lobstermen of the day set traps from Marblehead Rock to as far as the Outer Pigs. Older men were generally burned out by age forty from the strenuous activity required.

The weather patterns were the same then as now, of course. On the days when a morning north or northwest wind would turn northeast or east by midmorning, if a lobsterman was working downwind to the end of his string at the Outer Pigs, he was then faced with a long, upwind row back to the Cove. There was an alternative that the men would use for these conditions. The common practice was for all those out to pull in under Marblehead Neck at the point where the causeway meets the neck at the end of Devereux Beach. The bight formed by the neck going out to Flying Point becomes more placid the closer one gets to the beach. The men waited until all who were fishing in the bay west of Tinker's Island that day had arrived. This was generally five to ten dories and as many men or more. Then, as a group, they forded the causeway, launching the boats into the head of Marblehead Harbor. Depending on the wind direction, they rowed in the lee of the town or the neck back to Little Harbor. Ern had many other similar stories about the intricacies of scratching a living from the sea one hundred years ago.

The twenty-six-foot *White Horse* was the last boat he fished in his working life. The name came from the fact that he financed it from a floating find on Thanksgiving Day 1930. Ern was the only man out that day. Prohibition was in effect. He came across cases of whiskey in wooden boxes that had been jettisoned the night before by a rumrunner who must have been under intense pressure from the coast guard. Quickly filling his boat as full as he dared, he quietly made his way back to Little Harbor. He discreetly sold his "catch" in the days ahead, and by the time he finished, he had enough money for a new boat. Bill Brown (no relation to Bob) built this for him in his boat shop at Fort Sewall. The brand of whiskey was White Horse—thus the name of the boat that Bob bought.

One early summer day in 1955, we drove over to Beverly in Bob Brown's 1938, four-door Dodge he had bought that spring from our junior high school football coach and gym teacher, Henry DeNeis. Bob paid Henry

Ern Cronk near retirement.

thirty-five dollars for the car, which had seen better days. He constantly said he had "been screwed" on the deal. He usually added, "Henry got ahead of me on that one!" I had a 1947 Willy's Overland sort of station wagon for my wheels, not what I wanted to take out on dates with my girlfriend. I had to observe the ritual of asking my parents for the use of the family car for this. The "okay" always seemed to have a reluctant tone to it.

We were in Bob's chariot that day because we had learned that a Beverly lobsterman, Fred Bartlett, had two pogy nets for sale. We knew Fred only by reputation. He was well established, almost a generation older than us. Physically, he was well over six feet tall and seemed like a North Shore Paul Bunyan.

Bob told me to do the talking since I was a little older. Fred wanted seventy-five dollars for the two nets. I told him we couldn't afford more than sixty. He agreed to the deal. Driving back to Marblehead with the nets in the back seat, Bob asked me how I dared to talk Fred down to sixty dollars. I replied that my father once had told me, "Sometimes you have to drive a hard bargain."

In the years to come, Bob developed a well-deserved reputation for being very hard to deal with where money was involved. More than once I have wondered if this characteristic might have germinated from our purchase that day.

Later that summer, we built what turned out to be the last of the large lobster cars. A car was a holding container for live lobsters. In the 1940s and '50s and before, for that matter, there were no year-round wholesale buyers of lobsters in Marblehead. Barber's Lobster Pool was open from Mother's Day to Columbus Day. McClain's Fish Market on State Street and Quality Fish Market on Washington Street bought lobsters year round but in no great quantity. This meant that the men who caught substantial amounts had to sell out of town. Dunn's Lobster Pound on Juniper Cove in Salem

Willows was one of these. Dunn's had a dock accessible at better than three-quarters tide. They bought lobsters from Salem, Beverly and Marblehead boats. Lobstermen in Little Harbor would go to Dunn's on a daily basis, if the tide was right. If it wasn't, the catch would be put into a holding car in Little Harbor to wait for a good afternoon tide and then be taken by boat to Dunn's. I have nice memories as a ten- to twelve-year-old of going along on some of these trips.

Two or three men would put their lobsters in one boat, and often, Dave and I would ride along with them. While the lobsters were being weighed and checks written, one of the men would give us a dollar and send us up to Salem Willows amusement area for ice cream. On the ride back to Marblehead, we all shared. It was such a pleasant way to spend an afternoon. Other men would truck their catch to Lynn or Boston.

The common holding car of the day was the type Bob and I built. It was four feet high by four feet wide and ten feet long with a dividing partition in the middle. Doors on hinges formed the top. It was constructed with a frame of 4x4s and pine boards and was durable and sturdy. One-inch holes were drilled in the end and side boards for good water flow. Skids were added to the bottom for movement on land. The outside was painted with bottom paint to prevent marine growth. A bridle of half-inch chain was fastened on one end for mooring. There were several of these moored in Little Harbor prior to the 1960s.

When a lobsterman came in for the day, he dumped his catch in his car. Each side held several hundred pounds. Lobsters and bait were moved around exclusively in bushel baskets. A full bushel of lobsters weighed about thirty pounds, and a full bushel of bait, generally filleted redfish, weighed fifty pounds. The better fishermen kept separate piles of bushel baskets for each. Redfish particles and juice tended to make bait baskets have a distinctive aroma, even after being washed out. In hot weather, one quickly learned what maggots were. Bushel baskets were available from several sources, the best being the back part of a grocery store. There was an older man on Cowell Street, Gardner Martin, who satisfied this need with a small business he ran out of a barn behind his house. He spent a good deal of time scouring stores on the North Shore for bushel baskets. He sold them for three different prices, depending on their condition. I recall the best ones were ten cents each. Bob and I bought the cheaper ones. They were eight cents each.

When it came time to market held lobsters, the procedure was as follows. One stack of good bushel baskets was put in a punt, along with a dip net. The punt was rowed to the floating car, lashed alongside and the door unlocked and flipped open. The dip net, which held fifteen to twenty pounds, was put into the car, and a net full of lobsters was brought into the punt and laid across the gunnel. Each lobster was placed carefully in a basket until it was full. If it was sunny, an effort was made to keep full bushels covered with a canvas. When the car was empty, the punt was rowed in and the baskets loaded into a truck for transport or taken to a boat, if Dunn's was to be the buyer. During the late '50s, wooden crates holding ninety to one hundred pounds of lobsters were introduced around the North Shore, eliminating the large cars.

Before leaving for college, I had negotiated a deal with my sister, who was in high school. Her world revolved around sports and phone calls. The multiple conversations each night were whispered and usually only accepted in my parents' bedroom, where the more private of the two phones in the house was situated. While she continued her nonsensical discourse, no one else could contact us. I had heard there was such a thing as an operator interruption, but so far, nobody had been able to enact such an emergency. Her talk appeared to be endless. Anyone entering the room would hear an occasional loud comment such as "really" or "I don't believe it," but the reason for the reaction was never revealed. My father, who was still working in New York, became more and more frustrated as he futilely attempted to reach my mother. Finally, they got my sister her own phone number—not because they ever indulged us but because they needed to for their own sanity. Brenda was increasingly difficult during those years. Unable to have a vehicle at college, I "loaned" her my old Jeep, bought from some neighbors in Barnegat. I charged her three cents per mile and collected at the end of each semester. Math was never my strong suit, but at the end of my freshman year, the mileage seemed a bit meager. On closer interrogation, she admitted she had had one of her boyfriends disconnect the odometer cable. My father's only observation was, "You'd better sharpen your pencil!"

At college, I sat in study hall or the library and dreamed about the ocean, lobstering and sailing. I counted the days until I would be hauling traps again. I just couldn't get my mind off it.

The summer of 1956 came and went. It was similar to 1955. We were transitioning from being boys to men. Little Harbor was a great place to lobster in those days. There was a core group of ten or so full-time fishermen, a smaller number of part-timers, as they were called, and the "new kids," Bob and myself. There were some cliques, but everyone got along. Henry Briggs and his wife, Alvina, ran Barber's Lobster Pool. He called the Herrick

Grain Company in Beverly weekly for our salt order. We used large quantities of these one-hundred-pound bags to preserve our fresh bait. Frozen bait was unknown then.

Bait delivery was, from our perspective, a routine event, but as I think of it now, it was actually quite a spectacle. The scheduled arrival was meant to be mid- to late afternoon on Monday, Wednesday and Friday. However, you certainly could not set your watch by it. The truck had a two-and-a-half-ton capacity and was driven by an independent contractor, Jesse Main—and independent he was. Despite his lack of reliability, he was very likable and had two outstanding characteristics. One was his huge potbelly, and the second was the fish-like odor that exuded from his every pore. Redfish was the main species landed in Gloucester in those days; the remains after filleting (racks) made excellent lobster bait.

We were usually assembled at Little Harbor by 2:30 p.m. or so, waiting for Jesse to arrive. We couldn't afford to miss him, but he had a bit of a bad no-show record. Communication was different then, and waiting and worrying were the norm. As we sat on the bench in the shade of the bushes along the Hildreths' wall, we chatted and tried to casually await his arrival. Conversation ceased when we heard the squeal of his brakes easing the truck down the Orne Street hill. As he backed onto the beach, sighs of relief could be heard. The fishermen were now assured of bait for the next two or three days.

Jesse's truck had large holding tanks, mounted under each side of the body, to collect the fish juice from the filleted reds. His first act after parking at the top of the ramp was to back off the gate valves on each tank. The juice flowed down the sides of the ramp, discoloring the ocean water. No one dared complain.

Bait was bought primarily in fifty-five-gallon metal drums, which held six and a half to seven bushels. They were placed at the tail gate so Jesse's helper could shovel the redfish into individual drums. These were rolled aside to make room for the next man. The individual lobsterman forked his barrel's supply into bushel baskets. The wheelbarrows Ralph Conner had built provided transportation down the ramp to the waiting punts.

We all had wooden sugar barrels on our boats. There were two sizes, three- and five-bushel. Most of us had capacity for fifteen to twenty bushels. Bait kept longer in wooden barrels than steel drums, especially in warm weather. Unsalted, shelf life wasn't much more than a day. Three-day preservation required heavy salting. The new crop of young boys at the beach was eager to make a small fee rowing the new bait to a lobsterman's boat. Karl Pearson and Bill Montville, among others, did this for me.

Maybe we took it for granted, but it certainly was a necessary part of our trade. The aftermath sometimes included a cold beer, a social occasion with a silent toast to Jesse for showing up. Jesse would not always have enough bait on the truck to fill everyone's order. I never remember a time when we didn't easily agree to take a little less so everyone had a supply for the following day.

The fishermen were a true community, competing but cooperating for everyone's advantage. If a death of someone close to the group occurred, a collection was taken and flowers sent from "The Fishermen of Barnegat."

The bench accommodated an eclectic group—fishermen, neighbors and a few tourists. Times have changed, but the group of people then was of diversified backgrounds and ages. There seemed to be more time for listening and socializing and simply enjoying each other's company and the beauty of of our little cove. Most of the people from those days are gone. I miss them and how it was. It was a good place to be in the '50s and certainly a different world from Marblehead today.

Almost from the first day Bob showed up at Fisherman's Beach in the early 1950s, he became very friendly with Ralph Conner. Their relationship became almost like father and son. Ralph's daughter told me many years later, long after her father's death, that Ralph took a liking to Bob because "he was adventurous and hardworking." Ralph analyzed him early on.

Ralph was born in 1896 and had a common, hardscrabble Marblehead upbringing. His parents moved from one apartment to another. His father eked out a living lobstering and doing whatever else he could to support his family. He must have done something right because even though he never went beyond the ninth grade, Ralph went on to make quite a reputation for himself. By the early 1950s, Ralph, Henry Briggs, Ed Hawkes and Watson Curtis were considered the top lobstermen in Marblehead.

Ralph joined the army in 1918 and was on a troop ship ready to leave for Europe on the day the Armistice was signed in November 1918. He got off the ship and soon enough was back in Marblehead and lobstering with his father.

By 1924, Ralph had enough money put aside for a new lobster boat. Sam Brown designed it. It was twenty-six feet long and in the open style of the day. Bill Brown built it at his Fort Sewall boat shop. Ralph worked on it, and on weekends a Graves Boatyard employee, Charles Lawton, helped out also. Charles was known for his showpiece Lawton Tenders that he custom built during his days at Graves. By 1949, Charles Lawton was ninety years old and building his last boat before he went back home to Nova Scotia to spend his

*Star Dust.*

last years. That last boat was designed by Fenwick Williams and built over the garage at 10 Harding Lane, Marblehead, where I now live. My father named it *Star Dust*, after his favorite song, "Stardust." It was seventeen feet long with a cabin and two bunks. I spent many hours sailing the *Star Dust.*

To get back to 1924, Ralph Conner named his new boat *Junior* for his five-year-old son. The boat was built with no butt blocks. This meant that each plank ran the full length of the boat. It must have been well built, because Ralph lobstered with it until the late 1950s, when he sold it to Herb Dixey, who in turn gave it to his son. The boat went lobstering out of Little Harbor for over fifty years. I, like Bob, looked up to Ralph and admired his achievements and work habits. He was an extremely talented woodworker and taught me much. In the winter of 1960, we built a fourteen-foot punt together in the same shop in which the *Star Dust* was built. All his work was the finest kind, as the saying goes. Each year, the *Junior* was completely painted, just as a yacht would be. His traps and buoys were always in mint condition.

The *Junior* did not have a watertight floor, so the day's lobstering efforts would result in salt water and inevitably some kelp pieces and other debris ending up in the bilge. When Ralph put the boat on the mooring at the end of the day's haul, she would be immaculate. The bilge was painted with red lead. If you picked up the cockpit floor boards, you would see that the bilge had been hand pumped and sponged out. There was never a speck of seaweed to be seen. I could go on, but I think I have made the point that this was the type of man who became Bob's mentor. They developed a special bond—Ralph at the end of his fishing life and Bob at the beginning of his. I remember being sort of envious of how they related.

# Chapter 19

# Bigger Boats and More Knowledge

**D**uring the 1950s, Bob and I talked frequently about our desire to go out over the horizon and fish on grounds we had never seen. It was impossible during those days for two reasons: our small boats had no capabilities to go farther than a few miles from home, and we needed more knowledge. We didn't have a strategic plan to address these two restrictions, but in the early '60s, events unfolded that let us start to live our dreams of fishing offshore. Two new fishermen at Little Harbor were to aid us in our quest: Albert Hayes and Marty Sylvester. Albert was a generation ahead of us and migrated to Marblehead from Swampscott in 1955. He had a growing family and had lobstered and fished since a boy off Fisherman's Beach in Swampscott. Marty Sylvester was just a few years older. Recently married, he had two young children. I first remember him as the helper on the bait truck in the early '50s. He liked Little Harbor and started lobstering from a worn-out Novi boat the same year as Albert. By 1958, Marty and Albert had both purchased new thirty-four-foot Nova Scotia–built boats. They were a lot for the money and also had the capability for winter tub trawling.

Albert brought with him much practical experience. He could bait and haul trawls rapidly and knew the habits of fish in local waters. He helped Marty get started in 1959. Marty needed a helper to go with him and took Bob. That year and the next, he taught Bob the basics. I still didn't know the first thing about it, but it intrigued me.

By late summer of 1960, my college career and active army duty were over. I was left with two weeks of summer camp and weekly meetings for the next seven years. I felt free and ready to plunge ahead with fishing efforts. I painted the *Send'er* in Cloutman's Boatyard, where it had been stored, and by

September had my string of traps fishing; 150 seemed like a large amount at that time. If I was going to spread my wings, I had to address our two needs. First, I had Sam Brown design a thirty-three-foot lobster boat for me. I considered several builders and settled on Webber's Cove Boatyard in East Blue Hill, Maine. The yard promised the boat would be finished by April 1, 1961. They lived up to their promise. My boat was to be the last wooden boat they ever constructed. Webber's Cove was one of, if not the first, yard to try fiberglass construction. That tidal wave just about drowned all wooden boat builders.

During the same time, Bob had his father-in-law design a thirty-two-footer. He settled on a man named Ervin Jones in East Boothbay, Maine, as the builder. It was to be Ervin's first attempt at running his own shop, and construction started in early spring of 1961.

The year 1961 was the year of my first marriage. It was in February, and Bob was to be my best man. Sadly, his mother died three days before the wedding, so my father took his place.

The first weekend in April, my father and I brought the boat to Marblehead. We left East Bluehill at 7:00 a.m. on a Saturday in light snow. After stopping in Rockland for a compass adjustment, we arrived at Boothbay Harbor at 5:00 p.m. and spent the night in a motel. The next morning at 5:30 a.m., we left Boothbay, setting a course for the Portland Light Ship. It was a perfect early spring morning, crystal clear, with a light northwest wind. Mount Washington was plainly visible as we crossed the outer part of Casco Bay. I called my bride from Boothbay and told her when we expected to arrive in Marblehead. It was a great ride down the coast.

As we came into Little Harbor at 3:30 p.m., we received a reception that was only exceeded one other time in my life. As was the custom, a new boat was considered something special. Neighbors and fishermen were standing on the edge of the beach. Bill Hawkes had one of his largest cannons on hand and gave us several salutes as we slowed down and tied up at Graves's float.

My wife jokingly said that I cared more about the boat than about her. I named my boat *Mistress*.

If there was one person with more enthusiasm for lobstering and fishing than me, it was Bob Brown. He was to name his new boat *Sea Fever*. There were to be two more *Mistress*es for me and two more *Sea Fever*s for him. The year 1961 was when the ride really started for us.

# Chapter 20

# John Hawkes

On the edge of the Fisherman's Beach parking lot is a small plot with a granite stone, mounted with a bronze plaque that reads:

*In memory of John J. Hawkes*
*1923–1974*
*Given by His Friends*

I hope the following account will clarify the reason his friends, which certainly included myself, felt compelled to dedicate the memorial.

Looking back on my days around Little Harbor, I think kindly of all the men who had such an influence on me. There is one in particular, because of his outsized personality. He epitomized what was so special about Fisherman's Beach. His name was John Hawkes.

John, brother of Ed Hawkes, was born in 1923 at Mary Alley Hospital, the fourth of five children of Winslow and Elizabeth Hawkes. As a boy in the mid-1930s, John got "beach fever" and started hanging around the Cove in the footsteps of his older brother Ed.

Hauling traps in dories was still commonplace, and John got his first job rowing for a lobsterman named George Coffin. George was not exactly a high liner, as the top producers were called, but John was happy rowing a dory and enjoying the sights and sounds that went with it.

With the arrival of fall came the legal time for shooting seabirds. Besides rowing for George, John developed a growing interest in duck shooting,

John Hawkes's plaque.

which he indulged in when high school football allowed. He was considered a tough kid and became a starting lineman on the Marblehead High School teams of the late 1930s. His senior year, the fall of 1939, he was elected captain. Along with his strong body, his personality, which was to define him, was developing. John had an infectious way of communicating with people, leaving a lasting impression.

He enlisted in the navy at the beginning of World War II and served for four and a half years, several of which were on a destroyer in the Mediterranean Sea. He and his ship survived a lot of action.

After returning to Marblehead at the end of the war, John worked for the Graves Boatyard until 1949. That year, he bought an eighteen-foot, secondhand Grand Banks dory that had a one-cylinder Lawson air-cooled engine. He set out seventy-five traps and embarked on the life of a lobsterman.

When he was in high school rowing Coffin's dory, there was a saying you don't hear anymore. George liked a cold beer. When he was through hauling his traps for the day, off Cat Island, George would pick up a second set of oars in the dory and sit amidships, rowing with John for the return trip to Little Harbor. Two good rowers could make a dory really move. George would say to John, "There's a cold beer waiting in the shanty for me! Send'er!" "Er" (her) meant the dory, and "send" meant make her fly home as fast as possible. That expression is now in the dustbin but was common when I was young. John used that name for his new dory, and as far as I could tell, he included the cold beer in the bargain.

John's Lawson engine was temperamental and generally in a mood not to run, so John often rowed around to his traps, using the standing

John and Ed Hawkes in uniform. *Hawkes Collection.*

lobsterman style, except for long distances. He cut quite a figure, just as his older brother had. While not thin, he was in good physical shape, with biceps bigger than my thigh. He rarely wore a shirt during the summer, and on his right upper arm was a tattoo of a clipper ship with the words

John Hawkes landing lobsters.

"Homeward Bound" printed under it. He, like Watson Curtis, was someone Dave Hildreth and I admired. We considered Watson and John to be interchangeable, ideologically.

At the age of twelve, I was not allowed by my parents to row to Cat Island alone or even with Dave. When I explained John Hawkes to them, they said I could row with him wherever he had traps but that I couldn't stray from his whereabouts. Following him around gave me an opening to expand my boundaries—an overture to the future. As was true following Watson in his dory, rowing behind John in 1949 and 1950 is one of my all-time nostalgic memories. If I could live a day over again, one of my first choices would be to spend a morning doing that.

John was never a particularly early riser, unless it was to go duck shooting. He was single at the time and enjoyed a drink and often more than one, so the 4:00 a.m. rising time many lobstermen used was not to his liking. This was especially true if he had been out late the night before "playing," as he called it.

# The Rich History of a Small Fishing Port

Dave and I, together or individually, would often seek him out after we had hauled our own little string of a dozen traps. I knew where he went and would catch up to him by 9:00 a.m. or so. A warm greeting always ensued as I approached. Then I would fall in behind him. It never got boring; there was always the next trap, other lobstermen passing by in their powerboats with a greeting or a quick conversation and all the sights and sounds that made it a magical time for me. If John thought I was getting tired when rowing from Gray's Rock to Cat Island, he offered to have me tie my painter to his dory so I could rest while he pulled for both of us. With pride in my oarsman's ability, I never took him up on his offer, but that memory speaks of him. John was a strong man with rippling muscles. I would look at my scrawny arms and dream of having biceps like his someday. On arrival home in the evening, I flexed my arms in front of the bathroom mirror and wished for more than the small bump I viewed.

By midday or earlier, John had all his traps baited, and it was time to send'er for Little Harbor. Upon arrival, we went our separate ways. I never wanted the morning to end when I was following John.

By the spring of 1952, I needed a bigger boat for lobstering than the punt my father had built for me two years before. John had bought a twenty-six-foot, spray hood–style lobster boat from Dan Peach. He sold the *Send'er* to me for $100. This was to be my boat for the next three summers.

John's new vessel was named the *Green Hornet*. In early November 1953, there was a king-sized northeaster that lasted three days. In the middle of the night of the second day of the storm, the *Green Hornet* sank at its mooring, a total loss. There is never a fortuitous time to lose a boat you rely on for your living. The only small plus for John was that his brother Ed had gotten married and was leaving the fishing business. The *Lizzie H*, the boat Ed had built in 1947, was for sale in the winter of 1954. John bought it. It was still a Hawkes family boat. John fished the *Lizzie H* for the next ten years.

He was not necessarily a leader of Little Harbor men from a catch standpoint. John liked social times and wasn't usually the first one out or last one in. However, from the viewpoint of how to conduct oneself with his fellow man, John taught us much. He was one of the men who gave me some of my better values. He was always the first to step up and offer help in moving this or lifting that or doing anyone a favor, even if not asked. He was friendly without bias and had a townwide reputation for his generosity.

In the 1950s and 1960s, it was common for lobstermen to haul their own boats out for winter storage or spring painting. Wooden cradles that fitted a particular boat would be put in place on the beach at low tide and weighted down with rocks. This was done on a quiet day with little or no groundswell. As the next high tide started to ebb, the boat was brought in over the submerged cradle and tied in place, settling it into the proper location.

After the tide had receded enough, the rocks were knocked off the cradle. Then the boat and cradle were either jacked up with a mechanical jack or pried up with a crowbar or a long piece of 4x4 timber. Planks and rollers were placed under the cradle. There was a common pool of rollers kept at the Cove for use by all fishermen, with planks nearby. Then a block and tackle was rigged with power supplied by tying the end to a pickup truck. The boat was inched up the beach slowly but steadily. As planks and rollers came free behind the cradle, they were moved ahead.

I did this many times at the beach next to my parents' home. There we hauled my own twenty-eight-foot and later thirty-three-foot lobster boats or Stu Smith's boat. At the Cove during those years, I helped haul several boats using this method. They were tucked in a corner of the parking lot to be worked on by their owners.

I was taught by older, more experienced men how to use leverage and the many other little tricks that made this task easier. It was very interesting work, with a sense of accomplishment when the hauling was completed.

Azor Goodwin hauling a boat. *Peach Collection.*

Launching took place in the same manner. Since it was all downhill, so to speak, I learned that the whole process, if done properly, could be accomplished by putting some pressure on the cradle with a pry bar and letting gravity come into play. A line called a preventer was made fast to the cradle and up the beach to a "dead man" (some stable place). The person holding the end of this line gave enough slack so the vessel could move downward on the rollers gradually but never so much that it could "get away," as it was called. On level ground, a boat placed properly on rollers could be pushed and stopped by hand.

Moving boats in this manner is a thing of the past. It was really quite an art and nice to be part of. When one of these events was going to take place, you never needed to ask for help. Fellow fishermen and other beach visitors just appeared. People helping others was a common occurrence. No one told our generation how to do this; it was just what we learned when we were young by watching the grown men around us conduct business.

John was the acknowledged leader when it came to helping people. His style was "set the example." I loved to see him coming when I was moving my lobster boat. He was, of course, strong and powerful and had learned all the little tricks about boat moving years before. A typical hauling operation consumed a couple of hours. John helped frequently. You never paid others for this type of thing in dollars. Reciprocity was what was expected, and I hope and think I did pay back John and all the others who were so generous.

John assisted the elderly lady who lived near him on High Street for years. He took out bushels of bait for Ern Cronk during the last couple of years Ern fished. He was a frequent blood donor. The list goes on and on.

There is one story that I especially enjoy. I said his style was "set the example." On December 10, 1960, I woke up to a raging northeast snowstorm. It was cold, about fifteen degrees, and it had blown forty to fifty knots most of the previous night. A big sea had built up. I was concerned about my boat.

I quickly dressed and walked down to the Cove. My boat and Henry Briggs's were on the first two moorings out from the beach. Just as I got there, Bill Taylor, a fellow lobsterman, arrived from his home on Orne Street, equally concerned. It was snowing so hard at that point that we could hardly see. Shortly, the snow let up a little. Now Henry's and my boats became visible, as well as Bill's, which was the next one over from mine. Beyond that was where Bobby Brown's *White Horse* was moored.

Little Harbor was a rough place that morning, and as the snow let up, Bill and I could see that the *White Horse* was gone. We walked up through the

*White Horse* frozen in Little Harbor, 1961.

Hildreths' yard to the high rocks beyond. From there, we had a good view of Gas House Beach. The tide was quite low. Halfway up the beach, on her side, was the *White Horse*, her mooring chain hanging limply off the bow.

Bill went back to Fisherman's Beach. I went into Mr. Hildreth's house and called Bob with the bad news. Bob lived in an apartment at 218 Washington Street with his growing family. He quickly drove down to Little Harbor and met me. We walked back up to Molly's Rocks, where Bill and I had been twenty minutes earlier. The snow had let up enough so we could plainly see his boat—a sickening sight for owner or spectator.

Then we looked again. There was a man digging out stones and larger rocks from the skeg. It was fifteen degrees, snowing with a forty- to fifty-knot northeast wind blowing straight at him. This man was alone but knew that the boat would have to be moved before the tide came back in or it would be smashed to pieces against boulders at the top of the beach. The first step was freeing the skeg from the unwelcome weight.

Both Bob and I knew it was—you guessed it—John Hawkes. As the wind was coming straight at John, it was swirling around our heads, making it impossible to carry on a normal conversation. Bob looked at me with what had just been a long face. Despite his storm-inflicted pain, he smiled and shouted, "John Hawkes, what a man!"

# Chapter 21

# Nine Lives

In April 1961, my thirty-three-foot lobster boat, *Mistress*, was an advancement for me, but it was basically the same as boats of thirty-five and forty years before. Small-boat electronics were nonexistent or rudimentary at best compared to what was to come in a few more years. The big difference was the trunk cabin and pilothouse, which gave protection from wind and water.

The only accessory I had, compared to the men I had watched and learned from in Little Harbor, was a flashing fathometer. This instrument showed only the depth under the boat. Even this was scoffed at by many older fishermen, who felt it was unnecessary.

I had a 120-horsepower Palmer gas engine installed. Small-boat diesel engines were just coming on the scene. The first one that gained popularity among North Shore fishermen was built by Ford Motor Company. It had 100 horsepower and was reliable and quiet for a diesel. However, it was still considered too noisy by many.

Bob Brown's first *Sea Fever* was under construction in East Boothbay, Maine, that summer. The first two weeks of July, we went to Maine with our wives on the *Mistress*. This was the first time Bob had ever been beyond ten miles from Marblehead by boat, with the exception of one offshore dragging trip out of Gloucester with his uncle.

As my father had shown me, on that trip I taught Bob the basics of dead-reckoning navigation. I had learned that fog shouldn't stop you, but prudence, vigilance and a little luck were needed. I always enjoyed fog before the days of radar because of the satisfaction realized from dealing with it.

*Mistress I.*

In November 1961, I had the first of many close calls on the ocean. Bob, in his new *Sea Fever*, and I each had strings of 200 single-buoyed traps. Truthfully, I told him I had 200 but actually had 220 out. I suspect he did the same to me. We were friends but also rivals, each wanting to catch more than the other. With our larger boats, we moved traps beyond our traditional area, which was within two to three miles of the Marblehead and adjacent shores.

Except on weekend days, when often a school-aged boy would go out with us as a helper, we worked alone. One weekday afternoon in November, I was about five miles south of Marblehead. I had brought a dozen traps out from nearer shore to what we called "the dumping ground." It was sort of a hazy day, and there was no other boat of any sort in view. I was young and aggressive and had a habit of doing everything at as near top speed as possible. When I had gained hard-achieved experience and combined it with the wisdom of advancing years, I worked under strict rules when fishing alone. The first of these rules was: never try to gain time when setting out.

This November afternoon, I was twenty-four years old, believing I had more experience and wisdom than I actually did. I thought I was pretty much invincible. Instead of slowing the boat down to an idle and taking it out of gear when I was setting a trap, I ran the boat along at about half speed. I was throwing each buoy overboard, letting all the rope run out and then pushing the trap over. I did this for three or four traps. Then, inexplicably, I threw a trap over before the buoy and rope. Instantly, I said to myself, "I should not have done that!" I tried to move away from the pile of rope at my feet on the cockpit floor. In a split second, before I could make any voluntary movement, I was being pulled toward the stern of the boat. The boat was moving at five knots, with the trap trailing behind. I was entwined in the trap's line, its weight pulling hard on my leg. I could see two perfect half-hitch knots around my right ankle. Immediately, I was down under the small stern deck, only able to keep myself in the boat by bracing my feet under the deck and putting my hands against the combing. It took a good deal of effort to maintain that position. My mind started to work. I kept saying keep calm; don't panic. That took an exhausting amount of effort. First, I tried to pull on the line connected to the dragging trap. I hoped to get some slack and be able to free the half hitches around my ankle. I could still keep myself in the boat with my legs, holding the combing with just one hand, but I couldn't get any purchase with the free hand on the tight line. Briefly, I let my other hand go but could see I would be pulled out of the boat if I tried to pull on the line with both hands. My feet and legs just could not keep me in the boat by themselves. To go overboard was certain death. I was in peak condition, but my energy level was being drained at a rapid rate.

My mind raced. My father had taught me how to row, then to sail, then to navigate. All during his years of instruction he told me over and over, "Never go out in a boat without a knife in your pocket." I didn't always listen to him, but that piece of advice had taken firm root. I thought of the jackknife in my left-hand pants pocket. I knew it was my only chance. Holding the combing with my right hand, I carefully took the knife out of my pocket. I couldn't open it with only one hand but immediately put the knife in my mouth and opened the largest blade with my teeth, reached over and cut the line to the trap. I fell back prone on the cockpit floor and lay there for a few minutes, thought things over and said a prayer of thanks. I know my father's name was mentioned.

This is a good time to relate a story told to me just recently by an inshore Marblehead lobsterman named Steve Bird. Steve is my kind of guy, what I call hard core. He is a generation behind me but learned to lobster, as I did, working for a now deceased character and lobsterman named Joe Walker. Steve does his own thing, makes his own way and I think well of him.

Not too many years ago, Steve was hauling traps alone one day in his thirty-six-foot lobster boat *Cajen*, named for his two daughters. By this time, strings of traps or trawls were permitted in Marblehead waters. The days of single-buoyed traps only were gone. Steve was setting an eight-trap trawl in twenty feet of water, one hundred yards off the rocks northeast of the end of Preston Beach. The boat was moving toward the shore, and after three or four traps had left the boat, Steve felt himself being pulled toward the stern of his boat. The same two half-hitch knots I had experienced years before were around his ankle, a moment of carelessness with a likely bad outcome. Unlike me, he couldn't keep himself in his boat and was in the water, being pulled down to the bottom before he had time to do anything. Steve kept a cool head or, at the least, didn't have time to panic. I said the water depth was twenty feet. He was pulled right down to the bottom. The tension on his line was gone. He undid the half hitches and popped up to the surface. The story doesn't end there. The *Cajen* had continued on her way. The rest of the trawl set itself, and the boat went in until it hit the rocky shore. The shore there had a sharp drop-off. The boat nudged itself into an opening in the rocks and stopped with the propeller still churning away. Steve swam the one hundred yards or so to the boat, climbed over the side into the cockpit, put the boat in reverse and backed away from the rocks with no damage. He went in, moored his boat, drove home and sat in his easy chair looking out the window for three days!

# Chapter 22

# Line Trawling Starts

**I** had learned about the risk of setting gear haphazardly and was about to start what turned out to be much more of an addiction than catching lobsters. Tub trawling, as it was called, became my number-one calling. Gloucester sailing schooners in the 1800s started this method of fishing. The gear I used in 1962 was the same as that devised by fishermen one hundred years before, except that my line was synthetic and impervious to rot.

Bob Brown had acquired his trawling knowledge fishing with Marty Sylvester two years earlier. The previous winter, he had fished on a limited basis in the *White Horse*. By January 1962, he had his lobster traps on shore and was ready to catch fish. I was a greenhorn's greenhorn but eager to do the same. Bob had told me tales of how much money could be made from tub trawling in the winter. He advised me what to buy for line and the needed small anchors. Further, he showed me how to rig the gear. The ground line I purchased was three-sixteenths of an inch in diameter. I spaced my gangings nine feet apart. In the future, I also used six-foot rig.

Eight fifty-fathom lengths or "lines" made up one tub. The full length of each tub was just under half a mile and had a total of 270 gangings and hooks if it was a nine-foot rig. Each line was coiled into a wooden barrel three feet in diameter and thirty inches high. Commonly called tubs, the name tub or line trawling was thus given to this fishery. A small but important feature was a piece of rope spliced through a hole drilled near the top edge of the tub. When pulled through a hole on the opposite side and tied, a handle was created for carrying.

It took several days for me to rig eight tubs of my new gear. By the middle of January, I had it all put together. My freshly painted trawl tubs were stacked outside my Little Harbor shanty with the hooks ready to be baited.

Cut-up frozen herring, squid or mackerel was used for bait, as well as fresh sea clams. The first three were purchased in Gloucester and the fourth at a shucking business in Rowley, Massachusetts, called Savage Clam Company. The sea clams came in gallon containers. One of the big markets for them was a then-prominent chain of restaurants, Howard Johnson's. Cut into strips, they were sold as fried clams. For bait, we cut them into pieces the correct size for a hook.

It can't be stressed enough how different things were in the fishing industry before the days of electronic aids. Bob and I had flashing depth finders, and that was it! Dead reckoning navigation was key to our success or failure. Areas where fish were likely to be were found by landmarks. This house lining up with that water tower or Baker's Island lighthouse over Half Way Rock were the type of crosshairs used to find the desired bottom. These spots and appropriate bearings were passed on to Bob and me by older men who had trawled in their younger years. Line trawls required hard bottom to be effective. Setting trawls on soft or "slimy" bottom caused the bait to disintegrate, giving no chance for the fish to bite. When we started, we used the old-timer landmarks. Later that year, and in the future, we developed our own book of knowledge.

In 1962, the whole operation was conducted in the following manner. Weather was key. When the forecast was favorable, we baited up four tubs of trawl. To do this, each line of trawl was put on the workbench, and in succession, the hooks were baited. The ground line and gangings were then placed in the tub. One tub took either side of an hour to bait, depending on the skill level of the man and the condition of the gear.

We rowed our four baited tubs out to our respective boats. After leaving the Cove, we headed east-southeast or south from Marblehead Rock to our planned destination. We went no more than ten or eleven miles. Upon arrival, we threw over a high flier buoy, line and anchor. The baited tub was next to us at the helm.

We positioned the side of the boat from which we were steering, facing the wind and the waves. Putting the boat in and out of gear, we flicked each baited hook out of the tub, either by hand or with a stick. If there was a snarl, the boat was stopped. The wind blew the boat away from the descending ground line. Getting the trawl in or around the engine propeller was to be avoided under any condition. Setting this gear alone took patience,

A traditional wooden trawl tub in place to receive ground line when hauling trawl by hand.

finesse and skill. Each hook had to come out in order or a price was paid. If the gear hadn't been properly baited with the hooks in order, a mess of massive proportions was possible. Anyone who has set traditional gear for any length of time has had the disheartening experience of seeing most or all of a tub go out in a huge ball of hooks, gangings and ground line. The only way to clear this is back at the shanty, removing every hook and unsnarling the line. This could consume the better part of a day.

Generally, Bob and I made two separate sets and then returned to the Little Harbor, noting the course and time back to Marblehead Rock. The gear was left overnight. The reciprocal course and running time was repeated the next morning for hauling. Even in fog, we could find our gear with this method. If the weather report dictated, the second four tubs were readied to take out the next morning. Hauling was done 100 percent by hand, even the end lines and anchors. The winch used for lobster traps had the belts disconnected for the winter to save wear and tear. After the anchor was aboard, the trawl was hauled hand over hand with the ground line and hooks dropped, or "cartwheeled," into a nearby tub. Fish were slatted off into a fish pen.

Baiting hooks was a boring, laborious process, but hauling was the payback. Anyone, from a small boy at a pond with a pole on up, knows the rush of pulling in a line and waiting to see what is on the end. Hauling a line trawl by hand and, even later, with a powered line hauler magnifies that feeling over a longer period of time—it's exhilarating! When hauling, the tug and weight of fish can be felt from forty fathoms down or deeper, and multiple fish can be discerned. All the preparation, time and labor it takes to get to that moment of hauling is forgotten. I experienced that feeling thousands of times. When my fishing days are done, that's what I suspect I will miss the most.

In 1962, our results within sight of Marblehead were different every trip, but quantities of 500 to 1,200 pounds were common. When fishing alone, dressing the fish was normally done on the mooring. It was then rowed to shore in our punts and sold.

As a complete novice, I spent almost a whole day baiting up my first four tubs of trawl. Albert Hayes came in the shanty and, after observing my pathetic efforts, said, "It's piecework. You have to do it as fast as possible." I've never forgotten that piece of advice. The next day, for my maiden attempt, I made my first set only five miles out. Bob had had his operation underway for two weeks. Early the next morning, I was ready for my first haul back. A four-year-old on Christmas morning could not have been more excited. I knew the difference between a cod, pollock and haddock, but that was about it. At morning's end, I had close to five hundred pounds of fish aboard. I had also caught one large, blue-colored fish that weighed close to forty pounds. I wasn't sure what it was.

Bob was hauling his gear that morning a few miles farther out. On his way in, he came alongside just as I was finishing. We always gave each other an enthusiastic greeting on the water. He exclaimed, "How are you doing?" I replied, "Great! I caught a huge haddock!" (I didn't know it then, but haddock don't get any bigger than fifteen pounds.) He said, "Let me see it!" I held up the blue fish proudly with both hands; he took one look and said, "You Goddamn fool—that's a hake!" My fish knowledge had a new species added to it.

I got better at the whole thing as the winter passed. The Boston Light Ship, a permanently moored navigation aid ten miles from Marblehead, was still in existence. This one-hundred-foot vessel had hard bottom northeast of it that we prospected and started to set on. Fish were present there. This was too far for us to see landmarks on the North Shore, but we used time and distance from the lightship to keep track of our sets. Our larger boats and growing knowledge were working.

One day we went, each in our own boat, to Cape Ann Ridge, which was fourteen miles southeast of home. There was a buoy marking a dumping area eleven miles out that was a great navigational help to us. Here we set and hauled our gear back the same day. A few days later, we ventured to Middle Bank, twenty miles from Marblehead. We ran into similar-sized boats from Gloucester. This was a considerably large fleet. We knew there were more experienced men in these boats. Some of them were summer lobstermen like ourselves. There were a few who commanded the most respect and made their living year-round from catching only fish.

In summer months, when dogfish made line trawling unprofitable, they hand lined or "jigged" for fish. The dean of these year-round ground fishermen was Russell Wonson. He fished with one crewman in a thirty-five-foot boat named the *Guy R.* He was twenty years older than us. His ancestral fishing roots went deep into Gloucester history. He was a consistent high liner. Bob became very friendly with Russell in years to come and benefited greatly from his sound advice. Russell was the epitome of what it took to be a successful ground fisherman before the days of modern electronics. I still marvel at his knowledge and skill.

I look back on the winter of 1962 from the perspective of 1998 and think of how different things were, both the people and the equipment. A great deal has changed. That was where we got our start catching fish. The biggest significance is that today, I can handle a fifty-footer alone at age sixty. With the methods available when I first started, that would not have been possible. As for the thrill and enjoyment of feeling a fish come up before you can see it, that has never changed.

It took a while, but during the rest of 1962 and 1963, I began to wonder what economic life away from fishing would be like. It appeared that a man's best years were behind him in the fishing business by the time he was forty. I rather reluctantly planned for a future and a path away from where I was. My path became a detour, starting on April 1, 1963. I took a sales job with Westclox Division of General Time Corporation. Bob stayed with fishing full time. Our close friendship was to separate for a variety of reasons, not the least of which was that I was a part-timer. This made me a second-rate fisherman, while he was supporting his wife and three children by his fishing efforts.

We were never again to be as close as during the years from 1951 to 1963, but something stayed between us that never left. It's hard to articulate because we never talked about it. If I had to put it into one sentence, I would say we had a mutual respect for each other's accomplishments.

# Chapter 23

# A Trip to Tillies

**S**tarting in April 1963, I went to work with a suit and tie for the next several years. I fished sixty or so lobster traps in the summers with my thirty-three-foot *Mistress*. In the winter and spring, I set tub trawls on weekends as weather permitted. My fishing status was defined as a part-time "rag picker."

During this period, loran became more and more common for all types of mariners. It had been developed as a result of World War II, where it was used for military navigation. Charts began to have loran lines printed on them in the late '50s. The first sets that I heard of were military surplus, quite large and very crude by future standards. Cross bearings were acquired by counting the number of lines visible on a small screen. The radio waves that a receiving set showed were transmitted by sending stations in various locations. By getting two different bearings that crossed at an angle near ninety degrees and comparing these numbers to the printed lines on a navigational chart, a very accurate position could be determined, especially when compared to the old method of dead reckoning.

In the last three weeks of April 1962, Bob Brown and I ran a fifty-foot gill net boat out of Marblehead. This boat, now named *Horizon*, was built in 1952 for Watson Curtis. In 1960, Watson had sold it to a wealthy man who was an absentee owner. He had two men named Don Russell and Bill Whipple fish it on a catch/share basis. Both of them had other commitments that April. They convinced Bob and me that it was a perfect fit for us. We fished gill nets for cod in basically the same waters in which we had been tub trawling, using loran for the first time.

# The Rich History of a Small Fishing Port

Often, we left the gill nets overnight on Middle Bank, with the loran bearings of the high fliers noted. To be able to come back the next morning out of sight of land to the exact location where we had set was a revelation. We were slow to realize the significance of this. It wasn't until the end of the 1960s that loran became commonplace in small boats. In the early '60s, fish were prevalent in large areas. It seemed to me unnecessary to pinpoint a specific location. Dead reckoning still worked fine for twenty miles from shore!

My sales job was interesting, but I never lost my zest for catching lobsters or fish. I had what was known as a Hartman Converter in my company car. It was before the day of VHF radios, common as a means of marine communication in the 1970s.

Fishermen and yachtsmen talked on longer-range radios before then. Channels 2638 and 2738 were used for communication, and conversations could be heard from one hundred to two hundred miles away quite easily. In addition, there was another frequency known as WOU. Here, the marine weather was still given four times a day at 5:20 and 11:20, both a.m. and p.m. The channel had a marine telephone operator on twenty-four-hour duty. Ship-to-shore calls were handled from all types of vessels. The converter in my car enabled me to hear these channels while making sales calls in New England. I had observed that the older fishermen around Little Harbor never did much tub trawling after the age of forty. Hauling line trawl by hand was just too strenuous. Lobster traps were hauled with a turning winch, which took a good deal of the effort out of it, but I also noticed that lobstermen were less productive as their age increased.

By the mid-'60s, my wife and I were busy parenting. I reluctantly told myself that my full-time lobstering and fishing days were over. I consoled myself that at least I could catch something on weekends for the foreseeable future. I eased my anxiety by trying to convince myself that I would have much more long-term financial potential with something different from commercial fishing. "Besides, isn't that one of the reasons I went to college?"

It took a constant personal propaganda campaign because, in moments of weakness, I knew my heart and soul really wanted to be on the ocean trying to catch something. Weekend efforts were keeping my addiction under control.

Along with loran and future small-boat radar, the 1960s saw another advancement that was to have a huge impact on fisheries: the invention of the hydraulic line hauler. The first one of these I remember was brought around the North Shore on the back of a rack body truck by Marine

Hydraulic Engineering Company from Maine. The demonstration hauler had two twelve-inch tapered discs bolted together that gripped a line. It was powered by an attached hydraulic motor, with oil supplied by a hydraulic pump. During the 1960s, brass winches disappeared from lobster boats and were replaced with similarly powered line haulers. By the end of the decade, these had been adapted to make hauling tub trawls possible by powered means. The fishing world was moving under our feet.

During the years from 1963 to 1967, Bob and I stayed friendly, but our relationship was not as close as in previous years. He maintained the same fishing lifestyle as we had known in the early '60s. By now, Bob had made a name for himself both by how many fish he was catching (mostly haddock) and also by his risk-taking style of fishing in extremely bad weather, when other men thought better of going out. This was the time when people started using the nickname "Suicide Brown." Two stories will give a portrayal of this era.

The first involves a trawling trip I took with him on the thirty-two-foot *Sea Fever* in January 1965. That winter, I hauled my thirty-three-foot *Mistress* out for the month of January. I drove, as was my custom, into Little Harbor beach late one Friday afternoon. Bob had learned from his Gloucester fisherman friend, the knowledgeable Russell Wonson, that there were many haddock on Tillies Bank. Bob was not very familiar with Tillies. I, in my weekend forays, had never fished there. He asked me if I would go out with him the next day "to give Tillies a try." I jumped at the chance.

With two of us, we decided that we would be able to fish more than the four tubs he had been fishing alone. After supper that night, I went down to his shanty at Little Harbor and baited three more tubs of trawl. Bob went home for supper and a nap. The appointed hour to meet was 12:30 a.m., which meant no sleep for me.

We got the baited gear aboard the *Sea Fever* and departed, making our way along the shore to Eastern Point, Gloucester. After passing the whistle buoy, we headed east-southeast. I did catch a nap on the way out. We were steaming into a wind of ten to fifteen knots. I remember it was a sloppy ride.

Finding the proper fishing area without the help of electronic aids was substantially more difficult when out of sight of land, as there was nothing with which to mark the location. In addition to the compass and a watch, the only other means of assistance was a flashing fathometer, which showed depth only. Bob knew the course he wanted. He thought a run of an hour and forty-five minutes would be the amount of time to an area of deeper water known as "the gully." The gully was over one mile across and seventy fathoms deep. On the other side, the bottom quickly rose to forty fathoms. This was the accepted depth for setting, according to the information Bob had received from Russell. The whole thing was an art, not a science, and you had to keep your wits about you and hope for the best. The present-day fisherman, using loran and GPS, has no idea of the difficulty of finding the most advantageous location in an extremely small area using dead reckoning. It's so easy in modern times that it can be accomplished by an idiot.

The weather report for the day was for increasing southerly winds and rain followed by a cold front with strong northwest winds. To beat the northwest wind was the main reason we had left Little Harbor before 1:00 a.m. We arrived at what we thought was the right place at 4:00 a.m. and immediately set out three tubs.

By now, rain had started, and the wind had a little more heft to it. Even in pleasant weather conditions, when making more than one set, you had to be careful and keep track of the location of each. This was especially true with the poor weather we knew was going to be ours for the day. We ran a precise amount of time to the southeast that morning, about ten minutes or a little less than two miles, and made our second set composed of four tubs. The two sets gave us a total of three and a half miles of gear in the water. It was still pitch dark as we finished.

In the darkness and approaching rain and fog, it was necessary to keep our last set high flier in sight at all times. Losing sight of this would likely mean losing track of exactly where we were and would very possibly mean having to return on a clear day to find our buoys. The trawls would be retrieved with nothing but empty hooks. Parasites would have eaten all the caught fish in the interim. This was to be avoided at all costs. We took turns at the wheel, keeping the *Sea Fever* alongside the last high flier we had thrown. The man not minding the wheel had a mug up and could lie down for a while. As soon as dawn came, we started hauling back. One of us hauled by hand, while the other carefully coiled the trawl in "pin hooked" fashion. We worked fast because it was obvious that the weather was deteriorating.

By 8:30 a.m., the first set was in. From the buoy hauled aboard at the end of our set, we ran the reciprocal course for the short two miles back to the initial set made well before daylight. In the now very limited visibility, there was always apprehension about finding a buoy where we thought it should be. The buoys were very quiet. When our wristwatches said it should be in sight, it was right there. This brought out our usual comments about how smart we were—a form of pressure release!

Bob Brown in *Sea Fever I* at Isle of Shoals off the New Hampshire coast, 1964.

By 11:00 a.m., we had that set back aboard. By now it was raining hard and blowing southerly about twenty-five knots—quite nasty. The results of our effort were just over 4,000 pounds. There were a few cod and a stray cusk, but 3,900 pounds were haddock. We took turns steering and dressing the fish for the three hours back to Marblehead. It was a rough ride for the whole twenty-nine miles. Between the rolling of the *Sea Fever*, broadside to the sea, and trying to brace ourselves while gutting the fish, it was a slow process. The last 1,000 pounds or so we dressed at the mouth of Marblehead Harbor in the lee of Lighthouse Point. Just before we finished, Bob called Bud Noyes, the fish buyer from Beverly, on station WOU. We went into the Cove, tying up to Bob's mooring. It took two full loads in his punt to get our catch ashore. We spotted Bud backing his truck down the ramp as we approached the beach. We forked the fish into his truck, and Bud took them to his packinghouse in Beverly, now the Beverly Chamber of Commerce office, where he weighed, boxed and iced them for sale. When Bud left for Beverly, it was 4:00 p.m. After a fifteen-hour day of almost constant physical work with unsteady footing, we were very tired. That's the way it was! I doubt that a small boat will ever again land 4,000 pounds of fish in Little Harbor.

The next year, I installed an automatic pilot in my boat. This took away the need for a person to always stand at the wheel, which was a tremendous help. Automatic pilots were not unknown in the '60s but were not very commonly used in small boats. I was immediately happy with my investment.

Bob got one just after I did. The word started to get around among North Shore fishermen that we had installed these devices. We were pretty pleased with ourselves.

The top fisherman in Swampscott in the '50s and '60s was a man named Louis "Lucky" Williams. He was also called "The Chief" because he generally caught more than other fishermen. He fished a floating fish trap in the summer months off Dread Ledge. This was in front of the New Ocean House Inn, a very prominent hotel that burned down in the late 1960s. In the winter, Lucky fished gill nets, catching mostly cod, often on the Lightship Bottom. All in all, he was considered quite a successful man. In bad weather, he and some of his fellow Swampscott fishermen occasionally showed up at Little Harbor to visit people like John and Link Hawkes. There would be drinking, stories and good times. I first met him as a young boy. Since then, Lucky had always been friendly to me. He was the same way with Bob. We both liked and respected him.

A while after I had installed my autopilot, Lucky called me up and said he was thinking of getting one for his forty-foot Novi boat and asked my opinion. I gave him a completely positive answer and said he should go ahead. He replied, "That's interesting," because he had talked to Bob Brown, who told him just the opposite. In the years to come, he never forgot that bad information, especially if we were having a couple of cold ones. He would replay that conversation. Bob always sought a competitive advantage. He was perfectly willing to capitalize on Russell Wonson's excellent advice about fishing on Tillies but had consciously misled Lucky Williams with his advice on automatic pilots. Lucky was not even a direct competitor of Bob's.

*Chapter 24*

# Birth of a Fishery

y the middle of June 1968, there were a new *Sea Fever* and new *Mistress* sitting on their respective moorings in Little Harbor. These forty- and forty-four-foot fishing vessels were the maximum size that could be moored in and fish out of the confined anchorage. It's a fascinating story of how, within a very short time, the birth of small-boat offshore lobstering emerged from this tiny cove.

After 1966, I switched from selling clocks to becoming an investment broker. I didn't have a written strategic plan for my life, but I still constantly wanted it to have a fishing flavor. In my early thirties, I guessed that that might be ten or so more years. I now had a lovely wife and two small children. My offspring will forever remain my greatest accomplishment. I accepted the fact that I would never again fish full time. I was getting older by the minute, and the future of inshore fishing looked limited.

In May 1968, my wife took the children to see their grandparents. I had noticed an ad in the most recent issue of *National Fisherman* describing a forty-four-foot line trawler for sale in Chatham, Massachusetts. With time on my hands, the following Saturday, I drove down to Cape Cod to satisfy my curiosity. By 11:00 a.m. that morning, I owned this vessel, a very pretty boat. It cost me $17,000. It was built in Bass Harbor, Maine, in 1963, by a builder named Robert Rich. As we shook hands over the deal, the seller, a Chatham commercial fisherman named Sten Carlsen said, "Buying a new boat is the biggest event in a man's life!" I don't know if I would go quite that far, but it was exciting. The next weekend, I brought her home to Marblehead.

*Mistress II.*

During the fall of 1967, Bob Brown had come to the conclusion that his thirty-two-foot *Sea Fever* was limiting his potential. He had a vision. Wooden fishing boats in those days were being built in Nova Scotia for substantially less money than in the United States. There was a limit to the size that could be imported because of customs laws. About forty feet was the maximum allowed.

Link Hawkes, a jack-of-all-trades, had spent his youth during the 1930s around Little Harbor and, by 1967, was a sort of tarnished living legend. At the very least, he was colorful. Stories I heard or knew about him could fill pages. Among other things, Link had helped design Novi boats for fishermen from Marblehead and Swampscott, like Albert Hayes, Marty Sylvester and Lucky Williams. He envisioned himself as an expert in a lot of things. His opinions were certainly worth listening to. Over the years, he did many intricate mechanical jobs for others and me.

Bob took Link with him to Nova Scotia. They selected a builder, and Bob left a deposit. The new vessel was to be forty feet long and incorporate custom features. It would use all the extra money Bob had put aside.

One of the funniest stories I ever heard happened during that trip. According to Bob, they were able to find just one rooming house to stay in for the night. The only available room had a double bed. Before, during and after supper, several beers were consumed by both. Link could be "earthy" at times. Bob didn't want to sleep face to face with Link, and vice versa. To solve the problem, they backed up to each other. They both defended their limited territory very audibly—but not by using their vocal cords! Bob said that he gave it his best effort, but Link was an easy winner. He swore he would never sleep with Link again.

The new *Sea Fever* arrived in Little Harbor in June, and Bob was able to start pursuing his dream. In two separate trips, he took a total of one hundred lobster traps to Cashes Ledge, a large area of shoal water ninety miles east of Marblehead, almost in the middle of the Gulf of Maine. Bob's new boat had a loran, which helped him find the right bottom for lobsters and locating his gear. Individuals from Massachusetts and Maine had made attempts at lobstering on Cashes prior to loran, but the inconsistency of dead reckoning navigation had made sustained efforts unsuccessful.

During the summer of 1968, Bob made repeated two-day trips to Cashes. There, his traps were hauled twice, and the rest of the time was spent hand lining for cod and pollock. Catches of three to five hundred pounds of lobsters and several thousand pounds of fish were normal for each trip. Lobsters were sixty to eighty cents per pound, and pollock was three to six cents per pound, with cod a little more.

There was very little small-boat fishing on Cashes in those days. Large draggers in the eighty- to one-hundred-foot range sometimes were visible a few miles away in deeper water, pulling their nets over softer bottom. The only other small-boat fishermen Bob ran into were a couple of Italian hook boats from Boston. Earlier in the twentieth century, this was a large fleet that had dwindled down to a handful by the 1960s. These hookers commonly set forty to fifty tubs of trawl on a two- or three-day trip. Their wooden boats, about fifty feet, were of Mediterranean design, often built by an East Boston boat builder. The design had been brought to Boston and Gloucester by fishermen emigrating from Italy. In the not-too-distant future, Cashes would be fished heavily by New England gill net fishermen, and large draggers would gain technology that would also enable them to drag nets over jagged, hard bottom. However, for now it was a prolific, almost virgin fishing ground for small-boat fishermen who dared to venture that far. The *Sea Fever* generally was all by herself. When the fall weather pattern brought on much more wind, Bob brought his lobster traps in from Cashes and set them in familiar waters off Marblehead.

During the winter and spring of 1969, Bob went line trawling on Middle Bank and Tillies Bank. He and his crewman, Ben Doliber, had another very successful season. In the late spring of '69, Bob returned to Cashes with a load of lobster traps and picked up where he had left off the previous year. On his first trip, he noticed several inshore-type lobster buoys sporting a variety of colors. Soon it was learned that these had been brought out to Cashes by one or more of the Boston hook boats. They left Boston in the evening to arrive about daylight the next day to set their trawls. Coming along the shore off Nahant and Marblehead, they grabbed lobster buoys at random and took the traps with them out to Cashes. After a few such trips, they had a fair amount of gear out there. They didn't even bother to change the buoys to a different color—a brazen act of stealing, to say the least.

In the fall of 1968, I started going to Cashes on weekends with a crew of two or three boys or men. At dawn, after an eight- to nine-hour run from Marblehead, I jogged around until I saw fish markings on my fish finder. When I saw something promising, we ran up to windward, dropped the anchor and drifted back on the school. Hand lining three to five thousand pounds of mostly large pollock and cod was fairly common. We rarely had to move for the rest of the morning. A lead jig with three or four hooks or worms was used. A jig was a lead weight made to look like a fish. We made them ourselves by pouring molten lead into molds about twelve inches long. This mold and process were handed down to me by older fishermen from the Cove. The manual labor needed to boat several thousand pounds of fish by hand left us exhausted by midday. We would raise the anchor and head for Gloucester, about eighty miles away.

On Memorial Day weekend in 1969, my crew and I went to Cashes on one of these hand lining ventures. Bob had told me about the trap problem he was having. When we got there that morning at sunrise, it looked like a United Nations of lobster buoys. Some I recognized; some I didn't.

On returning to Marblehead, I discussed what I had seen with Bob. He said he was preparing to address the situation. He had made arrangements to take people out with him with the necessary police powers. He waited until the culprits were in place and the weather report was favorable. Neither he nor the people he suspected had radar. Bob timed the arrival of the *Sea Fever* for late afternoon on a bright, sunny day. He spotted the enemy boat, which looked like a speck on the horizon. Aligning the *Sea Fever* so she was directly in the path of the sun, he ran the boat toward his suspects. They came right up beside the thieves before being noticed. The hook boat was in the process of hauling some of the stolen traps.

That ended that, but it also ended Bob's lobstering for that summer at Cashes. His gear was then very vulnerable to retaliation, so he moved everything back to Marblehead.

This story was the talk of the waterfront at the time. Watson Curtis approached Bob and asked him why he didn't consider lobstering where he wouldn't have to worry about something like that happening again. Bob asked what he meant. Watson suggested, "Why not try lobstering on the Continental Shelf with the *Sea Fever?*" Watson said he would go with him if Bob would agree to try it. They needed a third good man, and Steve Goodwin, another Marbleheader, agreed. By August 1969, they were on their way to Oceanographer Canyon with their first load of traps. This was a 380-mile round trip from Little Harbor. To the best of my knowledge, it was the first time a boat that size had tried such a feat. The small-boat offshore lobster business was born. Steve Goodwin's life was to end tragically in less than seven years. But that year, Bob, Watson and Steve were being applauded for what they were attempting. Bob and Watson were both very strong-minded individuals.

Watson was born in 1928 and grew up as a young boy around Fisherman's Beach. He had taken a liking to Gerald Smith and often went out to haul traps with him in the late 1930s. He sat under the spray hood when it was rough or in the cockpit on calm days and plugged the claws of Gerald's lobsters.

As a youth, Watson had taken a familiar path to Bob and me. Soon he had a small dory and a few traps of his own. By the time he was fifteen, he had a small, powered lobster boat. After a stint in the navy at the end of World War II, he returned to Marblehead, as many other enlistees, anxious to get back to the ocean. His nickname was "Wonder Boy," partly because of his hard work and partly out of the envy and jealousy of older fishermen. He was also considered quite a talker or blowhard. When I was eleven, I found him extremely impressive.

In 1949, he contracted to have Albert and Bob Cloutman build him a new thirty-two-foot hard chine (V-bottom) boat for his endeavors, as well as nighttime drift netting for mackerel, a fishery that has since disappeared. An innovator, Watson was admired, envied and controversial.

By 1951, he had naval architect Sam Brown design a fifty-foot lobster boat for him. Newbert and Wallace, a shipyard on the Damariscotta River in Thomaston, Maine, built the vessel. Over the years, this firm built many large boats, particularly wooden draggers and scallopers in the eighty- to one-hundred-foot range. Watson named his vessel *Sea Dog.* When she arrived in Marblehead in the spring of 1952, I remember thinking that my dream would be to have a vessel of this size and type some day. Many thought he was out of his mind.

# The Rich History of a Small Fishing Port

With the *Sea Dog*, Watson could no longer moor in Little Harbor. The boat was too big for the confined anchorage. He moved to the main harbor and fished from State Street Landing or Commercial Street Landing for the rest of his working life.

In the 1950s, Watson was an innovator. Many of his achievements have been lost or forgotten. He went mackerel purse seining with the *Sea Dog* in the summer of 1952 with the help of a Gloucester man named Leo Favolora, a top seine fisherman. He made a trip the following winter and hand lined for red snapper off the southeastern United States as far south as Florida.

In the spring, he and his crew followed the spring run of mackerel up the coast with mackerel drift nets. The *Sea Dog* stayed near the nets each night as they floated with the cork lines on the surface. Either at or before daylight, they were hauled back by hand, and mackerel, which had been gilled, were removed.

This fishery took place in sight of land and every few days moved along the coast from New Jersey to New York, Rhode Island and the Massachusetts coast as the mackerel migrated in their spring movement north. When Marblehead was reached, they changed from drift netting to setting a floating fish trap. This was put in place off the southwest side of Tinker's Island. The trap was moored with several large, strategically placed anchors. A leader, or line of twine, was attached to the shore of the island. The leader had a line of floats on the surface with a row or fence of twine extending down to the bottom. It extended into deeper water, where the trap itself was anchored in place. Fish swimming along the shore followed it along and quickly found themselves in the trap itself.

The design of the trap kept the fish confused and swimming in circles. The trap was hauled by Watson and his crew of one or two other men early each morning. Their fish were brought into Marblehead and trucked to Boston or sold to lobstermen for bait, depending on the species caught.

These traps were common along the Massachusetts coast in the 1950s but became rare with the summer arrival of bluefish in the 1980s. Before that, bluefish were unheard of north of Cape Cod. The trapping season ended, and Watson switched to lobstering. Later on, the bluefish completely drove the mackerel from local waters and made fish trapping unprofitable.

The *Sea Dog* was large for lobster fishing in shallow water and bays, and Watson started venturing several miles off Marblehead with his traps. He found good catches as the fall wore on. Traps had always been between thirty and thirty-six inches long. I believe that Watson built the first forty-eight-inch traps himself, out of oak. In future years, this type of trap would become the preferred size for offshore lobstering. By 1960, Anderson Trap Company, in Maine, started to build these on a production basis. Watson can be credited with designing and first producing the four-footer.

He was a restless sort, and in 1960, he sold the *Sea Dog*. He had invested money in a couple of multifamily homes in Marblehead. Watson's career wobbled along in the 1960s, with his main effort being real estate investments. At one point, he became a game warden working for the state, but he always had his ear to the ground, and nothing much of waterfront news got by him. By 1968 and 1969, he was aware of large catches of lobsters by a couple of steel vessels (one hundred feet and up) fishing traps in the canyons of the Continental Shelf.

The Continental Shelf, off the East Coast of the United States, is the extension of the North American continent. The shelf, or plain, is the actual underwater perimeter of the East Coast. It increases from 40 miles wide off Virginia to over 150 miles off New England. At the outer edge of the shelf, there is a sharp drop-off of depth. This is known as the Continental Slope or edge. Indented along the edge of the slope are canyons with even more dramatic depth increases. Millions of years ago, both erosion and earthquakes contributed to the Continental Shelf's formation. As one gets farther from shore, the water gets gradually deeper until depths of 100 fathoms are reached where the edge commences. The canyons, or gorges, indent the edge of the shelf for a few miles. In these areas, the drops are huge, often going from 100 to 250 fathoms in distances as short as one hundred yards.

Draggers from Rhode Island, New Bedford and Gloucester, Massachusetts, had caught lobsters in the canyons in prior years. They dragged nets along the bottom with the same method they used for fish, operating mainly in the winter months, when they knew the lobster shells were harder and could endure the dragging method without too much shell damage.

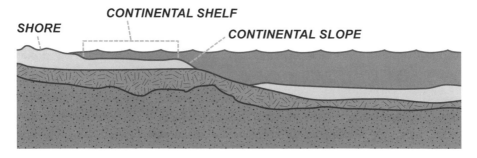

The Continental Shelf.

# The Rich History of a Small Fishing Port

One winter day in 1964, I was calling on a wholesale distributor in New Bedford. He was a customer of my line of Westclox timepieces. After the call, I migrated down to the waterfront of Fairhaven, Massachusetts, which is on the east side of New Bedford Harbor. There was, and still is, a large amount of commercial activity there. I parked my car and walked onto a nearby wharf with the name McLean's prominently displayed on the building. It was a lobster- and fish-buying business. A large white dragger was approaching from the harbor entrance. I immediately recognized it as the *Judith Lee Rose*, home port of Gloucester.

Just then, the dragger's skipper let out a couple of blasts on his air horn. One of the bystanders in the small crowd of people could easily see I was an outsider by my suit and tie. He told me in a knowing way, "The *Judith Lee* has a banner trip of twenty thousand pounds." A great story by a person who went on one of these trips on a dragger at the time is told in the book *White-Tipped Orange Masts* by Peter Prybot.

Landings of this size started some people in Gloucester thinking about using traps to catch lobsters in the canyons. Fishing traps in deep water (one hundred fathoms or more) was a trial and error business. A company called Deep Deep Ocean Products was started by Gloucester-based individuals. They acquired two older steel vessels in excess of one hundred feet. One was named *Red Diamond* and the other *Homarus*. Both were more than capable of withstanding the winter weather of the Continental Shelf. They had no pilothouse controls. Therefore, a person had to be in the engine room when any type of change was made in speed (forward or reverse). Commands were sent from the skipper to the engine room by a bell system. To set traps, a one-inch steel cable was put out off the winches, which were formerly used to tow the nets for ground fishing. Traps were attached to this wire with half-inch chain gangings and shackles. It is easy now to see the drawbacks to all these things, but the people involved were breaking new ground. At the beginning of this venture, they experimented with oversized high fliers, or end buoys, which were provided by a Marblehead fledgling float and mooring buoy maker. This little company was run by Watson Curtis. Buoys designed to be used to float mooring chain in Marblehead Harbor were adapted to make end buoys for the lobster pot trawls used by the *Red Diamond* and *Homaras*. These buoys quickly proved to be unwieldy and hard to handle. However, the sale of these monstrosities did give Watson a window to see how many lobsters Deep Deep was catching.

By August 1969, Bob, Watson and Steve were ready to leave the next day with their first load of four-foot wooden Anderson traps. The *Sea Fever* was moored in Little Harbor that evening with everything loaded and ready to go. For some reason, I rowed out to the *Mistress* to get something. As I passed by her stern, I remember saying to myself, "Bob Brown, love him or hate him; you can't say he doesn't have guts!"

By late summer, the three men, by trial and error, had perfected their methods and found a tremendous cache of lobsters near Oceanographer Canyon. They quickly found Cape Cod much more advantageous for a port of operation because of its proximity to the Continental Shelf waters. They tied up in Harwichport and started to cause quite a stir.

By Thanksgiving 1969, Bob and his crew had learned enough to have statistical results that looked much more than promising. It was a good bet that Watson and Bob, with their known personalities, would not stay compatible forever. Soon after Thanksgiving, they parted ways business-wise.

Shortly after January 1, 1970, Watson called me and asked for a meeting. He showed me the results of their previous efforts. I was flabbergasted! They had been going out for either one or two days of hauling, depending on the weather. Oceanographer Canyon was about twelve hours each way from Harwichport. On some trips, they had averaged twenty-seven pounds of lobster per trap hauled! A good ratio inshore was, and still is, one to one and a half pounds per trap.

I was now an investment broker with four years' experience. While still a neophyte, I did have one unique advantage: I knew the lobster and fishing businesses. Watson had visions of grandeur. He wanted the firm I worked for to underwrite a stock offering to raise money to build a large, offshore lobster boat. He was going to be the new corporation's president and become "Mr. Big" of the rapidly expanding offshore lobster industry. I thought the idea seemed possible and a good risk.

I approached the partners of my firm about the idea. They also thought it was sound. A limited offering was made to so-called sophisticated investors. I was the salesman. Initially, we raised enough money to build a new, seventy-foot shrimp-style boat rigged for hauling lobster traps. This was constructed by DESCO in St. Augustine, Florida. Named the *Sea Dog II*, this boat was followed in the next four years by three steel vessels between seventy-five and eighty-five feet named *Western Ocean*, *Western Wave* and *Western Sea*. The *Western Wave* is still fishing out of Gloucester rigged as a purse seiner.

I thought the whole idea was so great that I invested some of my own money and was made a director of the company called Western Ocean Resources. Business lurched forward and backward until the late 1970s. I resigned as a director about 1974. Watson had left before that. The only money I ever made from the whole deal was the commission I got from the initial offering. It was a viable deal that never got to the finish line.

As for Bob Brown, he made out just fine in those same years. After installing a brand-new Caterpillar engine in the *Sea Fever* in the winter of 1970, Bob started setting his traps near Oceanographer Canyon. His two-man crew of Perry Asher of Marblehead and Jerry Houghton of Swampscott were experienced inshore fishermen who were drawn to offshore lobstering by the rumors of its potential that were filtering through the North Shore fishing community. Two-day trips of several thousand pounds of lobster became the norm for the *Sea Fever*. Harwichport would be Bob's home port for several years to come.

It wasn't a totally smooth ride. Heavy trap losses resulted from large Russian fishing vessels dragging their nets where his traps were set, but by the end of 1970, Bob had an annual gross many times more than any inshore lobsterman had ever dreamed of. The risks of fishing 125 and more miles from shore in such a small boat were there, but a "gold rush" mentality took hold. This was to remain all during the '70s until the loss of lives and declining catches gradually resulted in a more sober assessment of the situation.

An extremely successful offshore lobster season for the *Sea Fever* in 1970 was followed by a profitable line-trawling winter fishery out of Gloucester. The year 1971 was another financial success for offshore lobstering. Bob now had money to buy personal extras for his growing family, as well as for reinvestment in the business. That meant a larger and safer boat. During the winter of 1972, Bob had East Boothbay, Maine boat builder Sonny Hodgdon build him a fifty-foot offshore lobster boat. This vessel was designed by Bob's father-in-law, Aage Nielsen. When I first saw it, I considered it the best-looking lobster vessel I had ever seen. Bob had grabbed for the brass ring and caught it. His newest acquisition was, again, named *Sea Fever*.

Starting in 1972, Bob's catches continued to increase. The boat proved to be a great success. I was reminded of the days almost twenty years before when he and I had talked about going out over the horizon from Marblehead and wondering what we would find out there. Bob was realizing those dreams and pragmatically increasing his checkbook balance.

I watched all this from the vantage point behind my stockbroker's desk. I was doing perfectly all right financially. My winter weekend line-trawling efforts and some late summer and fall fishing were paying for my boat upkeep, plus some left over. However, I could feel a restlessness taking hold, which built to a crescendo by 1973.

# Chapter 25

# The Red and Green Lights Were Just Right

**U**nless a person fishes alone, a big problem for any skipper is his crew. It takes a certain type of individual to be a commercial fishing crewman. It has elements of danger and risk, making it one of the most perilous occupations in the world. It can be very unpleasant in rough weather. However, it has its rewards. One of these is the satisfaction and enjoyment from a beautiful day with a good catch. Another one is the relationship between individuals that, from my experience, is different on a vessel out of sight of land compared to people working onshore. When fish or lobsters are coming over the rail, it is always a happy time on any boat I've been on. The main reason for this is most fishermen are paid on a percentage of the catch, or share. The more that comes aboard, the bigger the check at the end of the trip.

A few words are in order about the share system. There are many variations, but my method was similar to most. From the gross proceeds of a fishing trip, I would take what was spent during the time at sea. That would include bait, fuel, ice, food, gloves, etc. I would divide what was left in half, and half would go to what I called "boat and gear." From this, insurance, boat maintenance, new electronics or fishing gear would be paid. The other half would be "crew shares," counting myself as one of the crew. If there were three of us on the trip, the crew share would be divided by three. It was very basic and gave everyone aboard the chance to make an unknown amount. There was more work and longer hours with a bigger catch, but that was never a problem because we knew our share was growing in the process. It made for great teamwork.

Arthur "Sookie" Sawyer of Gloucester and John Zdanowicz, 1972. Two oddities of the trip: lobster and halibut.

During the years I was a salesman, I usually had a two-man crew, even though I was fishing only on weekends. I fell into the habit of having a full-time lobsterman looking for work in the offseason and a young boy, age thirteen to sixteen, for the other. The boys only worked for me until two things happened. The first was when my young crew discovered they really enjoyed the company of girls. The second was their acquisition of a driver's license. They lost interest when I told them I'd pick them up at 3:00 a.m. on a Saturday morning. I remembered my own feelings at that age with a touch of jealousy. From 1971 to 1974, my full-time crew for winter line trawling was a man named Ed Harbick. He was older than I and lived in Beverly but lobstered out of Little Harbor for many years. Ed was perfect for me. He enjoyed line trawling and was a very reliable and meticulous man. He had no interest in hauling trawls but didn't mind the monotonous job of coiling the gear back as it came off the hydraulic hauler. Powered haulers were now standard gear for any hook boat. Ed's coiling was always perfect and very easy to bait.

One Friday in February 1973, the boy who was to be my other crew called and told me he couldn't make it the next day. Typically, I left my Salem office early on Friday afternoons and, if the weather forecast was good for the next day, drove to Gloucester, where the *Mistress* had a winter tie-up at Beacon Marine. Ed met me, and we baited five or six tubs of trawl. That day, Ed suggested John Hawkes as a possible crew. John had crewed in Ed's place as my part-time crew not too many years before. Ed and John were good friends. John was now fifty years old and had "swallowed the anchor" and was a custodian at Marblehead High School, with an afternoon and evening shift. John wasn't a full-time fisherman anymore, but he was still a

John Hawkes "ready to go."

fisherman in his head and heart. He spent much of his spare time hanging around Fisherman's Beach and his old shanty. He had sold his powerboat, the *Lizzie H*, and had a small outboard skiff that he named *Rag Picker*. He also had a handful of lobster traps that he fished during summers. He seemed a happy man, but a trained eye could see that his fishing passion had never left him. On arriving back in Marblehead that evening, I found my way into the unlocked high school and located John. It was an easy sale, but when he called his wife, she seemed less than pleased.

I picked John up at his home at 3:00 a.m. the next morning and then Ed in Beverly. By 3:45 a.m., we were casting off from Beacon Marine, and by 6:45, we were setting trawls on the Peak of Jeffreys, about twenty-seven miles east-northeast of Eastern Point, Gloucester. It was a nice winter day, and we went farther up on Jeffreys and made a couple more sets. The three of us spent the day there, and it was a successful one. We lay to, baited and set a couple of extra tubs. It was after dark by the time we started heading back to Gloucester. By now, the wind was coming on a little from the southwest. The fifteen- to eighteen-mile-an-hour head wind made for a chop, but the *Mistress* was at her best going to windward. John, especially, had been rejuvenated by the day. We had a catch of 2,500 or more pounds of fish, common for the time. After we had the boat cleaned up, we sat around the pilothouse and talked. Everyone was tired but happy and pleased with the day we had spent together. The autopilot in the *Mistress* had the controls mounted on the right-hand side of the companionway into the forecastle. Every time an adjustment was made, a red or green light flashed to show which way the boat rudder was being changed. There was something special about the scene as the time passed. I thought how, as a young boy, I had gone out with these older men and now here they were with me telling them what to do. There was no resentment, just a nice day with everyone doing his job for a successful conclusion. It was an experience that could not be improved upon. I had a strict rule—no alcohol drinking while the boat was moving. By this time, we were almost abeam of Thatchers Island and three-quarters of an hour from Gloucester Harbor. I kept a quart of Seagram's Seven whiskey under the galley sink. There is an exception to every rule, and this was the time for it. I got out the jug of whiskey. We all took a healthy shot. Soon

Ed Harbick preparing to unload at Sonny Deltorchio's, early 1970s.

we were tying up at Beacon Marine, where we enjoyed some more and the remaining food we had. Then all settled in for a good night's sleep.

We arose early the next morning and went over to the fort section of Gloucester, tied up at Sonny's wharf and unloaded our fish. John drew me aside and talked about how nice the previous evening had been, with a shot of booze, the red and green lights flashing, the boat cutting through the chop and the three of us talking. He concluded by saying, "It was just perfect."

That was the last time I was ever in a boat with John Hawkes. He was shot accidentally by his wife eight months later. The whole thing was a tragic mistake. Sylvia was the one who pulled the trigger of a loaded gun John's cousin Link had foolishly kept in a desk drawer. Not knowing it was loaded with the safety off, she jokingly pointed it at John and inadvertently pulled the trigger. Sylvia and Link saw him slump over and die, a bullet through his forehead.

*Chapter 26*

# Hood Enterprises

**H**e learned to sew on his grandmother's Singer. International yachtsman, boat designer, sail maker and inventor, he landed at Little Harbor in 1954. Frederick E. "Ted" Hood, born in 1927, started his sailing career at the age of one month in a basket aboard his father's Friendship sloop. While other young boys were at the playground, Ted was working on model boats. With his father, he started racing at age seven. By age twelve, Ted was able to convert his original rowboat into a sailboat. Working in the cellar of the family's house in Danvers, he added a forward deck to house the mast, a centerboard trunk, rudder and floorboards. He obtained most of the hardware from the five-and-dime. Self-taught in sail making, he used a book called *Gray's Sailmaking*, which he got at the library, as his guide.

The family moved to Marblehead Neck during World War II. After a stint in the navy, Ted continued his education, paid for by the GI Bill. Summers were spent replenishing his finances by repairing and recutting sails. He obtained the referrals from the launch men at the yacht clubs. His bedroom on the Neck was his workshop.

By 1950, after a few years of using his parents' living room for the larger sails, he moved into a run-down boatyard next to the Boston Yacht Club on Front Street. Much of his early work involved making sails for International 110s and 210s, designed by C. Raymond Hunt. As Hood, Hunt was both a yachtsman and a designer, especially known for his deep V hull, an innovation in powerboats. He was best known for drawing the plans for the

Ted Hood, an innovator. *Hood Collection.*

Boston Whaler, a popular small boat. Billed as "unsinkable," it was based on Hickman's idea of the reverse-V bottom. Most boys in Marblehead viewed it as their idea of the perfect starter boat, and their parents tended to agree because of its safety and maneuverability.

The collaboration of the two men was further solidified after they raced together in Bermuda, winning the Amorita Cup, using Ted's IOD (International One Design), now fitted with Hood Sails. Soon after their return, Ray put a sign in his design office, a short distance from Hood's, saying, "C. Raymond Hunt and Fred E. Hood Associates."

Cotton, which had been used for sails since 1820, was being phased out by Orlon, an acrylic fiber made by DuPont. Its resistance to sunlight and moisture and its great strength made it a superior material. With pillowcase looms obtained from the old Pequot Mills in Salem (four looms bought for fifty dollars apiece), Ted began weaving his own fabric. Both Orlon and, later, Dacron, woven by Hood and used solely by his company, were a more tightly woven material, superior because of their higher stretch resistance.

His father, known as the Professor or "Prof," had a background in textile and chemical industries and was extremely helpful to Ted. Retiring after World War II, Prof was heavily involved in the production of all of Hood's fabrics, including the new polyester and nylon and his Duroseam chafe-resistant treatment. The father-and-son team had a close relationship, working together on innovation and boat repair.

During the early '50s, Ted Hood's sails started blowing the competition away. The Bermuda races of 1956, '58 and '60 were all won with Hood Sails.

In 1954, he purchased the remains of the Burgess-Curtiss Aircraft Company for $25,000. Using two sides of the original foundation, he frugally erected a new sail loft for $3 per square foot. However, whatever cost cuts he made in the actual building, he made up for in size. His new loft at Little Harbor would accommodate an eighty-foot sail for a 12-meter yacht.

I approached him in 1961 when I was looking for a riding sail for my newly constructed fishing boat. He quoted me sixty dollars—a price I found a bit too steep. Losing my order failed to hold him back, however. At his peak, he owned nineteen sail lofts in Canada, Argentina, England, France, Australia, New Zealand, Japan and the United States. He was a prolific innovator. Some of his most well-known inventions are the Stoway Mast and the Stoboom Sea Stay. To complete sail self-furling, he used the Sea Furl for jibs and headsails. The merchandising plan established by Hood was that by racing his yachts both nationally and internationally, he would attain "victories at sea."

People did notice. His sails were on every America's Cup defender from 1962 to 1977. The America's Cup is the most prestigious event in the sport of sailing. In 1974, he skippered the *Courageous* to a win, beating Australia. Since 1956, 12-meter yachts had been allowed to compete for the cup. The reduction of the waterline measurement of sixty-five feet, that of the old J-boats, to the forty-four-foot waterline of the 12-meters, was approved by the New York Supreme Court. Hood had been a part of the America's Cup scene since 1958, when he designed sail and ballast for the *Vim* and sailed with her. In 1962, he skippered the brand-new *Nefertiti*, built at Graves Boatyard, where Ted had worked during World War II building wooden landing craft. Hood Sails supplied the aluminum mast for $7,500.

When Hood bought the land in Little Harbor, his purchase included, along with the Burgess property, the remains of former boatyards. He kept the yard crew working, mostly doing repair work. During his competition in the U.S. Olympic trials in 1956, Hood's curiosity was aroused by the fact that of the thirteen 5.5-meters participating, the hull

Ted Hood at the helm, a great skipper. *Hood Collection.*

designs were extremely varied. With his idea of "design, build, sail and sell," he started his new venture. His first boat, *Robin* (aptly painted robin's egg gray-blue), turned out to be a winner. The next *Robin*, built in Osaka, Japan, started Ted's worldwide yacht building. The cost was half what it would have been if built in Marblehead. He was still experimenting with sails. Using a smaller mainsail with big overlapping jibs and, once again, his combination of himself as skipper, Hood Sails and improved yacht design, he proved victorious.

In 1961, he produced *Robin Too II*, with a new beamier hull, known as the "delta" or "whale bottom." His designs were now being referred to as "Hood style." In all, there were thirty-nine *Robin*s, different rigs, centerboard or keel, from forty to seventy-five feet, all tested by Hood. His production boat designs were used by such well-known names as Bristol, Tartan, Hinckley and Hatteras. They had been tested by Hood for racing capability and subsequently sold as he moved on to his next project. Eleven hundred of these Hood-designed production yachts were built.

Future boat building took place in Holland, Taiwan, China, Portsmouth, Rhode Island and, most recently, Poland and Turkey. More than 250 of these boats were built, ranging in size from thirty-five to seventy-five feet. Proving "It's not the arrow; it's the Indian," Hood won the Marblehead to Halifax Race in 1961 in a thirty-six-foot keelboat built in Japan and again, ten years later, in a fifty-foot sloop built in Holland.

His Little Harbor Custom Yachts, many built in Taiwan, included the *Palamar*, a seventy-five-footer for Tom Watson, the CEO of IBM. Another custom-built in Marblehead was the *American Promise*, which was used by Dodge Morgan to circumnavigate the world solo and break the previous record set by Knox-Johnston in 1969 (313 days). With two generators and two mainsails and jibs, he managed to shave 142 days off the Knox-Johnston time. The Stoway system and two of the Sea Furls, which he could operate from the cockpit, allowed one man to handle this sixty-foot yacht.

In 1986, with Ted's frustration over the shallow approach to his now-cramped Little Harbor headquarters and his inability to receive a go-ahead on any plans for expanding, he moved to a large tract of land previously owned by the navy in Portsmouth, Rhode Island. Marblehead suffered a loss in sailing preeminence with the departure of this quiet, talented yachtsman. He was a large part of what had made Marblehead successful as a major port in the second half of the twentieth century.

# Chapter 27

# First Trip to the Continental Shelf

he path to offshore lobstering on the Continental Shelf for me had a long incubation period.

My first job away from fishing was with the Westclox Division of General Time Corporation, visiting retail stores and promoting the Westclox line, which was a complete assortment of windup, electric and the new battery clocks. Their best-known products were Big and Baby Ben windups. My area was eastern Massachusetts, Rhode Island and southern New Hampshire. The clocks were in most retail outlets, including drug, hardware, jewelry, tobacco and the then increasing number of discount stores. Most manufacturing was done at a large plant in La Salle, Illinois. No products were produced outside the United States.

Within a couple of months, it became apparent that the New England district manager had a severe drinking problem. He was let go, and with no one else around, I fell into the job. A district manager had much more responsibility and money potential. I primarily called on the wholesale distributors who serviced our various retail stores. Four times a year, we had a new promotion of products or sales incentives. Westclox was a well-managed company, and I observed and learned a great deal about large corporate life in America.

By the fall of 1965, I had built a history of good sales figures but could feel a degree of boredom with the job. There were six regions of sales in the country, with ten to twelve district managers in each. I had started to receive overtures about becoming a regional manager. While the increased pay and responsibility would have been welcome, I did not relish leaving Marblehead, a necessity for a promotion. I began to think of another occupation. In addition, I had kept the thirty-three-foot wooden boat I had built in 1961 and continued with my part-time fishing.

By January 1966, I had interviewed and been accepted to be an investment broker with a Boston firm called H.C. Wainwright and Company. It was a member of the New York and American Stock Exchanges, which meant its brokers could receive commissions for purchases and sales of securities on the exchange. In this capacity, I could deal with listed stocks and all other securities, including mutual funds. Compensation was all commission based. Each broker was expected to build his own clientele. After a six-month required training period, that was what I did.

I started out walking up and down retail areas on the North Shore and going in and out of shops, businesses and gas stations. It was slow and sometimes discouraging work. Very slowly, I started to build a list of customers. My first order was from a man in Peabody at a waste paper business. He bought two shares of American Telephone—a gross commission of $6. My share was $2. Funny and interesting what something like that does to you. That was well over forty years ago but is as vivid a memory now as then. Four months later, I got my first sizable order from an owner of an automobile repair business in Ipswich. This was a $10,000 purchase of a mutual fund. My share was about $350. My enthusiasm was rising with my commissions.

The years went by, and in 1970, H.C. Wainwright closed its Salem office during a severe market downturn. I had become a member of the Salem Rotary Club and was starting to develop a presence on the North Shore. Not wanting to leave Salem, I moved to the only other firm in the city, a branch of the E.F. Hutton Company, a much larger and more impersonal firm based in New York City. You may remember their ads, "When E.F. Hutton talks, people listen!" At that point, several people would be shown with cocked ears, trying to catch a piece of invaluable investment advice.

During the early 1970s, influences in my life started to direct me to what had seemed impossible a few years before    returning to commercial fishing and lobstering full time. With the perspective of time, I realized there were three principal factors that were going to rule my decision.

The first was the words of my now-deceased father who, at various times in the past, had made the point that the time will come when you are going to reflect on your life. "When that time comes, you will want to have the satisfaction that you did the very best you could and made the most of your opportunities."

The second factor came from one of my closest friends, Bill Ardiff, whom I met in college during the 1950s. Bill was from Danvers and went to Dartmouth College and Cornell Law School. By 1970, he had become the prominent head of his own large law firm in Danvers. Bill referred many investment clients to me, and I reciprocated by sending people with legal needs to him. Bill would later have setbacks, sadness and an untimely death, but in those times, there seemed nowhere for either of us to go but up. Bill's office was in a lovely old building in the heart of Danvers Square, one of many pieces of property he owned in that town. In the early 1970s, a man named "Rocco" bought the property next door with the intention of putting in a pizza parlor. Bill fought this but was unsuccessful in stopping it. I believe he was mainly against the location of the exhaust fan, which was aimed at his second-story office. A resolution was achieved, and Bill and Rocco later became friends and Rocco a client. However, during the period of dispute, I couldn't resist a joking reference to how his law offices were going to smell once Rocco got in full production. We both enjoyed kidding each other, but one day Bill wasn't in the mood for it. He said something that sunk in more and more as time went by. His comment that day was, "Bishop [he always called me Bishop or Big Hugh], the people we are friendly with are bankers, accountants, lawyers or stockbrokers. It's people like Rocco who go out and invest in and start businesses. I have a lot of respect for people like him."

As the months went by, I began to say to myself, "In the brokerage and investment businesses, I am dealing with companies that other people are running. Maybe I should be thinking about investing in myself like Rocco did and seeing if I can produce something with my own mind and body."

At about the same time, the third factor came into play. Bob Brown stopped by my desk in the E.F. Hutton Salem office. Bob and I had our ups and downs, but we always had a unique friendship and would confide in each other in a certain special way. What Bob said to me that morning didn't have an immediate impact, but as time passed, it loomed larger and more frequently in my head. He talked about how well he was doing in the offshore lobster business. He went on to talk about what we called the old-timers at Little Harbor and other places, men generally in retirement or close thereto. He said many of the people talk about how they had a chance to do something in earlier years of their lives but never took it. Bob said, "This is my chance, and I know it."

That statement stuck in my mind and kept playing over and over. These three factors made me, over the next year or so, come to one unavoidable decision: I was leaving a successful business situation to strike out on my own. I was going to the Continental Shelf.

The first Monday in April 1974, after arriving at my office, I immediately went in and told the office manager I was leaving on Friday. After explaining what I was going to do, he looked at me in silence for a few seconds. Then he said, "I wish I had the courage to do what you are. Good luck."

I left the office early that Friday because I wanted to bait up my line trawls for the trip to Middle Bank the next day. I was high on life and didn't need or want the little going-away party the manager had planned for me.

The next morning at 3:00 a.m., the *Mistress* was steaming past Cat Island Bell. I had arranged for Frank Sholds, one of Dave Hildreth's crew, to go trawling with me for three weeks while I lined up all the necessary gear for offshore lobstering. I needed to order traps, line and buoys, besides hiring a two-man crew. It would be three weeks before I could get hauled out at Graves Boatyard to have a new engine installed. One-day line-trawling trips to Middle Bank would help provide some revenue in the meantime. That morning, there was a moderate southwest wind, and as was the custom, I took the first hour watch of the two-hour run and Frank and my other young crew, Dan Roads, took the second hour. They immediately sought a bunk and sleep.

As the *Mistress* passed Half Way Rock, about two miles out from Cat Island Bell, I put the boat on automatic pilot. I walked out to the back cockpit and looked across toward the lights of Boston and the choppy whitecaps in the foreground. I had, as it turned out, my only second thought. I remember saying to myself, "What did you just do? You threw away an excellent living. You had a great future in the investment business." The combination of the darkness and emptiness of the ocean before me caused doubts to rise. But there was no turning back.

As the day wore on, the wind died down. We caught over one thousand pounds of haddock and got a good price. The first small step had been taken on what was to be the defining decision of my life. I never looked back after that with anything but a smile and satisfaction.

The first three weeks in April 1974, Frank and I made three or four line-trawling day trips a week to Tillies Bank and Middle Bank. We enjoyed good spring weather and equally nice fishing for haddock and cod. A typical day's catch would be between 1,200 and 2,500 pounds of fish. We would leave Little Harbor about 2:30 or 3:00 a.m. If we didn't have all of the two thousand hooks baited previously, we finished baiting the gear on the way out. With the boat on autopilot and the pilothouse lights on, it was easy enough if it was calm, but with a sloppy chop, it became rather laborious. We hung on with one hand and baited up with the other—no fun! Frank referred to it as "Being back in heaven again" or "The romance of the sea."

When we arrived, about first light, where I thought and/or hoped fish would be available, we set the gear. People who have never fished for a living have no concept of how critical it is to set in the right place. The proper kind of bottom and depth make a huge difference. In those days, we didn't have the technology available today. Fishing electronics had advanced to the point where I had a fish finder that showed fish markings, water depth and the consistency of the bottom, to some degree. Where you set your gear was crucial and, over a period of time, determined whether a fisherman would be known as a high liner.

There was not a more enjoyable thing to do or place to be than on Middle Bank in April about midday. There would be a light sea breeze starting to set in. It was warm and sunny, enabling us to remove our oilskin jackets and roll up our shirtsleeves. By now, we had enough fish on board to know we would have a decent payday. It was line trawling at its best, a wonderful memory for me and I hope for all the good men I had with me over the years.

By midafternoon, we were on our way for the two-hour run to Gloucester. I sold my fish to Cape Ann Seafoods on the fort section. Cape Ann was owned by a Gloucester native named Sonny Deltorchio. Sonny was always a pleasure to deal with. He retired in 1989, but I still drop by his house to see my old friend.

After selling our fish, we made the one-hour run past Magnolia, Manchester and Bakers Island back to Marblehead and the comfort of Little Harbor. The boat was moored. Frank drove to Beverly, and I walked home to my wife and two children. The boat was comfortable but didn't include a shower and a beer. It was a great way to spend a day.

When I was not line trawling, I had plenty to do. Rope and buoys were purchased, along with 350 four-foot offshore lobster traps. A brand-new Detroit Diesel engine was ordered from Johnson and Towers Company, a marine engine distributor just outside of Philadelphia, Pennsylvania. Most importantly, I had to hire a top-notch crew of two. They were Steve Smith, a neighborhood boy whom I had known since he was born, and Rich Nielsen (no relation to Bob Brown's wife, Linda Nielsen), the son of a prominent inshore lobsterman from Beverly. Both men were in their early twenties, rugged and excellent workers. They had gone out with me on fishing trips as young boys at various times since they were twelve years old.

The author and Anderson traps.

By the end of April, Graves Boatyard was ready to haul out the *Mistress* for the preparation needed to handle lobster traps 190 miles from Marblehead. Steve and Rich worked with me on the boat and also in preparing rope and buoys as May progressed.

Graves Boatyard still had some very talented boatwrights who had spent all their working lives building and repairing wooden vessels. The dean of these men was a gentleman named Lester "Bucket" Barclay. Bucket was a very strong-minded, opinionated man who had a reputation for being hard to get along with. However, he and I got along fine, and I made sure he was assigned to work on my boat. Whatever his suggestions and ideas were to "strengthen this" or "change that," I took and never regretted them. The foreman of Graves was Milton Osgood. He was the opposite of Bucket in temperament, equally competent in knowing wooden boats, with a quiet way of seeing the bigger picture, a perfect fit for his job. He really ran the Yard, and I know any of the Graves men still living would sing his praises.

Milt oversaw what my crew and I were doing, as well as Bucket's work. One day, he made a very firm suggestion, which I had the good fortune to take. Milt said the pilothouse windows were unusually large for a forty-plus-foot boat and we should have some way to cover them with boards if the need arose. He didn't have to say it twice.

I made up two pieces of half-inch plywood that could be bolted over the pilothouse windows in an emergency. The bolts were put through the frame of the pilothouse windows, threaded ends out, and left permanently in place. The plywood had been pre-drilled with corresponding holes. Butterfly nuts, screwed on the ends of the bolts, would secure the window protectors. All fittings were bronze. I reamed out the drilled holes a little to make them fit easily, painted the boards and stowed them up under the pilothouse roof. I remember thinking as I finished the project, "That takes care of that; I don't ever expect to do anything with them again." Little did I know then that Milt's advice and my action would prevent my crew and me from having greatly shortened lives.

May seemed to fly by, and work progressed. Unanticipated problems were turned into opportunities, and early in June, the renovated *Mistress* was launched. By the middle of the month, all was in readiness for our maiden voyage. Another man from Marblehead, Manford Porter, had followed Bob Brown's lead and was also offshore lobstering in 1973. Manny was an old friend from fishing, as well as a high school football teammate from the 1950s. He attended Northeastern University, where he was an outstanding lineman, receiving many all–New England honors for his play. After a short stint at teaching, he had returned to lobstering and line trawling full time. Bob's, Manny's and my paths crossed many times in the years prior to 1974. There was a certain code, unwritten but very strong, that you had to stand on your own two feet as far as fishing accomplishments were concerned. Despite the fact that we were friendly and enjoyed a beer together, we had all been taught, since childhood, to keep our ears open and mouths shut when it came to fishing competition. Information would be shared only if you were sure it couldn't come back to haunt you in the future. Nothing was ever revealed about where you thought fish or lobsters were or little tricks about special types of gear. General information and friendly conversation always ensued, but nothing of any fishing value was ever offered. Particularly absent was any suggestion of a location for fishing. They considered me to be a new competitor who would be cutting into their own staked-out territory and possibly their income. I respected their attitudes and knew if the situation were reversed, I wouldn't volunteer either. More importantly to me, I was damned if I would lower myself to ask them for information, even if I needed it.

When it came time to set my first pots, I was clueless. I bought an offshore chart that showed the Continental Shelf from New Jersey to eastern Canada. I knew Bob and Manny were fishing somewhere near Oceanographer Canyon, so I ruled out any proximity to that area. I looked at Veatch Canyon, about fifty miles west of there, and saw that the contour lines were close together. This showed rapidly changing depth in a short distance, allowing me to set my traps for prospecting purposes. I made that my destination.

By the middle of June, it was time to start fishing. On the afternoon of Friday, June 21, we loaded seventy-two traps on the *Mistress*, along with needed rope, buoys and bait at State Street Wharf. By suppertime, we were finished and took the boat back to its mooring at Little Harbor.

At noon on Saturday, June 22, Steve, Rich and I rode out to the *Mistress*. We started the engine, cast off the mooring and idled out of Little Harbor to start the eighteen-hour run to Veatch Canyon. It was a beautiful early

Loading the *Mistress*.

summer day, and the afternoon sea breeze was just starting to ripple the water. As we jogged out through the One Design sailboats tacking out to their racing start line, I heard a few "good lucks" and "best wishes" from people I knew. Other people gave us a warm wave or salute. Just past Cat Island Bell, I put the engine in cruising rpm, and we were off. I remember feeling some trepidation, but overall I was eager and ready for what lay ahead. By early evening, we were abeam of Highland Light, Cape Cod, and altered our course somewhat more southerly for the run down the Great South Channel and on out to Veatch. The night was pleasant, with a light south wind and calm sea. The three of us took one-hour watches each. I was hyped up and barely slept. A gray dawn found us about ten miles from our destination. Steve was on watch at the time and in about twenty more minutes announced that there were six fishing boats ahead of us. I jumped out of my bunk. After ten seconds of peering through the pilothouse windows, my heart sank. They were fishing boats, all right—Russian ones. All were about three hundred feet long, a little over five miles directly ahead of us, which was almost exactly where I had planned to make our first set.

It was time for Plan B, which did not yet exist. The boat was stopped and the offshore chart perused. In desperation, I turned east to Hydrographer Canyon, about fifteen miles away. After running over an hour, we saw a tiny speck on the horizon ahead of us. When we got close enough for identification, I said to myself, "I recognize that boat." Lo and behold, it turned out to be the *Horizon*, formerly named the *Sea Dog*, built in 1952 for Watson Curtis, the same vessel Bob Brown and I had gill netted on in April 1962. By 1974, this vessel was owned by the father-son lobstering team of Fred and Tom Bartlett of Beverly. While they conducted their inshore lobstering, they had hired Jim LeBoeuf of Marblehead to skipper the *Horizon* in the offshore lobster business. Jim and a few of his friends were a few years younger than Bob Brown and I. Like us, they had grown up around Little Harbor, and Jim, at various times, had gone out lobstering and line trawling with both of us—a small world indeed! Jim was very helpful that day. He told me where his gear was set in Hydrographer so I could avoid it and wished us well.

Without further delay, we set out four strings of eighteen traps each. Before noon, we were on our way back to Marblehead, arriving and tying up at State Street Wharf shortly before daylight the next morning. After a short sleep, we hitched a ride to Brown's Restaurant on Atlantic Avenue for breakfast. I was on my way to what was to be an exciting and adventurous future.

*Chapter 28*

# A Day of Reckoning

**A**fter our first journey in June to Hydrographer Canyon, my crew and I made repeated trips from Marblehead and, later on, Newport, Rhode Island, with additional loads of traps. The run each way was about eighteen hours from Marblehead and twelve from Newport. By mid-July, we had our whole string of 360 traps in the vicinity of Hydrographer Canyon, where I started figuring the best way to increase our catch.

My old friends Bob Brown and Manny Porter remained in their roles as competitive rivals. They were tying up in Harwichport (on the Cape), and they knew I was just as determined as they to do well. However, they had a few years' head start. Manny sometimes offered a helpful hint, but Bob's lips were sealed when it came to fishing information. Bob had a way throughout his life of making you feel he was somewhat heartless and then, out of the blue, reversing his direction and giving a helping hand when most needed.

That summer, Manny, Bob and I ran into one another in Marblehead between trips once in a while. The two of them had traps set in Oceanographer Canyon. Bob also had some in Lydonia Canyon. This was many miles from my traps in Hydrographer, so I never saw them when out there. One day, Bob and I crossed paths in Marblehead, and he asked me how offshore lobstering was going. He had a particular knack of asking an innocent question when he was looking for information, so my guard immediately went up. My warning signals in this case were not needed. Bob genuinely wanted to know if I enjoyed fishing out of Newport and said he sensed I didn't. He was right, and I told him so. He said he thought I would be much better off in Harwichport, and with his help, I moved the *Mistress* there by August 1, 1974. Harwichport was a great location for me, partially because of its complete protection from bad weather but mostly because of the people we encountered. The harbormaster, Tom Leach, set me up with my own private docking slip and a fuel supplier. The other dozen or so fishermen were friendly, and the nearby Cape Fishermen's Supply in Chatham was an excellent place to buy gear. Last, but not least, the 400 Club was a friendly watering hole and restaurant with beautiful-looking female bartenders and waitresses. For the next six years, I felt I had found the ideal place from which to fish, because I had, and Bob was the one who got me there.

As I got my feet under me in Harwichport, Steve, Rich and I settled into a routine for each trip. It took about twelve hours steaming from Harwichport to reach our traps in Hydrographer Canyon. We normally left port between 4:00 and 6:00 p.m. to arrive at or before daylight the next morning. It took two hours to drive from Marblehead to Harwichport. I had Steve and Rich meet me at my house at 11:00 a.m. on a Monday. That summer, I bought all my bait, frozen redfish racks, in fifty-pound boxes in Gloucester from GMF Seafood, a frozen bait supplier. I went to Gloucester, put two thousand pounds of bait in my pickup and was back in Marblehead before 11:00 a.m. Steve and Rich would arrive, and we'd leave Marblehead shortly in separate vehicles. They generally went together and, I'm sure, discussed the skipper's plusses and minuses, among other things.

As soon as they arrived in Harwichport, they went to Stop & Shop and bought provisions for the upcoming trip. The menu was theirs to choose, and each took turns cooking. I went directly to the boat and started checking everything to make sure all was in good working order for an offshore run. By the time I moved the boat to the nearby fuel dock, they were there with the supplies. Fuel was topped off and bait loaded. It was then time to leave. If it was a hot day, we stopped the *Mistress* at the mouth of Saquatucket Harbor and took a quick, refreshing swim.

The southern tip of Monomoy Island was a seven-mile run. We then struck out across Pollock Rip Shoals and always made Great Round Shoal Buoy, fourteen miles to the southeast. Here, there were frequently draggers heading toward or out of New Bedford. Often this part of the ocean was foggy, and at night, extra care had to be taken for the vessel traffic near the buoy. Once this area was passed, we proceeded south-southeast across Nantucket Shoals and on down the Great South Channel toward Hydrographer. We each took one-hour watches. The night seemed to pass rapidly. When we were about five miles from the first trawl, we all got up, had coffee and generally cold cereal and got into our fishing gear. In the fall, that was oilskins, but in the summer it was light, waterproof aprons, shorts and no shirts. Some summer days were flat calm and cloudless. Fog, however, was frequent, and many times we saw nothing, except on radar, beyond our own high fliers and lobster buoys from the time we left Harwichport until our return. If the weather report was favorable, we would have left Harwichport to arrive one or two hours before daylight. Radar reflectors on our buoys enabled us to easily find our gear in good weather. We started hauling immediately. If the wind was twenty to twenty-five knots, we either arrived later or waited for daylight.

It was a full day's work hauling twenty strings of eighteen traps each. There was an eight-foot by four-foot-wide by four-foot-high tank in the middle of the cockpit floor that we had built out of plywood the previous spring. This had reinforcing steel rods for strength. The whole tank was secured with bolts through the cockpit beams.

Water was constantly supplied to the tank by means of a three-inch-diameter pump driven by a small diesel engine separate from the main General Motors engine. The tank could hold a maximum of five thousand pounds of lobsters

Traps were hauled, lobsters removed and traps baited and subsequently reset or moved to a new location. It was a big version of the inshore lobstering with which I grew up. The big difference was the size of the lobsters. A measuring gauge was almost never used. I remember coming in with five thousand pounds and having one, yes only one, chicken (one-pound) lobster. Seven-, ten- and twelve-pound lobsters were common. We were paid two separate prices. One price was for one- to three-pounders. This was generally $1.60 to $2.20 per pound, depending on market conditions. Three-pounders and up were the second category. They commanded less money, generally $1.00 to $1.40.

In the near future, trips would be three nights and two days. However, in 1974, with a few exceptions, trips were twelve hours out, twelve to fifteen hours of hauling and twelve hours steaming back to Harwichport. No two trips were exactly the same in terms of weather, total catch or other factors. Commercial fishermen live on hope and anticipation. When things are good, they are going to get better, and when things are doing poorly, they are also eventually going to get better. Once you get used to wondering what's in the next trap or coming up in the next net, it tends to take over your life, and you continually live for that moment. In the industry, it is what is known as the "fisherman's gamble."

# The Rich History of a Small Fishing Port

I have thought about it often, and when I define what's driven me for fifty years of lobstering and fishing, it always comes back to one word: anticipation. The anticipation of what will be caught next as a result of one's planning and effort. If I had known what I was going to catch before I went out, even if it was going to be a record, I would not have been motivated. It's the uncertainty and anticipation that is the driving factor.

As the summer of 1974 turned into fall, the planning and efforts were working. Our catch, while not up to the level of Bob's and Manny's, was decent, and we were making excellent money. There was enough that I wished more than once I had left the investment business behind sooner. As has always been the custom in fishing, we all were compensated by a share of the catch. The disbursement method was the same I had always used. A check was written to each crew member for the amount earned as soon as the results were known, along with the sheet showing the results of the trip. It's very simple and especially enjoyable when everything goes right. In the case of offshore lobstering, I did learn to keep a small portion of the crew's share until the end of the season, as insurance that they would complete the term.

As fall progressed, the wind became more prevalent, but the lobstering, which averaged eight to ten pounds per trap in the spring and summer, increased to where fifteen pounds per trap was not uncommon. Our gross catch of two to three thousand now often reached four thousand pounds or more for one day.

The forty-four-foot *Mistress*, while small even by the standards of the day, had taken us through all kinds of weather with runs at times in thirty-five knots of wind or more from different directions and many varying sea conditions. When I look back now, I see we were playing Russian roulette by fishing 120 miles from shore in an open-cockpit boat of that size. At the time, however, I won't say I was cocky, but I was confident we could handle anything that came our way.

I was about to experience a day of reckoning. This lesson took place over the first weekend of November 1974.

The weather report when venturing offshore is always a primary concern for any mariner. TV weathermen and offshore marine weather were constantly monitored when I was at home between trips. Information was exchanged between other skippers and myself about a possible upcoming "weather window."

During the summer, offshore lobstering could be conducted almost on a regular schedule. If we left Harwichport on a Monday, I would be back home in Marblehead by Wednesday noon. Thursday we had a day to ourselves. This four-day sequence was then repeated. It was a grinding schedule, but I loved it.

As storms with northwest gales behind them became more prevalent in October and November, the schedule became completely weather dependent. We knew we didn't have the appropriate boat for high winds, so we watched for the lull and placid conditions and tried to time our actions accordingly. It was, I have to say, a gold rush mentality. We were making great money and, in our minds, minimizing the risks.

A recent comment from a man named Bruce Deltorchio was certainly poignant. Bruce was the youngest son of Sonny, the Gloucester fish dealer I used for many years. I first remember him as an eight- to ten-year-old boy helping his father forty years ago. Now he is a hardworking lobsterman out of Gloucester. I ran into him recently, and we exchanged a few friendly words. He mentioned the irony of the *Mistress* and the *Sea Fever* both being built at the same location and now moored next to each other at a Gloucester dock. His quote was just about perfect. He said, "They were both top-of-the-line offshore lobster boats in the '70s, and now they seem so small. You guys must have been crazy!" He was right. The *Mistress* to which he was referring was fifty feet. The one that Steve, Rich and I used in 1974 was even smaller, at only forty-four feet!

We were well into the fishing "weather window" phase by the early afternoon of Thursday, October 31, 1974, when my crew and I arrived at Harwichport. As I recall, it was a gray afternoon, typical late fall Cape Cod weather. We all did our familiar assigned tasks. I remember going up to the Mobil gas station on Route 28 a short distance away from the parking lot and docks at Saquatucket Harbor. There, I blew up five or six balloons or buoys to replace any that were partially deflated. We used these to keep the high fliers from being dragged under by the tide. Like the previous people mentioned in the area, the owner was a friendly, nice guy who always greeted us with a smile. We tried to reciprocate by buying gas for our vehicles from him.

There were ten small lobster boats that fished offshore from two anchorages in Harwichport. None of us were locals, but we all coexisted well. Seven of us were in the area called Saquatucket. The other three, including Bob Brown, fished from nearby Wynchmere, separated by a quarter of a mile from the rest of us. Both harbors shared a common entrance over a sandbar. Manny Porter fished from Saquatucket and tied up next to me. Bob and his crew were preparing for departure, as well as Manny and his outfit. The only other fisherman present was a man named Ray Altivilla. Ray had one failing—his boat maintenance.

# The Rich History of a Small Fishing Port

At that time of year, warm summer nights are long past. The marina, which had a vast majority of pleasure boats, was now empty except for the seven offshore lobster boats. The whole scene, in fading light, was sullen and desolate. I am sure Bob Brown had already left. Shortly after dark, Manny and his forty-five-foot Beals' Island boat, *Donna Marie*, departed. During our last-minute preparation, I could hear a definite skip in the exhaust of Ray's boat, *Pegarina*, the sign of an engine not running properly. Shortly after that, we cast off.

The weather report that afternoon for offshore waters was "weak low pressure moving up the East Coast, northeast winds ten to fiteen knots tonight, increasing to fifteen to twenty knots Friday." This was long before the days of satellite observations.

As we passed over the bar at the entrance to the harbor, I could see only one light, which I knew to be Manny's. We proceeded on our usual path down the bay to the south end of Monomoy Island and then out to Great Round Shoal Buoy and on over Nantucket Shoals at a slightly reduced speed because the sea conditions were sloppy. This made it easier for those of us not on watch to stay in our bunks and get some sleep. The course and sea conditions made for a less than comfortable ride, but nothing unusual. The waves and swell were on the port side. We were not in much of a hurry because of the iffy forecast. We wouldn't want to start hauling until daylight, around 6:00 a.m. It wasn't going to be what we called a "bluebird day."

Initially, I had set my traps near the edge of Hydrographer Canyon. Fishermen always talk in fathoms, not feet, and 90 (540 feet) to 120 (720 feet) fathoms was a common depth to set traps in the spring. This bottom was only available on the edge of the drop-off of the Continental Shelf. The edge of the Continental Shelf itself runs for a very long distance from the southeast coast of the United States to off the east coast of Canada and periodically is marked by canyons that have even steeper drop-offs than the rest of the edge. When going from shoal water to deeper water, the area of bottom between 90 and 120 fathoms is very narrow, particularly in the canyons themselves. Commonly, the distance between these depths requires only a traveling distance of about 100 to 300 yards. Another distance of that size once again puts one in depths of 400 fathoms or more. Lobster traps set over 130 to 140 fathoms normally caught nothing but a species of red crabs.

The lobstering in 90 to 120 fathoms was best in the canyons themselves, especially on the west side. This quickly became common knowledge among lobstermen. It was fine in 1974, when there were still so few boats fishing these waters. However, as time went by, gentlemen's agreements to give each other space became nonexistent, and the lobstering developed into a cat and dog fight for the most desirable bottom.

Lobsters were caught in 60-, 70- and 80-fathom depths, but the "big" trips were between 90 and 120 fathoms, a limited area indeed as years went on. Jim LeBoeuf and the *Horizon* had moved elsewhere during the summer, but we kept some of our traps in these depths for the whole 1974 season. Throughout the fall, we had seen only one other boat, the *Fairwind*. She had a home port of Beverly, Massachusetts, and a fishing port of Newport, Rhode Island. The *Fairwind* was owned and skippered by a man about my age from Salem named Charlie Raymond. Charlie was a class act. I had first met him many years prior around Cat Island off Marblehead. I had traps there in the 1950s and rowed out in my dory when I was thirteen to fifteen years old. About the same time, Charlie came out from Salem in a lapstrake Amesbury wooden skiff with a small outboard engine. He lived at the corner of Herbert and Derby Streets in Salem in the family homestead. He often had his father with him, Sheriff Raymond, the head of the Salem jail.

I couldn't help but like Charlie, even if he was the competition. We developed a mutual respect for each other over the years, and in 1974, he also had traps in Hydrographer Canyon in the depths mentioned. Now, I was the new boy on the block since he, like Bob Brown, had been offshore lobstering for a few years and was very successful. In those days, there was room for both of us without stepping on each other's toes.

Moreover, in a conversation earlier that season, Charlie had tipped me off about shoal water. He said, "Hugh, it's hard to believe but the lobstering is often good about twenty miles inside the shelf's edge in thirty-eight to forty-two fathoms of water." I took his advice and moved six trawls about twenty miles nearer shore during August. I suspected that depth was where the *Horizon* had fished.

These were the traps we were approaching before daylight on Friday, November 1. We picked up our first high flier that morning at half light. By this time, there was a fifteen- to twenty-knot northeast wind with whitecaps and three- to five-foot seas, conditions we were used to. It took two men to boat a four-foot wooden Anderson trap comfortably. Steve and Rich alternated with me boating the traps and cleaning out one end. Lobsters were what we wanted, but crabs, fish and menacing-looking eels, about three to four feet long, were normal also. The third man slid the eighteen traps successively around the rail to the desired location for each one to be set back out.

Rich was first at the rail with me that morning. After hauling the first few traps, he looked at the gray clouds scudding across the sky in the increasing light of the dawn and said, "Those clouds don't look good." I said something like, "They are only forecasting fifteen to twenty," but Rich was a prophet.

By 9:00 a.m., we had hauled and reset our six trawls, 108 traps, in the shoal water and had about six to seven hundred pounds of lobster aboard. The northeast wind had increased slightly, now a steady twenty knots. What to do? A common question for fishermen offshore in small boats. Should we continue? It was two hours farther away from shore, now about one hundred miles away, to the rest of our traps. If we said, "The heck with it," our common expression, we would go back with a small paycheck for all.

Greed prevailed. I made the decision to head on out to the rest of our gear in Hydrographer Canyon.

Regular cruising speed of ten to eleven knots was possible as the northeast wind was exactly abeam or hitting us on the port side, so off we went to the southeast. As we steamed along, Steve noted that he could look to the southwest and now see the tops of the waves breaking, a sign the wind was increasing.

We reached our gear on the west side of Hydrographer at 11:00 a.m. and started hauling. The lobstering was excellent. The seas always seem to subside as product comes over the rail. The wind stayed steady at twenty-five to thirty knots for a couple of hours, and we had nine hundred more pounds aboard. We had the feeling, "This really isn't that bad." You get into a mode I experienced time and again. Even though you are 120 miles from shore and safety, your world is your little boat. You feel secure in your surroundings and enjoy where you are, especially when you are doing well, shutting out the reality of the situation. When I read or see stories about people climbing Mount Everest, I think that's how they must feel.

By about 2:00 p.m., it had started to rain, the wind increased to over thirty knots and I said, "The heck with this; let's go home." We started to the north-northeast. Rich and Steve were cleaning up, and we were going about regular speed when, suddenly, a switch was thrown. The wind went from thirty to fifty-plus knots in a matter of minutes, and the waves became bigger and steeper than anything I had ever experienced. We were in the heart of Hydrographer Canyon in an unforecasted, developing ferocious northeast gale.

We were on the edge of the Gulf Stream, which was flowing north; I'm sure the tidal flow was combining with it, and the water movement seven hundred feet below was going over the west edge of the canyon like a huge waterfall. To make matters worse, the sudden increase in wind was pushing against all this. We were the *Maid of the Mist* without a spectator platform. If there was one place you didn't want to be, this was it! The *Mistress* had to be slowed down to a creep. I looked back at Steve and Rich. Their faces, to say the least, showed concern. On any boat, the skipper's word is law, and I knew they were looking to me for leadership. As for me, I could feel fear coming up in my throat like I had never experienced. I knew myself well enough and had read enough about people in difficult situations to know that panic is a killer. I got myself settled down and thought, "You idiot; you got everyone here into this mess. Now you're the one that's responsible for getting them out." I felt much better!

The first thing we had to do was get out of Hydrographer Canyon. I've never seen waves like that before or since. They seemed to go straight up, like walls higher than the boat was long. Every once in a while, one would break. I felt like we were in a canoe. Fortunately, it was still daylight, and I could look to windward and see the future potential for a wave breaking over us and filling the cockpit. I maneuvered as best I could to avoid these killers. We drained the lobster tank to give us more buoyancy. By dark, we had gained five miles to the north, enough to get out of Hydrographer. Now the seas were huge but no longer a deadly "this is it" situation.

We were making some headway, about two knots, as evening descended and I debated my options. The course to Harwichport was north-northeast and more or less right into or just off the wave direction. I decided to try for Newport but gave that up after about ten minutes and two separate breaking seas almost swamped us.

Remember Ray and *Pegarina*? He had left Harwichport the previous evening sometime after us. His traps were set significantly nearer shore than ours. As we had, he started hauling shortly after dawn when his skipping engine quit. He called the local coast guard, who reached him by early afternoon while we were still hauling in Hydrographer Canyon. They took him under tow for Newport, which they figured would be their best chance for safety. The coast guard boat was an eighty-five-foot vessel designed to take heavy weather. The skipper later told Ray, after they reached Newport the next morning, that he had thought his vessel was going to roll over.

Bob Brown and Manny Porter were hauling traps in Oceanographer Canyon several miles north of our position. Both left for home about when we did. They got the increasing wind and seas sometime after us and, being farther north, had a somewhat more favorable heading for the conditions. They made Harwichport about daylight the next day after a very rough ride.

That leaves us.

After giving up on Newport, my world started to shrink right down to our little boat and the next wave. I gave up ideas about reaching port anytime soon. I remember thinking things like, "You're going to be a lucky man to see your front door again; you are way underboated. You are a fool!" We were out of Hydrographer but not out of danger by any means. By this time we were going, at the most, about one knot ahead, almost nowhere, and the wind was screaming—I'm guessing fifty to sixty knots.

After a while, I stopped feeling sorry for myself and developed a positive attitude and sort of said, "This isn't that bad. Use your head." In the meantime, the seas continued to build so that in the darkness the reflection of the running lights showed huge breaking waves going down each side of the boat. The three of us took turns at the wheel keeping the boat into the waves. The other two in their bunks held on with both hands to keep from being thrown onto the floor as the *Mistress* took on each wave.

About 10:00 p.m., I told Steve and Rich we had to get the boards on the cockpit windows to give ourselves a better chance. These were stored where I had put them back in May, under the pilothouse roof. Mounting them in a boatyard shed is one thing, but out there in the dark in a gale is quite another.

The *Mistress* had a flush (or flat) deck forward with an escape hatch in the middle of it. With his upper body half out of the hatch, a man could reach and mount the two separate boards in place on the bronze bolts. Each of the two boards covered half of the windshield. There were two bolts for each board with butterfly wing nuts on them. These had to be taken off the bolts. Each five-foot-long board had to be put over the bolts through previously drilled holes and then the wing nuts put back on the bolts and tightened. Steve volunteered for duty. I tied a rope around his waist and tied the other end to a post in the cabin in case a wave tried to wash him overboard. I had the boards ready to pass up to him from the cabin through the escape hatch.

It was impossible to do this with the *Mistress* heading into the wind. Our only chance was to head or jog downwind slowly and hope the wrong wave didn't catch us. I decided it was risky but worth it. Rich ran the boat on the required heading, and I passed the boards up to Steve, who did his job perfectly. During this very dangerous maneuver, I held onto his ankles with a vicelike grip. The whole procedure took about two to three minutes. We immediately turned back into the waves. The psychological effect was immediate. We couldn't see out the windows, but we didn't need to. The covered front windows gave us the feeling that we had a much better fighting chance. We continued easing into and up over the waves.

I was lying on my bunk about 1:00 a.m. Steve was at the helm. Suddenly, it sounded like someone had backed a five-ton truck full of huge boulders up next to the boat and dumped it on us. There was a huge bang and cracking sound. After it stopped, Steve leaned down into the cabin from the wheel and said with a laugh, "It's all right; we are still in one piece." A huge wave had broken over the *Mistress*. This was before the days of unbreakable lexan. The windows were shatterproof glass. Two of the four windows behind the boards were still in one piece but cracked in many places. The recently strengthened pilothouse was undamaged. God, in the persons of Milton Osgood and Lester "Bucket" Barclay, had prevented us from being at the mercy of the weather and an almost certain end.

The night wore on. That wave was the worst of it. The wind continued to scream and the waves were huge, but they started to get more distance between them, and conditions inside the boat actually became slightly more bearable.

When daylight came, the ferocity of the sea was awesome. I looked around at our little boat and my stellar crew. Gallows humor had helped sustain us all through that night. I remember noticing that everything that could move had found a new home. In my mind I spoke to my boat: "You got us through the night. Now, girl, take us home!"

With the sea lengthening between each wave, we could actually make some headway, and I started to figure out how far it was to the south side of Nantucket Island. By 11:30 a.m., we were twenty-five miles from there. Then, for the first time, I felt the wave heights were actually slightly less. I knew we would make it.

We got to the lee on the south side of Nantucket about 3:00 p.m. I went up as close to the beach as I dared. We dropped anchor about a quarter mile from shore. There was no sea here, but the wind was coming off the beach and blowing the little wavelets into a solid sheet of white spray. As soon as the anchor fetched up, I knew we were safe. We all fell into a deep sleep.

Just at dark, I got up to look around and saw blinking lights on shore. Neither of our radios would work because of blown antennas. The blinking lights were from a coast guard Duck, still in use in those days. They came out around us and, after seeing the name on the bow and transom, told us we had been reported lost. They went back to Nantucket and called my wife at home. Shortly thereafter, the death watch at the Gerry Veterans' Firemen's bar on Beacon Street in Marblehead was called off.

The next morning, the three of us woke up. It had cleared, and the wind had dropped to about forty knots, still from the northeast. We pulled up anchor and went up the channel between Nantucket and Martha's Vineyard Island and made our way slowly but steadily across Nantucket

Sound to the vicinity of Falmouth, where we were afforded a lee and ran southeast to Harwichport.

Steve and Rich straightened up the boat, we gave the 1,500 pounds of lobsters a drink with our pump and, by the time we reached our home port, except for the broken windows and still mounted boards and other minor damage, no one could tell what we had experienced.

The word had gotten out that we were coming along the shore, and as we idled into Saquatucket Harbor, we could see quite a little crowd on the docks. We backed into the unloading position and shut the engine off. Shortly, a man stepped forward and said, "I'm so and so, chairman of the board of selectmen, and I want to welcome you back to Harwichport." Then he said, "We didn't think you were going to make it!" After a brief moment of thought I said, "Neither did I!"

*Chapter 29*

# I'd Sure Hate to Be Paying for It

After our harrowing trip home from Hydrographer Canyon and the resulting damage to the boat, my crew and I immediately replaced the two windows with new safety glass. If there was emotional damage to any of us, we didn't talk about it but, rather, put our heads down and plowed ahead. We made our next trip as soon as repairs were completed and weather permitted. I don't recall any hesitation in going right back out.

As the fall wore on, the aggressive woodworms took their toll on untreated wooden traps. The fierce appetite of these parasites compromised the traps' strength. Every trip in November saw more and more traps fall apart as they were hoisted over the rail. It became almost normal by Thanksgiving for lobsters to spill overboard as the decaying trap was being boated. The first two years we fished offshore, we simply cut away what traps we had left by mid-December and brought the rope and buoys home. The next spring, we started with all new gear.

The four-foot-long wooden traps we used had what was known as a double parlor, with the kitchen in the middle. These oak traps were built by Anderson Trap Company in Yarmouth, Maine, costing $18.50 each. They were delivered to southern New England offshore lobstermen on a large flatbed truck driven by a jovial man named Charlie. Most days would see their truck, always with Charlie at the wheel, going south on the Maine Turnpike in the early morning and north after lunch. The company, now long gone, was a pleasure with which to do business. It was the main supplier from Rhode Island to Maine. Wire traps were used to some small degree, but

Charlie and Anderson truck, delivering traps in my driveway.

Rich Nielsen with halibut from winter trawling, 1975.

their catch ratio did not compare to Anderson's. By Christmas 1974, we had made our last lobstering trip.

The *Mistress* was quickly and easily converted for winter ground fishing. Steve, Rich and I started making one- to one-and-a-half-day trips out of Gloucester. We tied up at Beacon Marine Basin and sold our fish to my friend Sonny at Cape Ann Seafoods.

At first that winter, we set our gear within three hours or less steaming time from Gloucester, on Stellwagen (Middle Bank), Tillies and Jeffreys Ledge, my traditional area. As the winter wore on, we started venturing well into the Gulf of Maine, fishing around Fipponies, Sharer Ridge, Parker Ridge and Cashes. Here, if we found hard bottom in ninety-fathom depths or more, we just about always had excellent fishing. Four to six thousand pounds a day was normal for our eight tub trawls. Cusk was our mainstay, but cod, haddock and hake were also common. Draggers often fished nearby but usually didn't drag over the hard bottom, which was a necessity for our gear.

Dragging is conducted by towing a net connected to the vessel by wire cables. Heavy pieces of equipment, called doors, are connected to the cables. These are set up so that the strain on the cables from the towing vessel keeps the mouth of the net open to catch swimming ground fish. The bottom of the net scrapes along the ocean floor, and the top has a series of hollow metal balls on it to keep the top edge of the net floating. The work is dangerous, and the wear and tear on a dragging vessel is considerable. Ships used in this manner have to be ruggedly constructed.

By the 1970s, all serious fishermen had recorders and fish finders that gave an excellent indication of texture of the ocean floor. The hard bottom pieces we fished gave fish a sanctuary where they could breed and live. This was to change in the not-too-distant future.

One trip stands out in my mind. Rich lived in Gloucester in an apartment over the Blackburn Building on Main Street. This was the building used by the legendary Howard Blackburn as his tavern. Steve and I lived in Marblehead. We were to meet at Beacon Marine at 9:00 p.m. It was early April 1975. We brought along Gerald Smith. I considered him a real old-timer. Gerald was a Marbleheader who had grown up at the corner of Front and Union Streets. His father, a well-known boat builder, crafted Brutal Beasts in the 1920s and '30s. A favored craft of recreational sailors at the time, they were designed by W. Starling Burgess. The shop, behind his house, is still there on the left, going down the hill on Union Street to the Boston Yacht Club.

Gerald had the fishing addiction and worked out of the wharf near his parents' home as a young man. He talked often about the old days, and I enjoyed listening. When he was a bit older, he migrated to Little Harbor and fished for lobsters and dragged for fish. Along the way, he was a professional yacht captain, especially in the 1950s and '60s, when his bad back made commercial fishing impossible.

Gerald was almost a professional storyteller. Of his many tales, he told one about watching the launch of the ill-fated schooner *Columbia* in Essex, Massachusetts, in 1923. There is a much-publicized photo of this event. Gerald described to me where he and his father stood, saying that he was visible in the photograph. Lo and behold, the next time I looked at this picture, I could plainly make him out.

Slightly after 9:00 p.m., Steve, Gerald and I were on the boat at Beacon Marine waiting for Rich to join us. I knew from his storytelling that Gerald had never been farther than twenty-five miles from shore during his maritime career. This was a first. I assigned him as our cook. I could tell he was looking forward to the experience. Rich turned out to be a no-show, the first and last time in his career with me. We cast off the lines, and the three of us finally left Gloucester, striking out for Cashes Ledge eighty miles to the east. This was an eight-hour run.

Cashes Ledge buoy.

Getting ready to set trawl at sunrise.

It was a clear, calm, pleasant early spring night. We all, including Gerald, took one-hour watches. Daylight found us just inside Cashes. Steve and I set out our pre-baited tubs on a picture-perfect morning. We made three separate sets on the edge of Cashes and Parker Ridge. There were no other boats in sight. We hauled the gear back later that day, enjoying a fish chowder Gerald had made from a freshly caught pollock. We dressed and iced our fish. The weather report for the night and next day was favorable, so Steve and I baited four tubs with the extra bait we had on board. It was well after dark by the time we finished. At daylight the next morning, we set this gear on another "bluebird" morning, while Gerald cooked breakfast. We hauled the gear back and, by early afternoon, were on the way to Gloucester.

I remember well the results of that trip—six thousand pounds was our total catch. This consisted of five hundred pounds of halibut and the rest a mixture of cod, haddock, hake and cusk. We reached Gloucester that evening and all turned in. While we were selling our fish the next morning at Sonny's, Rich appeared rather sheepishly. He said he had run into "quite a woman" the night we went out. It turned out to be his future wife. When I first saw her a little later, I could see why he didn't show.

This trip was our last of the winter. It was time to get ready for the offshore lobster season of 1975. In April, we hauled the *Mistress* at Graves Boatyard. Everything was checked for readiness, and the boat was given a complete paint job. By late May, we once again started the setting process from Harwichport.

We fished Welker Canyon and the edge of the Shelf to the west. We set 360 traps, as we had in 1974. Since it took us about a month to get our entire string on the chosen grounds, it was quite a while before we started to turn a profit. We still made one-day trips. The season became a very lucrative one. We rarely saw another lobster vessel that year, and the only other gear we came across occasionally was that of Western Ocean Resources, a company with which I was very familiar. We never had traps any nearer to theirs than at least a half mile.

During one day in October, we had hauled eleven trawls (198 traps) by early afternoon. We had changed the lobster holding area to saddle tanks, built along the two sides of the cockpit. These tanks held 3,500 pounds. By 1:30 p.m., they had reached their maximum. We hauled one more trawl, filling four wooden boxes with an additional 320 pounds.

The weather was quite warm, and we had to start for home port because we had no way to keep any more lobsters alive for the twelve-hour steam to Harwichport. We put the fish boxes of lobsters next to the tanks on the cockpit floor, allowing the water to slosh from the full tanks, keeping our catch moist for the trip home. Lobsters will live up to three to five days if refrigerated but expire in a shorter and shorter time as the temperature gets warmer. The only way to keep them alive is to provide circulating sea water. The catch ratio for this trip was eighteen-plus pounds per trap—excellent and profitable.

By early fall of 1975, I could see I needed a larger boat for safety and increased productivity. Lobstering had been good to my crew and me. Enough money had been saved for a more than substantial down payment on a new vessel. First, I looked at a couple of secondhand possibilities, but nothing appealed.

Giffy Full was the foremost marine surveyor on the East Coast of the United States at this time. He was somewhat older than I, a good friend and had grown up in my neighborhood. He still lived in Marblehead, and I sought him out for advice. He said in that special, high-pitched voice of his, "Go see Walter McInnes; he's the best powerboat designer on the coast."

I did that. At that time, Walter was eighty-three years old and a living legend. He had designed all types of boats in his lifetime, included fishing draggers and all manner of yachts, both sail and power, up to and over one hundred feet. His designs always had a pleasing look to the eye. Walter is long since gone, but his accomplishments live on. He developed a type of hull that had a hard chine aft. This feature resulted in much less rolling. Forward, it had an entrance that prevented the boat from pounding when it came down off a head-on sea. He further honed this design so that when running before following waves, the boat handled safely and did not veer or "run off." This can be very disturbing and life threatening in bad conditions. Control of the vessel is lost, and in a worst-case scenario, rolling over can result.

After talking to Walter in September 1975, he convinced me this design would serve me well for a fifty-foot offshore lobster boat. His office was in downtown Hingham, Massachusetts. He shared the space with his son, who was his assistant but primarily a yacht broker.

I loved to visit Walter and discuss my new vessel. A definite dividend was listening to his many stories. Among my favorites was his description of designing fast vessels for the rumrunners during Prohibition. The coast guard, because of his outstanding reputation, also used him for designs to get boats that could catch the culprits. Sometimes the two factions would even rub shoulders passing in and out of his office!

With the design well underway, we discussed potential builders. The vessel was to be constructed of wood, and while wooden boat builders in the 1970s were on the way out, there were still several candidates. I visited a few of them between lobster trips. One of the possibilities was George "Sonny" Hodgdon. I knew Bob was pleased with the work Sonny had done for him on the *Sea Fever* in 1972.

Walter spoke highly of Sonny, exclaiming, "Sonny Hodgdon can build anything." After visiting his one-boat-at-a-time shop on the property of his home in East Boothbay, I settled on him as the builder. I met Sonny the day I visited his shop, never had any contact with his workers and did all the rest of the negotiations for the contract by phone and mail. His work crew had no idea who I was.

By October 1975, Sonny and his seven-man crew started construction. The engine was to be a 360-horsepower Caterpillar, which I soon purchased from a Cat dealer in Massachusetts.

I had told Walter I wanted a boat whose strength and construction I didn't have to worry about when it started to blow. Walter more than complied. The vessel was to be double-planked. The construction, when reviewed by any objective qualified party, would pass as exceptionally strong. All the fastenings were to be bronze and all metal parts and fittings stainless steel or aluminum.

One day in the middle of November, between lobster trips, I drove up to East Boothbay to see if there was anything to show for the outsized checks I had been sending that way. Sonny lived on Murray Hill Road in East Boothbay at the very head of Linekin Bay. His home was right on the water with a pier in front. The panoramic views extended down the bay and out to the open ocean beyond. His boat shop was capable of handling the building of a fifty-foot boat if a small, temporary extension was added.

Sonny was the tenth generation of Hogdons to build vessels. In boat building and the compound curves associated with it, Sonny was in a class by himself. He was a master at woodworking, possessing an artistry seldom surpassed. Wooden boat building was a centuries-old tradition in the Boothbay area, and Sonny's crew all had ancestors who had passed on their skills. They had great pride in their capabilities and history.

Neil Jones was Sonny's number-one man. He seemed to me just as skillful as Sonny. The rest of Sonny's crew consisted of his twenty-year-old son, Tim, John Hodgdon (no relation), Ken Rice, Wes Alley, Kenneth Pinkham and another colorful man.

I spent the winter of 1976 working on the new *Mistress*. It was a once-in-a-lifetime experience. Emotionally, at times I wondered if I was going to survive. By the end of the process, I was on life support financially. However, all in all, I look back on it as a great memory. As construction progressed, I went from working on the framing and planking to spending almost all of my time with Wes Alley.

These men were all the same in one respect. They were pleasant but very distant for the first three or four months. Fortunately, I knew enough to keep my mouth shut. Every Monday morning, I left my home in Marblehead at 3:45 a.m. to be there by 7:00 a.m. when the crew assembled. The drive was three hours. This gave me time for breakfast at the Miss Brunswick Diner. Every Friday evening, I returned to Marblehead.

After the first few months, even though I was the owner, I managed to develop a relationship that became more one of friendship. Wes Alley taught me a great deal. His specialty was installing machinery, piping, pumps, fuel lines and brackets. Wes was in his sixties and had worked on boats all his life.

Once the hull was completed, I spent most of my time at Wes's side handing him this or that, helping him and observing his work techniques. He moved at a steady pace, always making sure that what he was about to do would be done correctly. He had one favorite expression. If something went slightly wrong or he was stymied, which never lasted long, he would say, "Now let's not get excited!" I heard that time and time again until it finally made an impression. All I really wanted to do was get the damn boat finished so I could get back to lobstering. I tended to be impatient. With his demeanor, Wes helped me during that trying period more than anyone.

The real testimony to Wes was in his results. After launching and sea trials, we ran the boat to Marblehead and then made three back-to-back trips to the Continental Shelf with loads of 125 traps each time. We were going to fish 850 traps that season and were behind schedule getting started. These trips were about 120 hours of steaming time on a brand-new boat. Not one fitting or anything else Wes installed needed tightening or adjustment. Unheard of!

Construction of a new vessel, especially of wood, was considered quite a happening. During working hours, Sonny's shop was always open to the public. There was a constant stream of visitors. Some came almost daily, others not so frequently. Comments such as, "She's coming along nicely; she looks great," became commonplace. To me, with my dwindling bank account and the approaching 1976 lobster season, the progress sometimes seemed almost glacial. The work crew, while pretending not to notice these daily comments, took enjoyment from others complimenting their work. Often the people who came in the shop as onlookers were not known by anyone.

Early in November 1975, I had made a trip to Sonny's. His crew were still oblivious as to who I was. Someone was up in the mold loft working on patterns. Two men were at one end of the shop working on a large piece of oak that was going to be the stem. In the middle of the floor were two more large pieces being put together to form the keel. Three-quarter-inch holes had previously been drilled in the pieces, and a three-man crew was driving the keel bolts through, tying them together.

Of the three men, one was standing on a platform next to the keel pieces with a maul. A second was inserting each keel bolt in a hole and holding it. The third man had a few of the bronze bolts, which were three-quarters of an inch in diameter and about two and a half feet long, in his hands. I walked up and stood next to them and watched. The man holding the bolts was short, about five feet at most, give or take sixty years old. He wore a little white cap and white workman's overalls. Behind his wire-rimmed glasses, I could see his eyes squinting at me. He was just what one would picture as a seasoned Maine boat builder. The work progressed, and not a word was spoken for several minutes.

Not only did this gentleman look like he was out of a Hollywood studio's central casting, he had a name no one could possibly dream up. I found out later that his name was Rowser Watts! Rowser was eyeballing me, intending to get rid of this unknown person annoying him and the rest of the crew. He finally decided if he said something, I might get the hint and move on.

He looked up at me and then back at the bronze bolts in his hands and said in his thick Maine accent, "My God, that's some metal!" I looked down at him and said, "It sure is!" There was a pause. Then Rowser said, not knowing who the devil I was, "I'd sure hate to be paying for it!"

At that moment it fully dawned on me that this whole operation was on my nickel.

# Building the *Mistress* in East Boothbay, Maine

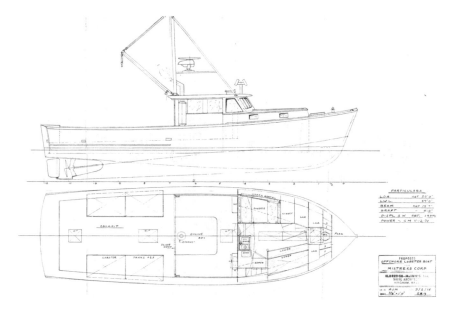

Drawing by Walter McInnis.

Neil Jones completing a wooden pattern prior to the pouring of bronze skeg. The bottom of the rudder shaft will fit in the round part of the left end.

Fitting the stem to the end of the keel.

Rowser Watts cutting keel bolts to length.

Rowser Watts (left), John Hodgdon (right foreground) and Ken Rice (behind) notching out the keel where the end of the frames will fit—a perfect picture of Maine boat builders at their craft.

The boat taking shape, with temporary ribbons in place.

Ken (left) and John cutting out an oak frame.

An oak frame being removed from the steam box after being moistened and heated for installation flexibility.

A frame being installed, with floor timbers visible at bottom right.

The Caterpillar engine being rolled into the shop.

*Above*: Planking starts. Rowser Watts offers sage advice.

*Below*: Helping build my own boat. Double planking took time but would prove very durable.

*Above*: Sonny Hodgdon, master wooden boat builder.

*Below*: My son Hugh, age eleven, spent February vacation 1976 putting bungs over plank
fastening heads.

*Chapter 30*

# Steve Goodwin

On February 2, 1976, a very powerful storm buffeted the East Coast of the United States. In many cases, experienced mariners who went through it in their vessels told of the biggest seas they had ever seen. Winds of one hundred miles an hour were recorded.

Among those in the middle of the maelstrom was a four-month-old sixty-foot steel lobster boat owned and skippered by Marblehead fisherman Steve Goodwin. Although only thirty-one years old at the time, Steve was already very experienced as far as maritime pursuits were concerned. He had started out lobstering with older men like Watson Curtis when he was twelve years old. By 1973, Steve had not only been one of three men who started small-boat offshore lobstering, but he also had run larger craft for absentee owners. In 1974, he acquired ownership of a fifty-foot wooden boat named *Queen*, previously owned by Marbleheaders Giffy and Jimmy Full.

With the desire for a larger, more efficient vessel, he had one built in Snug Harbor, Rhode Island, the following year. This steel ship was designed by Marblehead resident Walter Wales. Upon completion, Steve named her *Zubenelgenubi*, after one of two stars northwest of Scorpius, identified in ancient times as an outstretched claw of the scorpion.

By the time Steve's boat was launched in October, I'm sure he had his hands full with all the extra costs that always come with building. He started making longer trips than normal, often lasting several days, trying to improve his financial situation. He hauled some of his traps more than once and avoided the downtime that came from returning frequently to port.

# The Rich History of a Small Fishing Port

He left Newport, Rhode Island, on January 18, 1976, for one of those extended trips. His wife had not heard from him for several days. After the February 2 storm, she became very concerned and called the coast guard. They immediately commenced a surface and air search. Articles in the February 11, 1976 *Marblehead Messenger* tell the sad story.

> *"If bad weather comes up, I'll be late," Mrs. Jo Anne Goodwin remembers her husband telling her, before he left from Newport on January 18 for a 10 to 12-day lobstering trip, from which he and his three crew members had yet to return.*
>
> *Seemingly calm, Jo Anne said she was sure her 31 year old husband and the three crew members were alive and safe. Sitting in the living room of their Stacey Street home, which had been in the Goodwin family for too many years to count, Jo Anne tells her story with composure, which, one supposes, comes after years of being married to a man who makes his living from the sea.*
>
> *She admits, "This is the longest time he has been overdue, though he has been late before. He usually calls," she says. Sons, three-year-old John and one-year-old Jeremiah, don't really understand, but 13 year old Steven does. He came home from private school to wait with his mother.*

The last confirmed sighting of the *Zubenelgenubi* was on January 29 by a fellow fisherman, and the last known radio contact was by a Texaco tanker on that same day.

After five days and no sign of anything, the coast guard suspended its search. Two of Steve's crew were from the Newport area, and the third, Leroy Hanes, lived at 72 Naugus Avenue in Marblehead with his roommate, Peter Conway. Peter referred to Leroy in the article: "He's much more than a Sunday summer sailor." There was a large effort made to continue the search.

Pressure from many sources resulted in President Gerald Ford ordering the coast guard to resume. The first search resulted in coverage of sixty-six thousand square miles. The second attempt covered an additional twenty-seven thousand, farther away from shore and in the Gulf Stream, the theory being that Steve may have headed there to reach warm water to get rid of built-up ice. Not a single trace of Steve Goodwin, his crew or his vessel was ever found. The business that he helped pioneer had claimed his life.

*Chapter 31*

# Launching

The joys and frustrations of having a new, fifty-foot wooden vessel built are unique. The experience of seeing my boat come together in the winter and spring of 1976 gave me enough ups and downs for a lifetime. I would fluctuate from feeling elated at the way construction progress was advancing to saying to myself that same day, "Why did I ever get involved in this?" or, "I'll never make enough money to ever pay back all I'm borrowing."

I thought I had allowed enough financing to cover monetary contingencies, but some added new expense or problem seemed to continually land out of the blue. The boat was supposed to be completed by mid-May. When that date passed, launching was seemingly in the distant future. The contract was written so that the builder did not get any more money after a certain number of man hours had been billed. Sonny Hodgdon could see that deadline approaching. He supervised his crew very closely in early June. All of a sudden, within two weeks' time, everything seemed to mesh, and June 21 was set as the launching date.

They had moved my boat out of the shed. On Friday, June 20, it sat in the driveway on the Hodgdon property, gleaming in the sun. A man was carefully painting "*Mistress*, Marblehead, Ma" on the transom. My worry and anxiety of the past several months seemed to drop away as I stood and looked at what had been accomplished in nine months.

Early the next morning, a moving crew arrived and jacked up the vessel and its underlying wooden cradle. They placed wheeled dollies under it,

The *Mistress* waiting to float for the first time.

capable of handling its thirty-five tons. The boat had to be moved down the road about a quarter of a mile to a small beach at the very head of Linekin Bay. The moving crew was very capable, and by midmorning, the *Mistress* was sitting just above the low-tide mark. The rising water would float her for the first time. My wife, Annette, was in charge of the launching party, which was set up inside the boat shop. The front yard of Sonny's home overlooked Linekin Bay to the right. On the left sat the *Mistress*, plainly visible on the beach, patiently waiting. She would be towed and tied up for the night at a dock in front of Sonny's.

Annette had been in charge of invitations, and scores of people from Marblehead, the North Shore and other locations arrived for the celebration. I'm prejudiced, but it was the best party I ever attended. I remember well opening the present from Bob and Linda Brown. It was a brass Chelsea Ship's Clock engraved with "*Mistress* June 21, 1976."

By midafternoon, the *Mistress* was floating and towed to the dock, a crowd having gathered on the front lawn. My wife christened the *Mistress* with a bottle of champagne specially wrapped by Sonny's lovely wife, Margaret. The wrapping was a woven cover of red, white and blue satin ribbons. Later,

Celebrating at Sonny's wharf.

Neil Jones made a box with a glass front to store it in. It still sits on display in my home. The party rolled on. It was a marvelous day!

A Caterpillar mechanic came two days later to start the engine for the first time. After a couple of days more for finishing details, it was time to go to Marblehead for our initial load of traps, 850 of which were waiting in my yard. All equipment had been readied a few weeks before by my crew of Rich Nielsen and Peter Hayes. Tim Hodgdon, Sonny's twenty-year-old son, had made overtures of wanting to see some of life away from East Boothbay for some time. This boat needed a crew of three, plus myself. I discussed the situation and offered him the position. He responded enthusiastically.

One of my oldest friends, Charlie Foss, made arrangements to join me for the trip to Marblehead, a distance of one hundred miles. Just before leaving, I called my wife and told her my estimated time of arrival. Then, without my knowledge, she put together the plans for the welcome home party for the *Mistress* and me that I will never forget. With Jim Graves's approval, she brought food and plenty of liquid refreshment to the boatyard. She had quietly asked everyone with a connection to Little

Harbor and friends in Marblehead to come that evening. Somewhere in there, it sort of turned into an open house.

Charlie and I left East Boothbay a little late. Instead of arriving at 7:00 p.m., it was 7:45 when we passed the north end of Cat Island. Charlie was looking at the Cove with binoculars. He exclaimed, "You won't believe the people on the shore!" As we came into Little Harbor that evening, it was a repeat of April 8, 1961, with the first *Mistress*, only greatly multiplied. Bill Hawkes fired off several salutes with his cannon. Free food and drink had helped attract an overflow crowd. The evening was in the best tradition of past Little Harbor launching parties.

*Chapter 32*

# I Guess It Just Wasn't Our Turn

**A**fter our gala welcome home party on June 25, it was time to get to work. On June 27, 1976, we left Marblehead with our first full load of 125 Andersons. Departing at noon, we arrived the next morning just after daylight at Welker Canyon, where we set our first trawls, which took two hours. Immediately, we started the eighteen-hour steam back to Marblehead. In the middle of the night, we reloaded the boat. This took about five hours. Once the fuel truck arrived, we were off again. A third back-to-back trip had us starting toward profitability. After a fourth, smaller load, we returned to Harwichport, where we resumed our normal operations.

With the extra time needed to complete construction of the *Mistress*, we had lost at least a month of nice summer weather and its consequent good lobstering. By the middle of July, we were in full production. Catches were excellent. Trips of three nights and two days produced at least five thousand pounds. My checkbook was starting to go up for a change. We had 450 traps in and near Welker Canyon and 400 in forty fathoms, 20 miles nearer shore, north and northwest of Welker. We would haul "outside" (in the canyon) one day and "inside" (nearer shore) the next. With uneventful weather, our trips were on a regular basis. Overall, I was very happy with the performance of my new vessel. It was still comparatively small for fishing 120 miles offshore. The boat was comfortable and much more able than my previous craft.

One day in late August, we were hauling our inside traps on an absolutely flat calm day. It was so still that motion inside the boat was undetectable.

Loading the *Mistress* for her first trip.

About noon, I experienced the most traumatic event of my life—a story I was unable to talk about for more than fifteen years afterward.

Fog, which we experienced often, was as thick as could be. Even so, the sun was visible overhead. My crew of Rich, Peter, Timmy and I were very compatible. The three men rotated the job of cook for each trip. This was Peter's day. We started hauling our 25-trap trawls at 4:00 a.m. We finished hauling the 400 to 450 traps at about 8:00 p.m. To give ourselves a break, we stopped and sat down at the galley table for lunch, the recess being thirty minutes. Peter had gone below as we hauled the last trawl of the morning to prepare the food. Part of his cook duty was the post-meal cleanup.

Naturally, we had our radar going. It was always on, clear or foggy, from the time we left Harwichport until we returned. The radar screen could be set on different ranges. My radar had a maximum range of twenty-four miles. Our boat's position was shown in the middle of the screen. The following settings were available: one-quarter mile, one mile, two miles, six miles, twelve miles and twenty-four miles. With the twist of a dial, any range could be called up. At three-mile range, for example, with our position at the center, it was three miles to the outside edge of the circular radar screen. The

*Above*: Putting bait aboard in Harwichport.

*Below*: Taking out lobsters.

*Above*: Crew chatting on the stern.

*Below*: Crew having lunch.

Hauling lobster traps.

screen had markings, called rings, at three-quarter-mile intervals. It was easy to tell how far away a target was. We were lobstering in the likely path of large vessels traveling to several locations between Europe and the East Coast of the United States. These were of great concern at night or in the fog. It was possible to tell what direction a ship was traveling after watching the screen a while. If we were busy hauling, I frequently checked the radar. Between maneuvering the boat, boating the upcoming traps and clearing the lobsters, I found hauling in the fog extremely mentally taxing. The task of watching for potential danger was totally my responsibility. Radar was our eyes, be it fog, snow, rain or nighttime operations. I considered it our biggest single piece of safety equipment and had installed two identical ones on the new *Mistress* in case of mechanical failure.

On that particular day, we sat down and ate lunch, which took about fifteen minutes. Equal time was allowed for relaxation. I got up once while eating to look at the radar a few steps away in the pilothouse. I saw no big targets on the screen. Within the three-mile range, only a handful of our own high flier buoys was visible. After lunch, Tim and Rich lay down on the two upper berths for a short nap. They knew I would be cracking the whip soon. Peter started his job of cleanup. I should have taken another look at the radar, but I didn't. Instead, I sat down on a lower bunk. The combination of a full stomach, exertion from the morning trap hauling and the soothing sound of the idling Caterpillar engine made me drowsy. I said to myself, "Don't fall asleep." I looked up at the clock mounted on the front of the trunk cabin—the one Bob Brown had given me at launching—a good luck present. It said 12:46 p.m.

The next thing I remember was looking at that clock. It read 12:54 p.m. I had been asleep for eight minutes! Peter was still in the galley. I thought to myself, "I had better check the radar." Standing up, for some unknown reason, I started walking forward, away from the pilothouse and the radar. Up in the bow, or forecastle, of the *Mistress* was the area set aside for personal hygiene. There was a hanging locker for clothes and a sink. In the middle of the floor, as far forward as possible, was the head (toilet). Above this, there was an escape hatch that we had opened for ventilation since the day was so calm. If a person stood on the lid of the toilet, his torso would be about even with the frame of the open hatch. This offered a great view in all directions to the sides and front of the boat, but today, it was as foggy as it gets. Visibility was, at the most, twenty-five yards.

I thought to myself, "Why are you walking forward? You won't see anything from there today." Something made me keep taking the four or five steps to reach the forecastle. Then I stepped up on the head. As my head popped up above the bow decking, I heard something I'll never forget. Everything in me went on full alert. It was the distinct sound water makes in the form of breaking waves. At that instant, looking toward the sound, I saw the bow of a very large vessel. The waves were breaking off either side of it. Near the waterline I saw rust, but a few feet higher the bow, all black, disappeared up into the fog. It was headed right for us at a good rate of speed and was going to hit us just forward of the windshield.

Instinct took over. Running back through the cabin toward the pilothouse and the engine controls, I said, "Jesus Christ!" as I passed by Peter. I was not taking the Lord's name in vain!

I frantically reached the gear shift lever and threw it into reverse and instantly gave the engine full throttle. A big diesel engine receiving that much fuel takes a few seconds to adjust. I felt the engine start to turn the propeller and the *Mistress* start to move backward, ever so slowly. Looking out the windshield, all I could see was a huge, black mass emerging. I waited for the crash. The *Mistress* gained more speed. The black mass appeared to touch the bow of the boat, but miraculously, it missed. As the beam of the large vessel widened out, we backed out from underneath it. In much less time than it takes to read the last few sentences, we were out of its path.

Once I saw this, I ran out of the pilothouse to the back deck. Peter immediately joined me. We stood slack-jawed as the black side of a nine-hundred-foot container ship slid by us a few feet away.

The pilothouse for this behemoth was aft. As it passed, over two stories up in the fog, we could just barely see a man come to the edge of the bridge. He had on a white officer's uniform with gold braid. While it was not possible to make out his face, I'm sure there was alarm on it.

At the same moment, the ship let out a blast on its horn. We caught a glimpse of its transom as it disappeared into the fog. Part of the name, I think, was *Itel* or *Intel*. Then it was gone.

Peter and I walked back to the stern deck and sat down next to each other. I had not even come close to realizing fully what had just happened. We looked at each other. No words came out of my mouth.

Finally, Peter said one sentence I will never forget: "Well, Hugh, I guess it just wasn't our turn!"

The commotion woke up Tim and Rich from their naps. They came out into the cockpit. Everything was back to its pre-incident stillness. One of them said, "What's going on?" I was still speechless. Peter was, once again, eloquent. "Nothing," he answered.

As soon as I could speak, I altered the truth a little and told Peter the vessel was going to miss us anyway and I just backed up to be safe, but the real story was just as presented.

To this day, I still sometimes get a catch in my throat when I repeat the incident. I've gone over those few minutes in my mind many times. What made me wake up when I did? What made me walk forward when I said to myself, "You won't see anything from there today"? If I had gone up to look at the radar, by the time my eyes had adjusted we would have been run through. Why didn't I slip going up the companionway stairs to the pilothouse? Five seconds lost anywhere and I would not be writing this. I have my answer to these questions. God is a word that is often thrown around quite casually. You can call it whatever you want, but something was with me that day that was awfully powerful.

# Chapter 33

# Fifty Feet Is Not Long Enough

or a while during the late 1970s, it seemed that my fifty-foot boat was an excellent way to show a great investment return. Bob Brown had been very successful in his like-sized fifty-footer, *Sea Fever*. Several others in similar vessels from Cape Cod and Rhode Island ports were not doing badly either.

However, as time wore on, I began to have more and more doubts about what I was doing and the wisdom of continuing. This went beyond the gnawing feeling in my stomach, particularly in the fall when listening to weather reports and wondering whether to "go." One hundred twenty miles from shore makes for a long return. The morning of a potential sailing, four or five of us habitually called one another from our homes to try to build our courage. We didn't want to be foolish and go on borderline weather reports or be chicken-hearted and only go in placid weather. There were a few who waited for perfect conditions, but they never made any money for themselves or their crew. There was a constant concern to make the right decision.

It wasn't spoken of much, but we knew a fifty-footer was not designed or big enough to have a good chance of surviving extreme wind. The distances were too great to run for cover if the weather produced an unpredicted downturn. Over a three- or four-year period, incidences of pilothouse windows being taken out by large waves were not uncommon. In 1977, the sudden sinking of a boat the size of mine from Harwichport resulted in near loss of life. The same year, the *Frank J. Merriwell*, a fifty-five-foot steel vessel based in Newport, Rhode Island, and owned by Marbleheader Perry

Asher and Swampscott fishermen Lucky Williams and Jerry Houghton, had a frightening experience. Perry was at the wheel when a wave crashed through the pilothouse windows and showered him with glass. His face was a bloody mess. The coast guard was called, and a rescue helicopter took him to a Cape Cod hospital. One hundred stitches were taken to put Perry's face back in one piece. Accidents of this nature started giving me ominous thoughts. I still kept up a bravado of "It won't happen to me," but it took increasing effort.

Not only were our boats too small, but we also had a bad habit of severely overloading them at times. I dodged several bullets along the way that added to my uneasiness. The following are two prime examples.

The first came on September 8 and 9, 1978. We had traps set in Gilbert and Welker Canyons. In addition, we had moved eleven trawls (275 traps) thirty miles to the northwest and set them in thirty fathoms of water on the southeast edge of what is called Little Georges. Here, we found unbelievable catches of twenty to twenty-five pounds per trap. None of the lobsters was fewer than three pounds. The traps often came up full with as much as one hundred pounds. Well over half of what we caught were egg-bearing females, required to be released by law.

On September 8, we got to these traps just before daylight after running all night from Harwichport. It was cloudy but just about flat calm. The weather report at 5:20 a.m. was "clearing with northwest winds becoming fifteen to twenty knots." A weak, low pressure was moving out over the Georges Bank area, to be followed by a cold front and building high pressure. This created the potential for intensification, with the northwest wind on the back side of the low increasing dramatically. That's exactly what happened. About midmorning, a line of clouds with blue sky beneath it could be seen approaching rapidly from the northwest. At the same time, an eastern rigged dragger (pilothouse aft) passed a couple of hundred yards to the north of us, heading to the westward. This was an older vessel with traditional schooner-like lines, a green hull, white trim and orange mast, seventy feet long. With the clouds and blue sky forming a background for this handsome vessel, the scene was like a painting. It was one of the beautiful sights I call "a fisherman's special dividend." There was just the first sign of ripples on the glassy sea. I enjoyed the scene to its fullest.

Within thirty minutes, the wind was northwest fifteen knots; within an hour after that, it was twenty-five to thirty knots. By noon, the wind had further increased. We were stacking our twenty-five-trap trawls inside the cockpit prior to setting back out. This was our rough-weather procedure.

Female seeder lobsters must be returned to sea.

By 1:00 p.m., we could only move from trawl to trawl at idle speed. I considered it too rough to haul anymore. We prepared for what we anticipated would be a very uncomfortable night. Everything was lashed down and secured as tightly as possible. I would guess by now it was gusting at least to fifty knots. We could drift comfortably laying broadside, which we did. We then all lay in our bunks, with me getting up periodically to look at the radar.

Another perspective comes from a story entitled "Overdue," written by a man named Greg Cook. Nick Parisi, skipper of the Gloucester dragger *St. Nicholas*, fishing in the Georges Bank area that day, recalls hauling the nets aboard his ship at 9:00 or 9:30 a.m. on that Friday, September 8. When the crew set out the nets again some time before 10:00 a.m., the water was flat as a table, Parisi says, "but half an hour later it was blowing fifty miles per hour. That's how fast it came down. It came down quick."

On the *Mistress*, the afternoon passed without any problem in our drifting state. Just before dark, I heard the loud hissing or sizzling sound of a wave breaking upwind of the boat. From my vantage point on my bunk, I was looking at our diesel-fired stove with the teakettle on its top. There must not have been too much water in the kettle. As the wave broke over the boat with a roar and a loud bang, I watched the teakettle go up in the air, do a 360-degree turn and come back down on the stove. I took that as a signal.

After that, we kept the boat into the wind by letting it fall off thirty degrees to starboard and then putting it in gear until it was almost directly into the waves before letting it fall off again. We did this over and over, for ten hours, until 4:00 a.m. At that time, there was a noticeable lessening of waves and wind. We drifted again broadside. By midmorning, the wind had dropped to light.

It had been a wild night with breaking seas down both sides of the *Mistress*'s pilothouse. A good boat and a few prayers along the way had helped us sustain no damage except our loss of sleep. By this time, we had been pushed twenty-five miles to the southeast. We were near our Gilbert Canyon gear, which we hauled for the rest of the day. By dark, we had finished all our trawls. The conditions had returned to flat calm. The weather forecast never did come close to what we had experienced.

Just as we were setting out our last trawl, I saw a large target on the radar approaching from the east. Moving very rapidly, it was going to pass close to us. After the last trap went off the boat, we stopped to watch this leviathan before we started heading for Harwichport. It was so close, we could hear a band playing. With the glow of the ship's lights, I read the name with my naked eye. It was the *QE 2*. I've told you all this because, after getting home and reading the newspaper the following Tuesday, I learned two things. The first was that an eighty-foot dragger from Gloucester named *Captain Cosmos* was missing, with six men aboard. They had been fishing in the Georges Bank area, not that far from our location. After an exhaustive search for many days, nothing was ever found of them.

In the same paper, there was another reference to the same storm that quoted the longtime captain of the *QE 2*, the ocean liner that had passed by on Saturday night, September 9. She had just arrived in New York. He spoke of a one hundred-foot wave, the biggest he had ever seen, that had dented the bow of his bridge on September 8. The *QE 2* had been well to the east of us when this happened, but it still gave me pause. I reread these stories, looked out the window and thought for quite a while.

The second story was of a different type, two months later. We were working to get our traps back to shore. The plan was to try to have this all completed by early January at the latest. At the season's start, 125 dry traps made a full load. When bringing them home when they were wet and much heavier, 100 traps were as much as we could handle. In addition, the boat had to carry the normal catch of lobsters in the water-filled tanks.

It was the second day of our trip, and since noon, we had been stacking the traps. The weather the day before had been fine, with a moderate northwest breeze and clear. This day, so far, had been flat calm with a gradually increasing cloud cover, a classic weather breeder. By 5:00 p.m., we had our quota of one hundred four-foot wooden Anderson traps aboard. I climbed up on top of the pile to check the lashings. Everything had to be bow-tight to prevent any movement and shifting of weight that could lead to serious trouble. I had a good crew, but I always felt better if I checked everything again myself, especially when sloppy weather was forecast. The previous 11:20 a.m. forecast had been, "Southeast winds increasing to fifteen to twenty-five knots after midnight with rain." This wasn't ideal but was very manageable, even with our overloaded situation. Darkness was descending as I sat on top of the pile for a few minutes, surveying the scene. The *Mistress* was rolling slightly in the gentle groundswell. The smooth idle of the Cat exhaust was a comforting background sound. In our lobster tanks, we had several thousand pounds that were going to give all of us a good-sized

A load similar to that on the *Mistress* leaving Welker Canyon.

paycheck. For a short time, I took that all in and thought of where I was and how satisfying it was to be here. By now, it was 5:20 p.m. From where I was sitting, I could easily hear the report coming from our long-range radio. The update was, "Offshore gale warnings for southeast winds increasing thirty-five to forty-five knots after midnight with rain." My enjoyment of the past few minutes evaporated. I was not counting on this dramatic change. Immediately starting for Cape Cod, I wondered what the night would bring.

By 8:00 p.m., the wind was light southeast. The first six hours were routine. We kept our regular watches as the night wore on. It was a smooth, placid ride. Just after midnight, my watch concluded. I could see the wind freshening and white caps and a chop building, but it was a following sea and still very comfortable. The skipper of any vessel doesn't sleep as soundly as the crew. My apprehension kept me tossing restlessly on my bunk. During the next hour, I could feel the boat's movement gradually increasing. About halfway home and northeast of Asia Rip, we were approaching Nantucket Shoals. I took the watch again. I had to make a decision.

Both departing from Cape Cod and upon return, we always passed close by Great Round Shoal Buoy. This marker had a flashing light. It was fourteen miles southeast of the southern end of Monomoy Island. It marked the entrance of Great Round Shoal Channel, used by vessels passing through the water between Nantucket and Martha's Vineyard Islands and the mainland. The preponderance were fishing vessels going to and from New Bedford, Massachusetts. We often passed close by them near the buoy as our courses intersected. Over the years, I heard us referred to over the radio as "those crazy guys from Marblehead in their little boats." This was a definition not far off the bull's-eye.

From our position at 1:00 a.m. that morning near Asia Rip, I had two choices. I could take a somewhat circular route and a north-northeast course, staying outside Nantucket Shoals in water depths of twenty fathoms. When we were fifteen miles from the buoy, I could then turn to the northwest and cut across a small area of shoal water and pass by the buoy, continuing on to Monomoy.

The other option was to take a course just west of north and head directly for the buoy about forty miles from our present position. This was the normal route in good weather. Care always had to be taken to stay well east of Rose and Crown Shoal, which was close to this route and no place to be—even in good weather. This second option would save up to an hour of steaming time but would have us pass over much shallower water, with some areas being only four fathoms or less. Either option would still have the southeast wind behind our beam and favorable. The surface chop had built, but there was still not much underlying groundswell from the developing storm.

I decided on what proved to be the wrong choice—the second option—and headed west by north. The first hour went fine. By 3:00 a.m., the much stronger wind created greatly increased adverse sea conditions.

I can assure you that Nantucket Shoals is no place to be in a forty- to fifty-knot southeaster in an overloaded fifty-foot lobster boat. The combination of tide against the wind and the periodic shoal water made for confusing seas, which came at us from varied directions, causing complete confusion. As time wore on, the action became more and more violent. It was pitch dark. The approaching sea changes could not be seen. The only thing in our favor was that the wind was blowing from behind us. A few times, it felt like we were white-water rafting through rapids. Often the boat would surge forward and down at the same time. Many times, I reduced the engine speed to gain better control of the boat's erratic movement. I considered cutting away the traps but decided the risk of putting my crew up on the pile for the job was just too great. In my mind, I considered our survival extremely uncertain. I knew the boat better than anyone and had the most experience. With me at the helm, we had the best chance to make it. Finally, about 6:00 a.m., we passed Great Round Shoal and its flashing light. It was the first positive sign in the last few hours. The remaining fourteen miles to Monomoy were rough but not as severe as earlier. After rounding the tip of the island, we were in much smoother water with just a windblown chop. I now considered it safe to turn the boat over to one of my crew.

I woke the men on the seven-mile run up the bay to Harwichport. I practically needed help prying my fingers off the wheel. It had been five and a half grueling hours for me at the helm—a white-knuckle ride!

Chapter 34

# 1979—A Retreat

The offshore lobster season of 1978 came to a conclusion at the end of December. More and more, I wrestled with the reality of how great the risks and chances were with which my crew and I were dealing. The boat I had was very strongly built and well equipped, but the inescapable fact was that fifty feet was too small a vessel to be going where we were fishing. I had accumulated the wherewithal to finance a new, steel seventy-foot boat but knew that this would mean longer trips and more time away from my wife and two children, now thirteen and eleven years old and growing up fast. By spending so much time in my boat, I was missing a great deal. I knew I couldn't go back and revisit it later.

The winter of 1979, I put together a top crew for the line-trawling season. One man was Frank Sholds, who had been my first mate for the 1978 lobster season. He was in his twenties and had grown up in nearby Beverly. Dave Hildreth had his own saga of offshore lobstering and, by 1974, had a boat built that he fished out of Newport, Rhode Island. Frank was Dave's crew for three years, and in the spring of 1978, wanting a change of scene, he asked me for a job. I had just lost my number-one man. Frank was as good as you could get. Beverly born and bred, he was smart and hardworking. He took the initiative and became someone on whom I could count. He replaced Richard Nielsen, who wanted to join his father in Florida. His father had been a successful lobsterman who fished out of Beverly for many years prior to moving south in the early '70s. The spiny lobsters were his initial prey. By 1978, the elder Nielsen had switched from lobsters to catching fish with traps of his own design. In the years to come, Richard and his father became two of the pioneers in the golden crab fishery. With their own hands, they built a new fifty-foot boat suitable for this new endeavor. Based in Port Everglades, Florida, they set strings of traps for these crabs in the deep waters between Florida and Bimini. For his work in development and helping set up rules and restrictions to make this fishery sustainable, young Richard won one of the annual honors given by *National Fisherman*, a prominent industry magazine. This honor was called the High Liner Award.

My relationship with Richard began in 1969, when his father called me from Beverly and asked if I would take his son out on one of my hand-lining fishing trips to Cashes Ledge. Richard was a short, pudgy boy, less than five feet tall and fourteen years old. He grew to be a big man—over six feet tall and three-hundred-plus pounds!

For his first trip with me, I drove to Beverly late one Friday afternoon to pick up Richard. We were going to leave from Marblehead for the nine-hour night boat ride. He was obviously excited, and on the ride back to Marblehead, he said, "I spent all day looking out the school windows watching the trees to see how hard the wind was blowing." This was spoken like the good future fisherman he was to become. I was impressed. In the four years he would lobster offshore with me, we pulled thousands of traps over the rail together. I think of him often.

Richard died in a tragic accident while fishing for golden crabs in the 1990s. His several trawls were composed of fifty crab traps, which were set in deep water about four hours' steaming time from Port Everglades. This was in the middle of the Gulf Stream. They didn't use a floating buoy system because, between the currents caused by the stream and the tidal flow, it was impossible to keep the buoys on the end of the trawls from being pulled under the surface. They used a grapple made of a heavy piece of steel with prongs welded to it to retrieve the trawls. The grapple was dragged across the bottom, where Richard had written down the loran bearings of his set trawls. If all went well, the prongs snatched the ground line between the trawl's first two or three traps. His hauler would bring the traps to the boat, the trawl hauled, cleaned out, baited and reset.

To make this work in the one hundred or more fathoms of water and the swift-moving current, a very heavy grapple of one thousand pounds was used. One day, Richard and his crew threw the grapple overboard. He was standing near the carefully placed coil of heavy line that was flying out as the grapple descended. Unfortunately, he was a little too close. A loop of the line somehow caught around his arm, and in an instant, he was pulled out of the boat and down. The crew managed to get the line in the trap hauler and retrieve him, but it was too late. A good man gone and a sad day for me when I got that phone call from his wife. Besides his wife, he left four young children.

My other lobster crewmen in 1978 had no interest in line trawling. Frank Sholds had a recommendation. His closest friend was a man named Bill Garnos, who was one of the crew on Charlie Raymond's offshore lobster boat, *Fairwind*. Bill would be available during the winter when the *Fairwind* didn't go out. I signed him on.

It was a great winter. We made one- or two-day trips, depending on the weather. We normally fished eight tubs of the traditional trawl tub gear. We were fishing in the Gulf of Maine at least 60 miles from Gloucester. After fishing 120 miles from Cape Cod during the lobster season, this sort of felt like inshore fishing. When the shore is 70 or 80 miles away, it is a much more comfortable feeling.

Frank Sholds (left) and Bill Garnos, winter of 1979.

Leaving Salem Harbor, 5:00 p.m., March 29, 1979.

The season was capped off by the biggest one-day line-trawling trip I ever had. On March 29, 1979, we left Hawthorne Cove Marina in Salem, where we moored for the winter. It was 5:00 p.m. and cloudless. As we left the Marblehead shore behind, the sun set. We were bound for an eighty-eight-fathom spot 120 miles to the southeast, a couple of miles off the northern edge of Georges Bank.

A young man from Marblehead, Roger Bakey, was making quite a name for himself in the line-trawl fishery. He now owned the previous *Mistress*, built by Robert Rich. He had converted my lobster-rigged boat into a line trawler. Roger had suggested the eighty-eight-fathom spot as a good bet. I wanted to try it.

After steaming for eleven hours, we arrived at this spot just at daylight. It was still flat calm and clear. We quickly made a two- and three-tub set of our eight baited tubs. I never would set all my gear in one location in case the fish there wouldn't bite or what I had thought were fish on my recorder turned out not to be. The fish recorder that morning showed a healthy potential, but we still ran a few miles to the east to set some gear on a hump that showed on the chart. I spent over an hour trying to find that hump but came up empty. Not knowing what else to do, I broke my own rule and went back

Setting out on the morning of March 30, 1979, north edge of Georges Bank.

and set three more tubs parallel to our first two sets. The eighty-eight-fathom hump we were on was just wide enough to set the extra one and a half miles of trawl without getting into deeper water and the soft bottom where the bait would not stay on the hooks.

After a quick nap and breakfast, we started hauling back. I have never seen anything like it before or since. As soon as the first hook was in sight, large fifteen- to thirty-pound cusk started to appear. Every once in a while, a large cod would come along. By the end of the first set, it was obvious we were onto something. My crew and I talked it over. We all agreed we would probably not get back out to this spot again that spring, at least on such a perfect day. We had brought extra bait and had a modest amount of ice aboard. We decided to go for it. We each baited a tub of trawl and then made another three-tub set. We repeated this process after the second set was aboard. When pulled up from deep water, large cusk often have their bladders expand from the pressure change. That day, there were fifteen or twenty cusk floating the trawl ground line to the surface out ahead of us. The day stayed calm and clear. It wasn't until late afternoon that a light southwest wind rippled the water.

Discouraging seagulls.

Bill Garnos, late afternoon, March 30.

The morning of March 31, heading for Gloucester.

A truly golden day! It was 11:00 p.m. when the last hook was over the rail and properly coiled. We had very little bait left and had used up our ice. We started for Gloucester. By the time we had all the fish dressed, everything stowed away and the boat scrubbed down, it was 4:00 a.m. and the first glow of light of the next day was in the eastern sky.

We arrived at Sonny Deltorchio's Gloucester wharf by early afternoon. We took out 12,500 pounds of fish—10,000 pounds were cusk, and 2,500 pounds were cod.

A couple of days later, Frank and Bill stopped by my house for their checks from the trip. We had a beer together and decided we couldn't top that trip. After a second beer, we decided it was time to start preparations for the offshore lobster season.

A couple of weeks later, the foundation was laid for a new path for my working life. I was friendly with the manager of the Atlantic Lobstermen's Cooperative in Saugus, Massachusetts. His name was Fred Wilson. We met when we had both worked at the same investment firm in the '60s. Now, life was moving on for both of us.

The old Barber's Lobster Pool on the shore of Little Harbor had been expanded and was now in the end of the Graves Boatyard building. It had undergone new ownership and been given a new name, Barnegat Seafood. The blizzard of '78 had devastated the place. It had sat idle until the spring of 1979. Fred wanted to downsize from his job as the cooperative manager. At a bank foreclosure auction in April 1979, we acquired the assets and formed a corporation for our new venture, which Fred was to manage. We named our company Marblehead Lobster Company. I was a silent and ignorant partner. Selling was a lot different from catching.

By June 1979, the offshore lobster business was in full swing. Our eight hundred traps were set in Welker, Gilbert and Lydonia Canyons. I knew something had to change for me in the near future. My old Marblehead friends had expanded. Manny Porter now had two new fifty-five-foot fiberglass boats. Like me, he had started in a wooden forty-five-footer. Bob Brown now had a new seventy-foot steel-hulled *Sea Star*, along with the *Sea Fever*. In addition, he had bought and renovated a sister ship to the *Sea Fever* and renamed it *Sea Holly*. I wrestled with what my plans would be for the future.

As the late summer came and went, the weather pattern took its familiar turn of more and more windy days. There were still plenty of nice days in September and October, but the good days were fewer. Allowing for the time needed to get back and forth and the time needed to haul enough traps to make a profit, it was often necessary to start or end a trip in borderline conditions. As the fall wore on, I would have to psych myself up more and more to get past the worrying. The question "What if the weathermen are wrong?" was constantly on my mind.

Late in October that year, a young man who I had never heard of called me. He identified himself as Robert Thayer. I believe he lived in Hamilton, Massachusetts. He wanted to know if I might need a crew for offshore

Frank and Bill scrubbing fish pens after unloading.

lobstering in 1980. I told him that I wasn't sure of my plan for the next season and suggested he try Bob Brown or Charlie Raymond. I added that they were the skippers who would make him the most money. A few months later, I heard that he had secured a site on Charlie's *Fairwind*.

In November, I made my decision. The next year, I would fish lobster traps in my home waters off Marblehead. Line trawling in winter out of Gloucester would get me away from shore. I would relieve Fred at Marblehead Lobster and learn about selling. Most importantly, I would be sleeping every night in my own bed, enjoying family life and not missing so much of my children's activities. I've never regretted that decision. It most likely contributed to my longevity.

# Chapter 35

# Even Fifty-five Feet Was Too Small

**M**y transition to inshore fishing in 1980 went smoothly. My income was nowhere near what it had been from offshore lobstering, but I was home more nights and enjoying it. Beyond lobstering locally, I worked at times with Fred at Marblehead Lobster Company, slowly acquiring knowledge of how to sell wholesale and run a retail fish market.

After Labor Day, I ran into David Berry, a young man I knew from a well-known Marblehead family. He was now a crewman on my old friend Charlie Raymond's boat, the *Fairwind*. Charlie was overseeing the construction of a larger vessel. The skipper of the *Fairwind* was Bill Garnos, my former line-trawling crew. David also told me that day that another member of the crew was Rob Thayer, a fellow who had called me ten months previously looking for a job. Rob had followed my advice when I had suggested that he contact Charlie. In that same conversation, David also asked if he could go line trawling with me in the upcoming winter, when the *Fairwind* would be idle for a few months. I knew his good reputation and said "of course." One Sunday morning in November, I was sitting at home reading the *Boston Globe*. A story jumped out at me from the front page about two Cape Cod–based, offshore lobster boats. The first one mentioned was the *Sea Fever*. The paper reported that a man had been lost overboard and the vessel was drifting disabled. The second was the *Fairwind*, which hadn't been heard from following an un-forecasted, one-hundred-knot northwest gale. I immediately called Bob's wife. She didn't know much more than what the newspaper had writ. However, she had talked to her husband, who was some miles away from t.

*Sea Fever* in his seventy-foot *Sea Star*. Bob had told her that their son, Peter, was not the man who was lost.

When I hung up the phone from Linda, I started thinking back. I had set traps in Lydonia Canyon the previous October and November and was the only boat fishing there for most of that period. In my conversation with David Berry, he had told me that, among other places, the *Fairwind* had traps set in Lydonia. Charlie Raymond and Bill Garnos were gentlemen, as were most other offshore skippers. We never encroached on each other's territories. There was enough room that there was no need to crowd anybody. That was to change in the years to come. I surmised that the *Fairwind* moved into Lydonia in 1980 because they knew I was no longer there.

My worst fears of prior years seemed to be materializing. The area had been subject to the same vicious weather we had experienced in 1978, when the *Captain Cosmos* from Gloucester disappeared. A normal northwest wind had been felt along the coastal waters, but one hundred miles offshore, winds far in excess of hurricane force from the same direction had blown for many hours. This was an offshore lobsterman's worst nightmare. Running through my mind that morning was the visualization of what might have happened. In the days to come, the news sadly became clear.

The *Sea Fever* had been thrown on its side. The man at the wheel crashed through the pilothouse, went overboard and drowned.

The fifty-five-foot *Fairwind*, built of steel and much heavier, was a few miles away, attempting to survive the giant building seas. An enormous comber pushed the bow to the side, and the vessel started to slide down the wave. Before control could be regained by the helmsman, a second huge sea picked up the stern and "pitch poled" the boat, end to end, turning it upside down. The fate of the *Fairwind* is known because, amazingly, one of the men survived. In the tumult and ensuing disorientation, that man spotted light from an open door at the back of the pilothouse. Instinctively, he dove down and swam through the opening, surfacing just before his breath ran out. Of the other three men, one was below in his bunk and the other two were in the pilothouse. None escaped. The whole story and one man's survival is extremely well told in the book *Fatal Forecast* by Michael Tougias.

The men who drowned on the *Fairwind* were Bill Garnos, David Berry and Rob Thayer. I had a strong connection to all three.

# Chapter 36

# Marblehead Lobster Company

The two days after the initial news about the *Sea Fever* and the *Fairwind* were spent in ominous suspense by people of the North Shore. On the first day, I was working at Marblehead Lobster Company. Late that afternoon, one of our lobstermen came in with his catch for the day. He was Peter Berry, one of David's brothers. It's hard to know what to say to a person in Peter's position. He was downhearted but trying to stay positive. We talked for a few minutes. The phone rang. It was a TV reporter from a Boston station. He asked a lot of questions. Peter sensed to whom I was talking, looked at me and shook his head as if to say the last person he wanted to talk to was a TV newsman.

The next morning, our fears started to become reality. I was out in the *Mistress* that day hauling my inshore lobster string when word came over the VHF radio channel 19, used by most North Shore lobstermen. The report announced that a life raft from *Fairwind* had been found. That gave us a ray of hope. A few hours later, further word arrived that there was only one survivor. This news was not only a major blow to our fishing community but also had a great impact on me because I knew and had worked with these good men.

It was only one year ago that I had been lobstering in the same waters as the deceased. I remembered the weather report on the day the *Sea Fever* and *Fairwind* had sailed from Hyannis, Massachusetts, the day before their tragedies. I might have gone on that report, or I might not have. It was one of those borderline forecasts. For sure, I knew that this loss could have been my crew and me just as easily. I have reflected on that ever since.

In 1979, my sister, Brenda Booma, moved back to Marblehead from North Carolina. She needed a job. Fred hired her at six dollars an hour. A year and a half later, Fred wanted to sell his share of the company. In an amicable transaction, Brenda and I bought him out. For the next fifteen years, the two of us worked together to build up our little company.

Here I was again, back on the shore of Little Harbor scratching out a living by selling lobsters instead of catching them. Brenda brought a woman's touch and was very instrumental in building up our retail counter. She learned to tread on equal ground in a man's world. With frequent trips to the Boston Fish Pier, she acquired the knowledge of available products, as well as the respect of the male vendors. Starting with only three trays— haddock, cod and flounder—she gradually increased the selection to a full line of seafood, two full cases, with over fifty items. Little Harbor was still full of active lobstermen in the '80s. As our wholesale customer base increased, we bought the catch of more and more men. There was an unwritten agreement that if you took on a new lobsterman, you would buy everything he brought in, whether you needed it or not. Eventually, we bought lobsters from all the Little Harbor producers, many other Marbleheaders and a few from Swampscott.

To help our sales, we put together a joint venture with a similar-sized company in Saugus, Massachusetts. Together, we hired a salesman who worked for both companies on a commission basis. He sold lobsters by telephone to customers all over the United States, and we shipped them by airfreight. Within a few years, we had hired a full-time fish cutter named Ron Stevens. Ron was the kind of person you want on your team if you are choosing up sides. He was always at work on time and was superb at his job. He would obligingly fill in at any other task he was asked to do. Having Ron enabled us to cut our own fillets, a cost-cutting measure. We could then buy fish from local gill netters: Peter Fadden, Dave Rogers and Jerry Houghton Jr. They primarily caught cod. I was fishing in the *Mistress* and sold my haddock and cusk to go along with the cod. We supplemented with whole fish from Gloucester and Boston. The local boats gave us "day boat" fish, one day out of the water, the very best. With Ron's cutting ability, we had the freshest possible fillets for our retail trade. We supplied local restaurants and the wholesale United States air shipping trade as well. Though small compared to the big operators in Boston and Gloucester, we made a distinct place for ourselves in the marketplace.

Over the years, we had a great group of employees, never having to put a want ad in the paper for help. The existing group recommended their

Brenda Booma and Hugh Bishop displaying a twenty-five-pound lobster.

friends for interviews. The work was strenuous, but there was always joking and non-malicious pranks.

The highlight of each season was our Christmas party. After one particularly successful year, we hired a five-piece Dixieland Band. When I lined them up, I had intended they would play in the retail room by the lobster tank. The bandleader asked if he would have to play with a snorkel on. I decided to change their site to a space backing up to the freezer. He then seemed pleased, saying the cold might solve his hemorrhoid problem.

It was necessary to learn how to sell lobsters, our mainstay. Water pumped in constantly from Little Harbor kept the crustaceans alive in our holding tanks, which had a capacity of ten thousand pounds. From July until November, we commonly bought two to five thousand pounds per day. In the winter, when local catches were small, we still had to have lobster to supply

We were noted for our pretty retail girls.

our local customers and air trade, so we bought from Nova Scotian dealers and Maine suppliers. We were open seven days a week all year, closing only for Thanksgiving, Christmas and New Year's.

At peak season, with lobstermen arriving every day and a limited capacity, the product had to be moved. Individual catches vary. How many are caught each day depends on factors like water temperature, sea conditions and tidal ranges, among other things. When lobsters were being caught in quantity in Massachusetts, there were likely to be good catches in Maine also. Sometimes a market glut resulted. Wholesale prices reacted quickly in the environment in which we were functioning. I soon learned the beauty of free market operations, how prices adjust to a level where both buyers and sellers can survive. Politicians and government bureaucrats should spend a month behind the desk of a lobster dealer before they are allowed to make their statements about economics.

An increased customer base allowed us to buy from more lobstermen, but it made moving the excess in times of large catches more of a problem. Brenda learned how to handle the wholesale part of our business as time went along. She ran the place in the winter. I was line trawling and seldom around.

# The Rich History of a Small Fishing Port

For moving lobsters, we had our retail counter, but this provided a minimum amount of the volume needed. In addition, we sold to caterers, fish markets and supermarkets, as well as the air shipping trade. We also sold back and forth with other dealers like ourselves in eastern Massachusetts. Whether buying or selling, prices were marked up minimally for these trades, as it was a way for buyer and seller to adjust their constantly changing inventories. In short, we were dealing with a supply of perishable goods over which we had no control. It made for a challenging business existence.

As Brenda got more experienced, she learned how to deal with the individuals in a macho male-dominated business. One story illustrates this well. A dealer we developed a relationship with was Mortillaro Lobster Company in Gloucester. This was run by Vince Mortillaro, a hard worker but a bit rough around the edges at times. He drove a hard bargain, but he was fair and left room for us to make a decent profit, especially as he got to know that our word was good. We sold him primarily rock-hard chicken or one-pound lobsters. He used these to sell to customers in Japan. It was a long ride, and the lobsters had to be the strongest possible. When we had extras, we called him first because, in addition to the premium he paid, a check came back with our driver or arrived in the mail in a couple of days.

One day, Brenda called Vince and told him we had some hard-shell chickens for sale and asked if he wanted them. Vince commonly used the F word in his conversations. Brenda was repulsed by it. Vince replied, "Send them up here but make sure they are f---ing hard!" Brenda replied, "Don't worry, Vince, they will be f---ing hard." There was a long, pregnant pause. Finally, Vince said meekly, "Good." They always got along very well after that.

Brenda and I learned much from our years together at Marblehead Lobster. There's nothing like running a small business to understand our economic system. At least one of us was always there. During busy times, our day started at 4:00 a.m. or before to get our air shipments ready for early morning flights.

We had good times and bad, funny and sad experiences and made a decent living but never got rich. Along with my acquired experiences, it left me with many nice memories.

By 1995, the constant lifting of 140-pound crates of lobster and heavy boxes of fish was starting to take its toll. This plus the demanding nature of the business reluctantly made us decide to sell. It was time for both of us to move on. Brenda has an interesting story involving a trip she took with me soon after our sale:

Brenda and one of our friendly
customers.

*I never quite realized during our years of fish purchasing exactly what was
involved in the actual procurement of the product before it got to our scales.
In 1996, I decided to take a trawling trip with Hugh.*

*Although I had been lobstering with him many times, I was
unprepared for what I encountered. I had a small bag of provisions
with me and knew enough to wear my orange Grundens. These pants
had been standard garb at the Lobster Company. There is no way to
minimize the discomfort of wet jeans in a place as poorly heated as our
building on the Cove. This wonderful Swedish outerwear provided the
necessary waterproof insulation.*

*Adorned in my flattering attire, I boarded the boat. We left the Little
Harbor at 3:00 p.m., arriving at Cape Pond Ice in Gloucester an hour
later. They loaded a ton and a half of ice into the hold. Picking up a
mooring in the outer harbor, we cut the mackerel and squid and baited
the gear. This was a painstakingly time-consuming process, an extremely
repetitive three-hour job. The small fish had to be cut into chunks. Then,
each nugget was impaled on every one of what seemed like thousands of
hooks. As darkness enveloped us, Hugh announced it was naptime and
that we would head out for fishing at 11:00 p.m. I guess he was used to
the routine, because in no time at all, he was snoring. I, on the other hand,
wasn't the least bit tired. I guess I finally drifted off, because the story I
was reading became a blur, but in what seemed like no time, he was on his
feet, ready to leave. I cautiously attempted to find the correct location on the
Mistress for whatever my presence might be able to provide.*

*I wondered if I would be allowed to steer, remembering that the captain had once allowed me to dock his vessel returning from the fireworks at the main harbor on July 4 —a heavily coached performance. Amazingly, he announced I would have the second watch on our way to Platt's Bank, sixty-five miles away. He showed me the radar rings and explained that when he was alone, sleeping or awake, it would be on. It had an alarm that could be set to warn of approaching craft. After several successive watches, we reached our destination.*

*Quite honestly, I had been able to assist in the baiting, because wielding a knife was familiar territory, but setting out the gear was not in my realm. Hugh managed that with very little noticeable effort. Although it took a considerable amount of time, he seemed to have endless stamina and patience. Not bad so far, I thought to myself. I was pretty strong from lifting those one-hundred-plus-pound crates at our business but had no idea how much more taxing standing can be when combined with the motion of the boat. Many of the necessary muscles, in my case, were evidently untapped. I never sat down in our nine- to ten-hour days at work but found myself perching occasionally on a fish box or anything else that was not in the way of the captain.*

*Letting the set "set" gave us time for another short nap. This time, I dozed off quite rapidly. Hugh began hauling, removing the cod and haddock from the hooks to be sorted into nearby fish "totes," and sent the rest of the fish down the chute, still attached. I assumed my assigned position. The haddock and cod were easy, since he had already extricated them from the hooks. They were put in their respective boxes to await dressing. The cusk were a bit tricky. Our friend and part-time business associate from Saugus, Dusty Traill, had devised a clever instrument for removing the cusk. The motion required to "detrawl" them was a quick twist of the wrist with the metal tool inserted in their mouths. Any one of them, still able, was more than glad to go for one's hand. Three miles of hooks might seem easy to land, but by the end of the day, I still stood, alternately gutting (during slow times) and removing hooks when the catch was plentiful. I discreetly tried to peer over the starboard side to see if there was literally an "end in sight," preferably a buoy.*

*After what seemed like an eternity, carpal tunnel challenging my wrist, I finally realized that we were closing in on it. Hugh had actually suggested we might take a break and eat. I guess he was cook for that trip, as he baked some true "day boat" haddock with a can of tomatoes, his favorite on-board recipe. I wolfed it down.*

*I knew better than to get too relaxed. Ten more minutes of sitting, and we were back on deck. Hugh was tossing boxes of fish around like they were sacks of potatoes. From the depths of the fish pen, ice appeared and restacking commenced. Every fish not already cleaned had to be dressed and the entire catch washed. Separated by species, they were then iced and once again loaded into the fish pen—not a job for the faint of heart.*

*When we had finished, or so I thought, I heard Hugh announce he thought he'd stay out for another day. I swallowed hard and picked up a knife, barely cool from the afternoon and early evening workout. The deck lights illuminated the work area. When we finally finished, it was close to 10:00 p.m. I was whipped. Hugh appeared fresh and cheery, with enough enthusiasm for both of us. Removing my Grundens took all my remaining energy reserve.*

*As busy as we had been, with the stern well illuminated, I had hardly had time to notice the spectacular scene. Now, with only the required vessel lights showing, the moon and stars watched over us. The big dipper, its ladle pointing at the North Star, was clearly noticeable, just as it had been for early mariners who used it as a navigational tool. There was a perfect sort of peace not possible ashore. From where we stood, with the Mistress idling, I knew the land, where cares resumed, was not visible over any part of the horizon, day or night, a strange feeling to the uninitiated.*

*We had been gone for almost twenty-four hours. Despite my exhaustion, I seriously doubted a decent sleep with the drone of the engine easily audible below, but I was out the minute I hit my bunk, fully clothed. The gentle rock of the boat acted as a soporific. I woke up once to see my brother checking the radar. Sleep for the skipper is always light, the care of his vessel and crew constantly on his mind.*

*The rest of the trip went as the captain planned, but I had a new appreciation for Hugh and certain justification for the high prices the Lobster Company was paying for fish.*

# Chapter 37

# At the End, I Was Alone

**F**or the thirty-six winters between 1962 and 1998, there was only one when I didn't go trawling. The year 1976 was the exception, when I worked all winter at Sonny Hodgdon's boat shop helping build the fifty-foot *Mistress*. In all those years, my body went from a muscular, young man of twenty-six to an older man of sixty-two who, thanks to good health and a keen interest, could still catch fish.

Lobstering inshore and offshore was always enjoyable, but hook fishing was my passion and what I will remember the most fondly. I saw very significant changes of all sorts that affected ground fishing during those thirty-six years. For the first two-thirds of that time, there were no restrictions on an individual's efforts, except the limitations of his boat size, weather, body and personal ambition. Sadly, younger fishermen today will never enjoy what my contemporaries and I knew. The whole present-day situation has had much written about it. The vast majority of so-called facts has come from people who have never been out in a boat and/or have never invested a dollar of their own money in a risky venture.

I began to be aware of how technology was changing ground fishing. Loran made accurate positioning possible during the late 1960s. It's important for a non-fisherman to know that fish are not everywhere out there. Different types of fish are on different kinds of bottom at different times of the day and year. A good deal of the challenge and satisfaction of making a living from the sea comes from finding and catching the mobile fish. An old-timer once told me, "If they didn't have tails, we would do much better." Fish are

The author boating cod.

a moving target. Any successful, experienced fisherman has a storehouse of knowledge of where to go when. That, in itself, is still no guarantee of a good catch.

Somehow, zealous environmentalists have managed to use their money and media savvy to portray commercial fishermen as some of the worst people on the planet. While not all are saints, the men I have known over the years were not only supporting their families but also providing one of the three basic necessities of life—food. People have to eat.

Loran made it possible to return to the same location time and again. Better sonar equipment showed not only depth but the consistency of the bottom and, even more importantly, concentrations of fish. Radar and GPS followed. When we first saw new technology, we would say, "Oh boy!" Now, I look back and I wish some of these things had never been invented.

In years past, draggers, which caught fish by towing their nets over the sea floor, avoided the harder bottom and jagged peaks because their nets would tear and the fish would escape. This also meant loss of fishing time to mend the tears. Conversely, these areas of hard bottom and peaks were what hook fishermen looked for. The gear set there was safe from getting destroyed by the draggers, and the areas themselves served as sanctuaries for fish. Hook gear did not (and still does not) destroy the habitat. The fish could also swim away and eventually be caught by draggers and others. After 1980, dragging gear became more sophisticated, allowing the captains of those boats to tow over just about any kind of bottom, including what were called church steeples, the sharp peaks that looked like towers on fish finders.

I experienced much sadness when going to the places where there once was consistently good hook fishing—with no draggers present—to seeing draggers blanketing those pieces of bottom and no fish left to catch anymore. To me, it was a case of shooting holes in both our feet at the same time. By destroying the habitat and catching the fish simultaneously, there was nothing left for any of us. As I lived through the '80s, I was complacent. There were still fish to catch; I just had to go farther and work a little harder. I felt that since hook fishing was the most selective and environmentally friendly, I wouldn't have to worry. However, there were growing signs of government intervention. As it became obvious that some types of regulations were necessary, I welcomed them, figuring that hook fishing would be favored.

Skid Miller with halibut.

Boy, was I wrong! I learned a lesson I should have known: don't count on government to have common sense and be aware of the obvious.

Gear technology came to hooking also. Evolution of line-trawl methods had changed little since its inception. In 1982, a friend of mine got me interested in a hook-fishing system he had heard about in Barnegat, New Jersey. Hooks were set on racks and then dragged through a trough filled with cut-up pieces of bait. A piece was snagged on the way by. This was supposed to bait up 90 percent of the hooks involved. There was a little more to this technique, but not much. Hauling back the gear was at the same speed as previously, but baiting up was done in a fraction of the time.

We drove to New Jersey one day, and each of us bought a system. I bought enough equipment to handle twelve tubs of our previously fixed gear. From a company in Rhode Island, I purchased the proper amount of ground line. The whole setup let us put four thousand hooks in the water. Additionally, I purchased a hydraulic-powered bait cutter, which eliminated hand cutting. A dozen spinning discs cut whole herring, mackerel or squid with amazing speed. It was no place to put your fingers. The system worked.

That winter, I had a two-man crew of local lobstermen friends, Ben Doliber and Perry Asher. We fished mostly in the Gulf of Maine on hard-bottom patches. We tried to set in ninety-fathom water or more. Shortly, draggers started to beat on these spots with their improved "rock-hopping gear." Our last few trips, in early May, were in the Cashes Ledge area just before the dogfish showed up on their annual migration. We had two-day trips with catches in the range of eight thousand pounds. The dogfish put us out of business by May 12. Ben and Perry went back to lobstering, and I retreated to Marblehead Lobster Company.

The next year, I assembled the same crew, and while not as profitable as 1982, it was acceptable. Late one afternoon at the end of a trip, I was coming by the end of the Gloucester breakwater in the *Mistress*. It was a clear day, with a moderate northwest wind. I noticed a small, thirty-foot boat under the shore on the west side of the harbor. It had a furled-up riding sail, and one man appeared to be dressing fish on the stern deck. I knew every hook boat in those days. This was one I didn't recognize. When we got to Sonny's, I asked him if he knew the boat. He said, "That's Jeff Tutein." I'd never heard of him, but he was to become a fishing friend who gave me much good advice and then a personal friend in the years to come.

I met Jeff in person later that winter. He seemed like a loner, a very quiet type. He, indeed, was a hook fisherman. His wooden boat was thirty-one feet long with a gas engine, very basic electronics and no radar. He reminded me

*Above*: Crew working the snap baiting system.

*Left*: Ben Doliber and large cusk.

of myself twenty years before. He also had a method of fishing I had not seen previously. He had his ground line in a big box on the deck. His hooks were circular with a monofilament line and a snap device on the end of the three-and-a-half-foot ganging that he clipped onto his line. It was the first time I had seen monofilament and snaps.

The next year, I bought some of these snaps just to try them. In a way, I felt it was a step backward, because each hook had to be baited by hand, just like the old, fixed gear. With the snag baiting system, I thought my old age would be free of this tiresome process. We experimented fishing with the new type of gear on the ends of some of our snag gear. The snag gear would have no fish and the mono gear would have some, or the snag gear would have some fish and the mono gear would have three or four times more for the same number of hooks. By the next season, I had completely converted to monofilament. I've baited hundreds of thousands of hooks since then, but it's been worth it. I still use this system today.

When I first met Jeff, I had a two-man crew, and my winter fishing was always profitable. During the 1980s, fish became more and more scarce. It was obvious that I had to take some type of conservation measure. My crew was reduced to one. The National Marine Fisheries Service, in collaboration with the New England Fisheries Management Council, tried different methods to limit fishermen and conserve fish. I agreed that sensible regulations were needed. I will say that I never feared the potential measures because I felt hook fishing was the most conserving method in place, and no matter what, I would survive or at least be the last man standing. Jeff always fished alone. Watching him, I was inspired by his one-man operation. As I got to know him, I learned of his extensive background. In years past, he had experienced dragging, tuna harpooning and tuna seining, Scottish seining and sword fishing. We confided in each other with our fishing knowledge, which is something neither of us did lightly. He had a wisdom beyond his years, and by 1998, he was one of my closest friends.

The restrictions on fishing became more and more onerous. The last straw was an edict called the Western Gulf of Maine Closure, initiated in May 1997. This shut down, for supposedly three years, 90 percent of the area where I had been line trawling. I then had to run forty miles to an area northeast of Cape Cod to find suitable hook-fishing bottom or fish on the limited area of Jeffreys Ledge not included in the closure. Party, or "head," boats were allowed in the WGMC area to appease the tourists. At a meeting with the district chief of the National Marine Fisheries Service, Jeff and I were told this was because "they don't have anywhere else to go."

Fishing the *Mistress* alone.

Hook fishermen didn't have anywhere else to go either, but the NMFS didn't care about us. Another ridiculous comment made by the district chief was the party boats "do not sell their fish." Since these party boats could catch several thousand pounds of fish a day, how was that a conservation measure?

My response to the tangle of contradicting restrictions came from watching Jeff and his operation. "If he could fish alone," I said to myself, "so can I." With rare exceptions, I started to take the *Mistress* out with no crew. By 1998, I was very experienced at it. There was extra risk attached, but I only had to think of myself, with the dwindling resource. When it came time to figure out the crew shares, I only had to divide by one. I started out in 1949 at twelve years old setting my first two lobster traps by myself, and forty-nine years later I was back working alone.

# Chapter 38

# Memorizing on Jeffreys

On January 15, 1998, I set and hauled my line trawls on Jeffreys Ledge, twenty-three miles east-northeast of Gloucester. It was a unique and rare day for me. It was one of the few times over all the years that my heart wasn't in fishing. My memories and reflections and Bob Brown's present status dominated my thoughts.

Bob's relationship with me had been cordially distant for the past fifteen years. Now we were both married to second wives. When I got home that evening, I called Bob's wife, Suzanne, to get information beyond what Jeff had told me on my VHF radio early that morning. She said Bob had fallen from the top of the wharf ladder while leaving the *Hannah Boden*. There was a telephone pole moored between the vessel and wharf pilings to help keep the *Hannah Boden* lying in her berth. His head hit the log at the bottom of his fall. She said he was in Massachusetts General Hospital with a severe injury but she seemed cautiously optimistic. I thought of all the risks through which he had lived. I could never imagine him dying before me and just knew he was going to be fine.

Only a month before, my new wife, Judy, and I were driving in Gloucester when we saw the *Hannah Boden* tied up at the Star Fisheries Wharf, where her trip of red crab had just been unloaded. Red crabs were caught with traps in water over 150 fathoms along the edge of the Continental Shelf. This was another new venture for Bob. The previous few times our paths had crossed, I had sensed a slight mellowing in Bob's demeanor. It seemed more pronounced that day. As he showed Judy around the boat, he seemed like the close friend he had been forty years before. When we left, he asked

A last look at the *Sea Fever* underway.

us to a Christmas party he and his wife were having two weeks hence at their West Gloucester home.

The party was fun. There were old friends and acquaintances from many previous years. Among other things, Bob and Suzanne said they couldn't imagine why anyone would read the new book *The Perfect Storm*. They asked Judy and me to take a trip with them to a Caribbean resort later in the winter. We accepted. At the party, Bob and I enjoyed talking about some of our memories around Little Harbor back in the '50s. Shared experiences of forty years can't be bought for any price. I left the party with a positive feeling. I had not seen or talked to Bob since then. Now I wondered if the southern trip would ever take place.

Bob showed signs of improvement for the next two weeks. He could talk, but his recovery was far from certain. On January 28, he took a turn for the worse and died. Suzanne called and asked me to speak at his funeral at the Old North Church in Marblehead. I spent some time preparing my remarks and decided to end them with a poem. I felt the effect would be much better if I could recite the whole piece from memory.

The day before the funeral was a beautiful winter's day. I once again was line trawling on Jeffreys. I had written the poem out on a piece of paper and took it with me. After I set my hooks that morning, I taped the piece of poem-covered paper over the pilothouse window. From where I stood during haul back, I could easily read it. Before noon on that sunny, calm day I had the poem solidly in my head for the service. Its message spoke about life and death and was especially significant for Bob. The poem was entitled "Sea Fever."

*I must go down to the seas again, to the lonely sea and the sky*
*And all I ask is a tall ship and a star to steer her by*
*And the wheel's kick and the wind's song and the white sail's shaking*
*And a grey mist on the sea's face and a grey dawn breaking.*

*I must go down to the seas again, for the call of the running tide*
*Is a wild call and a clear call that may not be denied;*
*And all I ask is a windy day with the white clouds flying,*
*And the flung spray and the blown spume, and the sea-gulls crying*

*I must go down to the seas again to the vagrant gypsy life,*
*To the gull's way and the whale's way where the wind's like a whetted knife;*
*And all I ask is a merry yarn from a laughing fellow-rover,*
*And quiet sleep and a sweet dream when the long trick's over.*

# Epilogue

**BOB BROWN**—At the time of his death, Bob owned the fifty-foot *Sea Fever* and the ninety-five-foot offshore lobster and crab boat *Hannah Boden*. In addition, he had a lobster-buying business in Vinalhaven, Maine. There, from a newly constructed building next to the ferry terminal, he bought large amounts of lobster from the local lobstermen. He also owned tidal holding areas nearby called lobster pounds, which were used for storage to supply lobsters during the winter when landings were light. These assets were run by his wife, Suzanne, with a Herculean effort after he died until they were liquidated.

**RALPH CONNER**—Ralph died in 1966 at age seventy. He lived a full life of lobster fishing and boat building.

**WALTER "WATSON" CURTIS**—At the top of his game in the 1950s and '60s, everyone in Marblehead at least knew of him. He spent his last working years as an inshore lobsterman out of Marblehead. On his retirement in 1992, he and his wife, Virginia, spent the next fourteen years traveling the United States in a camper. He died in 2006 at age seventy-eight. A sign of life moving on is that recently, when his name came up in conversation, a young lobsterman in Marblehead said he had never heard of Watson.

**JOHN "SONNY" DELTORCHIO**—Sonny sold his wholesale fish business, Cape Ann Seafoods, in 1990. Now eighty-nine years old, he has spent the time since quietly with his wife, Ruth, between a condo in Florida and his home in Magnolia, Massachusetts.

**GRAVES BOATYARD**—This Little Harbor facility passed out of the Graves family over twenty years ago. It is now called Marblehead Trading Company, owned and very successfully run by a capable man named Ralph Anderson.

**ED HAWKES**—Ed Hawkes and his wife, Jean, moved from Marblehead to Falmouth, Massachusetts, in 2011 to be near their younger relatives. At ninety-one years old, Ed still produces hand-carved, high-quality duck decoys and has not lost any of his sharp wit or sense of humor.

**DAVID HILDRETH**—Now seventy-four years old, Dave is retired and rides out Maine winters in his home in Bucksport. In summer, he spends as much time as he can rowing up and down the Maine coast in a sixteen-foot dory, very similar to a Chamberlain design. It is rigged with a removable canopy, which permits him to sleep aboard. The accommodations are somewhat Spartan.

**LITTLE HARBOR**—Little Harbor remained a location with ten or a dozen active fishermen well into the 1980s. In more recent years, these fishermen have dwindled until, in 2011, there are only four left. Most of the people passing by in their kayaks and center-console outboards are naturally oblivious to the boats and men of the past. I am not. I appreciate the rich experiences I had and all that those hardworking men taught us.

**MARBLEHEAD LOBSTER COMPANY**—Our old business is now a small retail lobster and seafood business.

**MANFORD "MANNY" PORTER**—My old football teammate, friend and competitor lives in Gloucester, Massachusetts, where he spends his time helping his son, Craig, who is a full-time gill net fisherman and lobsterman. Manny is still a colorful character.

**CHARLES RAYMOND**—Charlie still owns and manages the seventy-seven-foot offshore lobster boat *Kristen and Michael*, named for his two children. This vessel, built in 1981, was under construction when the *Fairwind* and three of its crew were lost. Charlie has a captain run the boat out of Gloucester, Massachusetts, where trips of several days are made to Georges Bank and Continental Shelf waters.

**FRANK SHOLDS**—My former first mate and friend lives in Manchester, Massachusetts, and lobster fishes with a thirty-six-foot boat full time out of Beverly. We often pass close enough to each other for a "fisherman's wave." When we get a chance to talk, it is always enjoyable, with an occasional reference to the way it was.

**JEFF TUTEIN**—Jeff and his wife, Jane, live in Rockport, Massachusetts. He is a full-time inshore lobsterman fishing out of nearby Pigeon Cove. He is an intrepid fisherman, close friend and the person I lean heavily on for accurate weather forecasting.

# FINAL THOUGHTS

For several years, from 2005 to 2010, my former fifty-foot *Mistress* and Bob Brown's *Sea Fever* were berthed seventy-five feet from each other at the Gloucester State Fish Pier. Often, before or after golf, I felt drawn to a spot in the large parking lot where I could view both vessels The irony of these two vessels, both built by Sonny Hodgdon well over thirty years ago, being next to each other always amazed me. After spending a few minutes with my memories, two thoughts would run through my mind.

The first was of Sonny and his boat-building crew; they got a sincere mental "tip of the cap." The second thought was of my crewmen through all those years—the many sunrises, rough and calm weather, good trips and bad and all the other things we experienced trying to catch something. These good men went with me and fished by my side. We had wonderful times. It was a great ride!

Coming up Gloucester Harbor at sunset.

# Bibliography

Ferguson, David L. *Cleopatra's Barge*. New York: Little Brown and Company, 1976.

Fisher, Captain R. Barry. *A Doryman's Day*. Gardiner, ME: Tilbury House, 2001.

Hood, Ted, and Michael Levitt. *Ted Hood Through Hand and Eye*. China: Mystic Seaport, 2006.

Lindsey, Benjamin Lindsey. *Old Marblehead Sea Captains and the Ships in Which They Sailed*. Marblehead, MA: N. Allen Lindsey & Co., 1915.

*Marblehead Messenger*. "Busy Airplane Factory Was Once Operated Here." November 13, 1974, 1, 5.

————. "Steve Goodwin and Crew Are Feared Lost at Sea." February 11, 1976, 1.

Masefield, John. *Poems*. New York: Macmillan Company, 1925.

Morris, John N. *Alone at Sea*. Canada: Commonwealth Editions, 2010.

Probate Court, Salem, Massachusetts. asst.

Registry of Deeds, Salem, Massachusetts. asst.

Roads, Samuel, Jr. *History and Traditions of Marblehead*. Marblehead, MA: N. Allen Lindsey & Co., 1897.

Stetson, Mildred Graves. "The Graves Yacht Yards." *Marblehead Magazine* (January 1987).

Thomas, Gordon W. *Fast and Able*. Gloucester, MA: Cape Ann Ticket and Label Company, Historic Ships Associates, 1968.

# About the Authors

**H**ugh Bishop and his wife, Judy, live in Marblehead, Massachusetts. He handles a modest string of lobster traps from a small lobster boat (named appropriately *September Song*), fishing in the same waters where he first set traps over sixty years ago. Other interests include a significant amount of time playing golf.

**B**renda Booma, raised in Marblehead, grew up with a deep respect for the ocean and a love of the small area called Barnegat. Having moved away in her twenties, she raised three children while playing and teaching tennis. When she moved back, she became involved with the seafood business, with which she was affiliated until her retirement in 2010. Golf, gardening and grandchilddren are her new passions.

Visit us at
www.historypress.net